P9-DIY-078

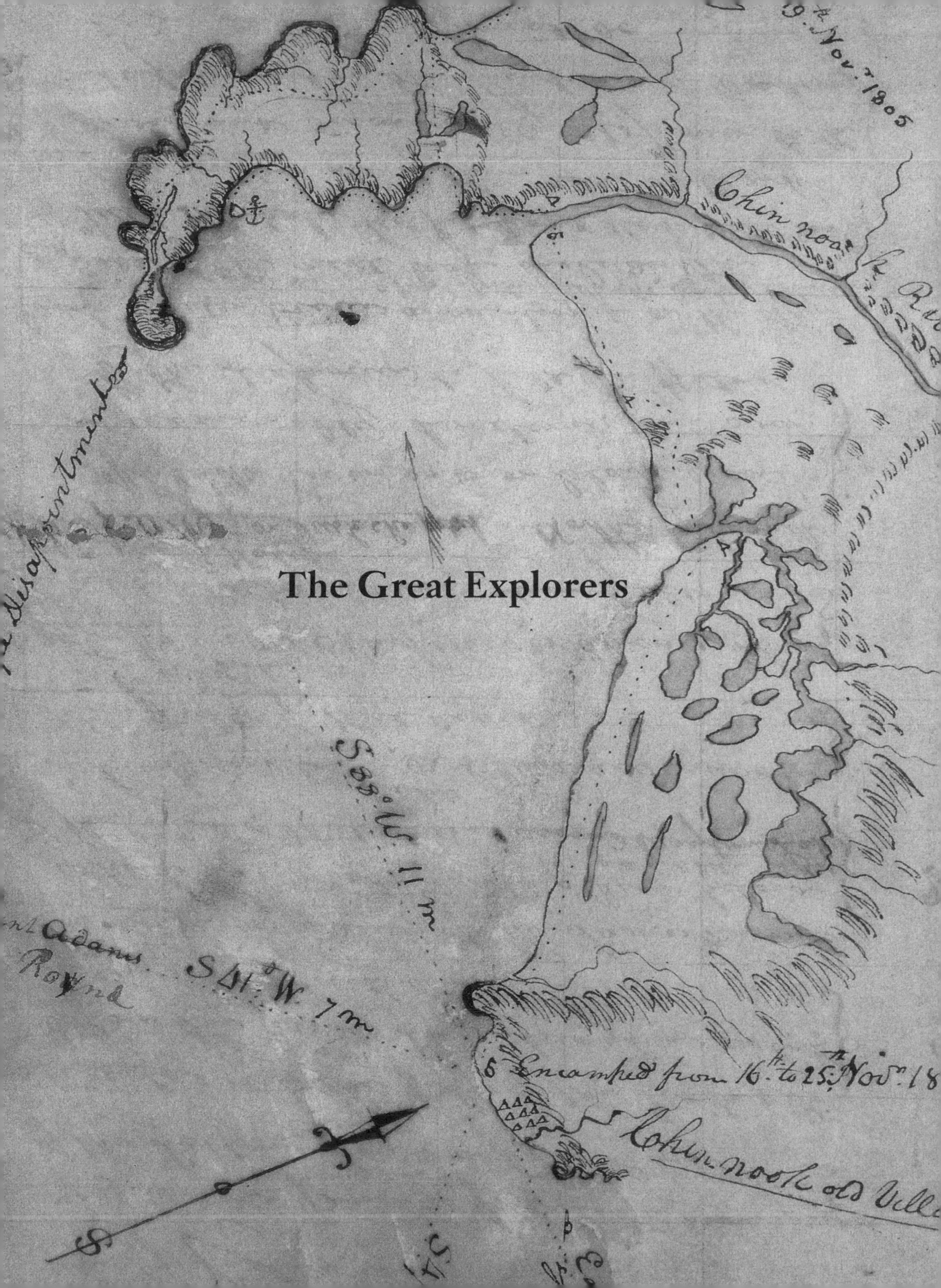

The Great Explorers

The Great Explorers

EDITED BY ROBIN HANBURY-TENISON

With 204 illustrations

Thames & Hudson

CONTENTS

Half-title: William Clark's map of the mouth of the Columbia River, from the Lewis and Clark expedition of 1804 to 1806.

Title page: Alexander von Humboldt and his companions stride towards Cajambe volcano in Ecuador, 1814.

First published in the United Kingdom in 2010 by
Thames & Hudson Ltd, 181A High Holborn,
London WC1V 7QX

© 2010 Thames & Hudson Ltd, London

Designed by Karolina Prymaka

The right of Robin Hanbury-Tenison to be identified as the editor of the work has been asserted by him in accordance with the Copyright, Design and Patents Act 1988

All Rights Reserved. No part of this publication may be reproduced or transmitted in any form or by any means, electronic or mechanical, including photocopy, recording or any other information storage and retrieval system, without prior permission in writing from the publisher.

British Library Cataloguing-in-Publication Data
A catalogue record for this book is available from the British Library

ISBN 978-0-500-25169-0

Printed and bound in China by C&C Offset Printing Co., Ltd

To find out about all our publications, please visit
www.thamesandhudson.com.
There you can subscribe to our e-newsletter, browse or download our current catalogue, and buy any titles that are in print.

SEARCHING BEYOND THE HORIZON

When you set out on your journey to Ithaca,
pray that the road is long,
full of adventure, full of knowledge.

C. P. Cavafy, 1911

Great explorers are different from other men and women. Throughout the ages, certain people have excelled in their geographical endeavours to an extent that has changed the world. These are the people who, through their explorations, transformed our perception of our surroundings – they revealed the planet to us and opened our eyes to the physical, natural and historical world around us. It started long ago and it continues today. It has always been mankind's gift, and curse, to be inquisitive – this is what makes us unlike all other species. Without this curiosity we would all have stayed at home. Since we developed the brains we have today, perhaps at least 100,000 years ago, we have viewed life differently from other creatures. We have looked beyond our immediate surroundings, to the possibilities that each new territory has to offer, and we have felt an urge to go further and explore, not just for food, space and land, but also out of curiosity.

Never has it been more important to recognize where our curiosity has led us, what it has brought us in knowledge and understanding, and what it can tell us about our responsibility to this planet. Once, it was a new and unknown world. Now, while most of the wonder and diversity are still there, we are just beginning to realize, at the last dangerous moment, that there is still so much we do not understand and so little time to get it right. The urgency to explore has never been greater.

Ever since we emerged from the Rift Valley in Africa, where it is now generally accepted that *Homo sapiens* originated, we have explored. The earliest pioneers, who

In three epic voyages, James Cook discovered more of the earth's surface than anyone else; this detail of a painting by William Hodges shows Cook's arrival in Matavai Bay, Tahiti, in 1769.

A boat's compass used by David Livingstone on his first journey down the Zambezi in 1855–56.

rapidly spread out to occupy most of the habitable and accessible land, were the original great explorers. No one can ever again replicate the experience they had of setting foot for the first time on swathes of diverse, pristine landscape, from deserts to tropical rainforests, from mountains to fertile plains. There have, however, been many since who have been driven to explore the limits of the worlds known to them and to their societies. A few, whose curiosity and courage led them to reveal what lay beyond the horizon, stand out from the crowd as giants. These were the Great Explorers and, from the many who qualify for inclusion, this book describes 40 of the most interesting. These were the men and women whose biographies reveal not just their dogged ambition, which drove them to go the extra distance, but also their other strengths and weaknesses, their greed, courage, authority and individuality, and, above all, their spirit of inquiry. Often it was an obstinate belief in themselves and their dreams that made them succeed where others failed.

Crossing Oceans

The great era of recorded exploration began – as this book begins – with the oceanic journeys of around five hundred years ago. When Columbus reached the New World, his journey was arguably the most cataclysmic in human history. No other geographical discovery unleashed so much change on so many, nor had such a lasting effect. The known world was effectively doubled in size at a stroke. Soon after Columbus sailed west, Vasco da Gama, one of the few explorers to die successful and rich, opened the route to the east. Spices, such as pepper and cloves, were until then obtained only through the expensive and rare cargoes which survived interminable overland journeys. Suddenly, Europe found itself sitting between two vast sources of wealth. From then on, for the next few centuries, the majority of exploration was focused on finding better ways and faster routes to capitalize on these riches.

Magellan, another ruthless and determined man, demonstrated in his search for a western route to the Spice Islands that the world could be circumnavigated, though he himself did not survive the journey. Thereafter, gradually, the oceans were conquered until virtually no habitable place within them remained unrevealed. At first Spain and Portugal concentrated on looting and destroying the incomparable empires of the Americas and jostling for possession of the Spice Islands. Then other important naval world powers, Britain and France, began to push the boundaries further to the east, discovering new islands and founding colonies. Their finest captains, such as Bougainville and Cook – perhaps the greatest navigator of all time – were enlightened men, who sought knowledge rather than riches, and in that sense were very different from the conquistadors; but the changes they brought to cultures unprepared for western diseases and attitudes were almost as devastating.

EXPLORING CONTINENTS, BY LAND AND RIVER

On land the challenge was to penetrate to the deepest parts of the interiors of the unknown continents. In the New World, there was the enticing prospect of mythical cities of gold, which drove conquistadors such as Hernan Cortés, Francisco Pizarro and Hernando de Soto to commit many excesses. Later, there was the prospect of new land to settle, which led President Jefferson to send Lewis and Clark to the west of North America. Unusually, these two men managed joint leadership of a major expedition without acrimony, but their success was to be followed by the massive American migration which displaced the Plains Indians.

Thomas Baines made this sketch of himself drawing from a precarious viewpoint near Lake Ngami, in present-day Botswana, in April 1862. Baines was a born artist and explorer, who brought to life the wonders of Africa and Australia for those who remained at home in Europe.

Africa, of course, drew many explorers to uncover its wonders and secrets. Before the days of photography, skilful painters such as the modest Thomas Baines, who travelled for a time with Livingstone, recorded scenes that amazed and informed the Londoners and Parisians who bought them. Complex characters including the mystic Richard Burton, who travelled in Arabia as well as Africa, became the celebrities of their day, lionized and listened to. In Asia, the Great Game (the struggle for supremacy between the Russian and British empires) was an excuse and a cover for many explorations of epic length. The Russians had the redoubtable hunter Nikolai Przhevalsky, after whom the wild horse is named; the British had soldiers and dreamers such as Francis Younghusband and dogged, reserved men such as Ney Elias and Nain Singh and other Pundits. They vied with each other to influence the course of history, while mapping vast unexplored areas. Once again, among them were those whose spur was their insatiable curiosity to measure or to understand – such as the determined and dogged Aurel Stein. Reading about these extraordinary men we learn what it is that drives a rare few to push the limits of travel beyond the bounds of possibility.

Often there were huge rivers running from a mysterious source, driving men mad in their desire to reach it. With so much life along the river banks, it seemed to make sense to believe that once the river was conquered and understood, the rest would fall into the colonizers' hands. In both North and South America it was the rivers that first led into the interior. Some, such as the Frenchman Samuel de Champlain, were wise enough to watch and learn from the indigenous inhabitants; they prospered and were able to secure large areas of land, in Champlain's case Canada, for their colonial masters. The idea that there might be a river passage across the American continent that would provide a route to the Far East continued to drive many, including Robert Mackenzie, an immigrant Scottish trader, to extremes, as he paddled further and further up unexplored rivers in pursuit of his dream.

The Nile was, from the dawn of time, a magnet for explorers. The first from Britain, the mighty James Bruce, was not believed when he returned to tell of discovering the source, albeit of the Blue Nile. Later, the Royal Geographical Society sent many expeditions to locate and map its headwaters and the search for the real source became a matter of intense rivalry, pride and shame – the failure to find it being known as the 'opprobrium of geographers'. Such competitiveness and obsession also brought tragedy. John Hanning Speke died on the morning he was due to debate with Richard Burton whether he had indeed discovered the Nile's source.

Members of the Tibet Mission Force escorting Francis Younghusband's punitive military incursion into Tibet in 1903–04 along the Kyo Chu river near Lhasa.

The charismatic Mungo Park solved the mystery of the direction of the flow of the River Niger, and returned to London from his first trip a hero, but longed to retire; like so many of these driven men, however, he found the lure of Africa and adventure too great and returned there, only to perish. It was religious zeal that first drove the great missionary explorer David Livingstone, who covered immense distances in order to convert the natives and stop the slave trade rather than to gain wealth. He was convinced that rivers, especially the Zambezi, held the key to opening up the continent to legitimate trade. Some, like the Welsh orphan turned American journalist, explorer and finally British member of parliament, Henry Stanley, went further and discovered how much of Africa was ripe for exploitation. It was the explorers who showed the way, the colonizers who followed. And it was the same in the Far East, where the prospect of finding new routes for trade with China initiated French colonization in Indo-China, as the diminutive but feisty and determined Francis Garnier and his companions forced their way up the Mekong and through to the Yangtze.

Edward Wilson travelled with Captain Scott on two expeditions to the Antarctic, including the tragic attempt to reach the South Pole. As well as being a doctor, Wilson was also a fine naturalist and artist, faithfully recording the wildlife he encountered, such as this Emperor Penguin.

Arctic landscape in moonlight – a photograph taken on 20 December 1893 during Fridtjof Nansen's North Pole expedition of 1893–96; barely visible in the background is a polar bear trap.

ICY WASTES AND SEARING DESERTS

The inhospitable polar wastes then fired with enthusiasm those who wished to go beyond and to discover and understand the nature of what lay there. The Norwegians such as Fridtjof Nansen, who went on to win the Nobel Peace Prize, and Roald Amundsen, first to the South Pole and first to fly over the North Pole in a balloon, excelled in this environment. Although the heroic efforts of men like Shackleton and Scott captured the public's imagination, it is Edward Wilson the loyal, eclectic scientist, naturalist and doctor, who travelled with both, who is included here because he typifies so many of the heroic qualities that make an explorer great. Extreme cold travel reached its peak with Wally Herbert and his amazing transpolar expedition. His tenacity, which saw him and his three companions through 15 months of sub-zero temperatures, was matched by his skill as a painter. The lure of polar ice survives in the brave men and women who still test themselves to the limit reaching the Poles.

Deserts have always held a particular fascination for mankind. Most of the major religions were born in the silence to be found there and they have attracted some of

Heinrich Barth was a great scholar and linguist who made detailed studies of the people among whom he travelled; this plate is from his account of his voyages through North and central Africa.

the toughest as well as the most visionary explorers. Usually, desert travellers were inspired as much by romance as by any thought of reward. Many wrote about their experiences in some of the finest and most passionate exploratory prose. The Sahara was an immense barrier to entry into Africa and most of those who tried to cross the endless wastes perished. Heinrich Barth was the first to survive extensive travels and to record meticulously what he saw. He applied scientific discipline to his exploration, a trait which was to become a feature of 19th-century expeditions.

The interior of Australia is one immense desert, but it was once widely believed to contain an inland sea and rich grasslands. Charles Sturt did more than anyone to reveal the truth: that there was nothing much there. The Arabian desert drew many into its harsh beauty, including some remarkable women, such as Lady Hester Stanhope and Lady Anne Blunt. But it was Gertrude Bell who left the most substantial legacy, including the somewhat tarnished credit of having effectively created Iraq. The Empty Quarter in Arabia attracted men who strove to be the first to cross it and there are several who contend to be called the greatest. Harry St John Philby was a flawed but fascinating character, who probably understood it best. Wilfred Thesiger's classic book, *Arabian Sands*, was accompanied by some of the most evocative black-and-white photographs of desert people; and these from a man who professed to despise photography. He famously said '... to have done the journey on a camel when I could have done it in a car would have turned the venture into a stunt'. His contemporary, Ralph Bagnold, had done just that in the Sahara, where his experiences on motorized expeditions to study archaeological remains and the behaviour of sand dunes led directly to the Long Range Desert Group in the Second World War.

The Quest for Knowledge

It took a long time for science to supplant religion and conquest as the prime mover in generating expeditions. But when it did, mainly in the 19th century, a whole new breed of dedicated polymaths emerged, who revealed an unknown and infinitely varied biosphere. From the indefatigable Alexander von Humboldt, a driven man if ever there was one, whose punctilious recording of everything he saw and heard has never been surpassed, to the pensive Alfred Russel Wallace, who conceived the theory of evolution while lying fever-ridden in a hammock, the pursuit of scientific collections in the most inhospitable surroundings drove some remarkable men and women to superhuman feats of endurance. For both Marianne North, who only began her journeys at the age of 40 – and this in the Victorian age when it was not quite done for women – and for Frank Kingdon-Ward, it was a fascination with the world's richly varied flora that provided the motive for travel and exploration, though, as always, they pursued it with an exceptional energy and dedication that sets them apart.

For a time it seemed as though it would be possible to harness mankind's skills and knowledge to master the planet and exploit it without limit or fear of consequences. Gino Watkins combined a romantic thirst for adventure with a practical aim: he helped establish the air route over Greenland that opened up today's era of easy transatlantic air travel. But it is only in the last few decades, as we begin to plumb the remaining depths and reach for the stars, that have we begun to realize how little we truly understand about the workings of nature and how much more remains to be done. There are those, like Yuri Gagarin, the humble son of a carpenter who found himself thrust into space and fame, who have been a part of these colossal changes almost by accident. And there are still today those who are driven to seek the remaining unknown places left on earth: the Cousteaus, who virtually invented submarine research and brought the wonders of the deep to so many; and Andrew Eavis, a cave explorer committed to probing the secrets of the 90 per cent of subterranean passages still undiscovered. The new great age of exploration may be just beginning. It may be too late to prevent many of the ills that threaten our world, but there will always be people with the single-minded vigour to go to the limits and to inspire us all.

THE OCEANS

Columbus sets the standard for what constitutes an explorer. He set out to find a route that no one had travelled previously and with no certain way of returning; and through his determined leadership – even if he was deluded about what it was he had discovered – he changed the world. The story of this 'Genoese upstart' who became so famous has inevitably become surrounded with myth and legend. This was an epic era, when visionary merchant-adventurers conspired, co-operated and competed to discover two new and unimagined continents.

Barely five years after Columbus sailed west, the route to the east was opened by Vasco da Gama, who pioneered a sea-passage to India by sailing around Africa. In 1493 the Papal Treaty of Tordesillas, having divided the unknown world between Spain and Portugal by drawing a line on a map, had effectively given this eastern approach to the Spice Islands to Portugal. By the time Ferdinand Magellan crossed the Pacific from the west in the first circumnavigation of the globe, the Portuguese were well ensconced, although he was able to claim the Philippines for Spain.

The consequences of the surge of exploration in the last decade of the 15th century were, perhaps, as significant as any in human history. From then on, Europe looked outwards and the major powers began to build their empires. The world would never be the same again. Wealth beyond the dreams of avarice lay waiting to be plundered, and plundered it was, ruthlessly, for the next 400 years. Today, as we begin to reap the dreadful harvest of our greed, it is worth pausing to consider how different the world would be if peaceful trade instead of violent conquest had been the guiding principle. If the often long-established nations encountered by the explorers had been recognized for what they were and treated with respect instead of contempt, it is possible we could have avoided the shameful atrocities wreaked upon unsuspecting

An atlas of 1519 reveals how well the Portuguese knew the west coast of Africa. While the Spanish sailed to the Americas, the Portuguese were the first Europeans to cross the equator, to round the Cape of Good Hope and to reach India and the Spice Islands beyond. They also 'discovered' and colonized Brazil, which lay 3,000 km (2,000 miles) across the Atlantic.

MARE ATLANTICVM
ISPA NIA
DORIA
LVSITAN
ISPA NIA BETICA
AFRIC
GVINEA
CANCRI

The French physician and botanist, Philibert Commerson, took part in Bougainville's 1766–69 circumnavigation of the globe. Here we see a selection of his tools, including microscope and razor, as well as his books and herbarium of pressed plant specimens.

peoples and the egregious destruction of so many pristine environments. There were some who did recognize, albeit often only dimly, the common humanity of those whose lands they encountered, but they were virtually always overruled by others with more immediate and venal aspirations.

Another national trait which, had it been different, would have changed the political map of the world for ever, was the extraordinary reluctance of the Chinese to look far beyond their borders. There was a brief moment when it might have been otherwise. In 1405 the outward-looking Yongle emperor assembled the most prodigious fleet the world had ever seen. Under the Grand Eunuch, Zheng He, 63 vast ocean-going junks set out to assert Chinese suzerainty over the known world. Having invented the compass 500 years before its general use in Europe, with ships 10 times the size of Columbus's *Santa Maria* and with 28,000 men on board, the Chinese were unassailable. On six more voyages they visited at least 35 countries and may even have reached South America, although that is disputed. Whatever the truth, this moment of possible empire-building passed, and, 50 years before Columbus sailed west, China returned to its traditional isolationism, which has continued until today.

For the next three centuries after Columbus, the oceans continued to provide the main means of discovery and conquest. As both the sailing and navigational techniques pioneered by the Portuguese, and the conditions and nutrition of sailors, improved, long journeys were made to the furthest corners of the earth. Once Magellan had proved that the world really was round, mapping rapidly advanced and it became possible to fill in many blanks. Australasia remained elusive for another hundred years and Polynesia for even longer, but gradually remote societies on isolated islands were encountered one by one, often to have their well-established lifestyles shattered by the introduction of disease and Christianity.

Louis-Antoine de Bougainville was a rare French member of the British Royal Society. He was also rare in another way: explorers tend to be a rather puritanical lot, quite a high percentage never marrying, but Bougainville provides a wonderfully Gallic contrast, being an inveterate womanizer, with a strong *joie de vivre* combined with the acute mind of a scientist. He was the first Frenchman to circumnavigate the globe and, unwittingly, he took with him the first woman to do so, Jeanne Baret, who had disguised herself as the valet of the expedition's botanist.

James Cook has rightly been described as the greatest of all explorers. A true Renaissance man, he led epic voyages of discovery and claimed Australia for the British Crown. His prodigious navigational skills took him and his crews to an astonishing number of then still unknown places in the Far East and the Pacific – journeys equivalent in distance to sailing to the moon. In spite of searching diligently for the fabled Great Southern Continent and coming within 120 km (75 miles) of Antarctica, it was not until after his death in 1779 at the hands of the Hawaiians, whose islands he had encountered in 1778, that it was reached. By this point, much of the world's oceans had been charted – but vast tracts of the continents were still unknown and unexplored.

A flywhisk handle from the Society Islands collected by James Cook on one of his voyages. Such objects would have been given freely to the sailors, while a single iron nail would buy sex with a Tahitian woman.

Christopher Columbus

THE MAN WHO CHANGED THE SHAPE OF THE WORLD

(1451–1506)

Now I observed the very great variation which I have described and because of it began to ponder this matter of the shape of the world. And I concluded that it was not round in the way that they say, but is of the same shape as a pear ... or it is as if someone had a very round ball, and at one point on its surface it was as if a woman's nipple had been put there; and this teat-like part would be the most prominent and nearest the sky; and it would be on the equator, in this Ocean Sea, at the end of the Orient.

Christopher Columbus, explaining his third voyage

Explorers are well known to be elusive, contradictory characters. Perhaps they have to be to generate the necessary will to make their journeys, and the bravado to persuade people to follow them. But of all the great explorers, Christopher Columbus must be a prime candidate for the most paradoxical. He was at the same time a brilliant navigator who was consistently mistaken in his calculations and theories, a snobbish social climber with a messianic sense of destiny, a greedy obsessive and a religious maniac.

What is so fascinating about these apparent contradictions in his character is that there are also paradoxes in sorting out fact from fiction in his own history. We have copious examples of his diaries and self-justifying letters, yet there are no contemporary portraits of him and there remains a whole library of bizarre theories about his identity. Columbus has been variously hailed as Italian, Spanish, Jewish, even American, and has been painted most recently as an aristocratic Portuguese spy. But an exhibition organized in Genoa to celebrate the 500th anniversary of his birth demonstrated the overwhelming documentary evidence that linked the man calling himself Cristóbal Colón with the Christopher Columbus born there, the son of a cloth weaver and political activist named Domenico Columbus, in 1451 – 18 months before Constantinople fell to the Ottomans, cutting Genoa off from its lucrative colonies in the Black Sea.

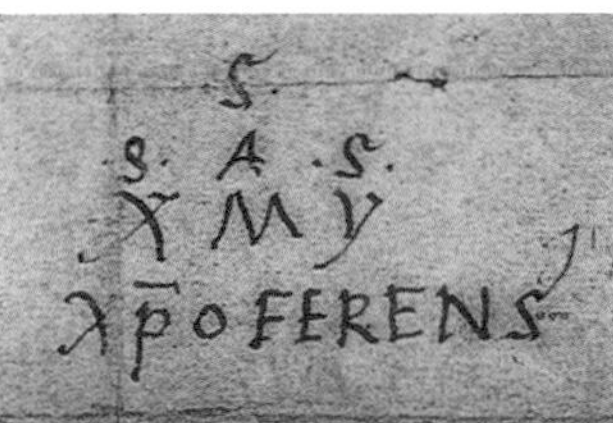

ABOVE *There is no reason to believe that any of the portraits we have of Columbus was painted by people who had actually ever seen him, but tradition suggests that this one – by Ridolfo Ghirlandaio – is the most accurate, though painted after his death.*

LEFT *Columbus began signing his name with a mysterious cryptic set of symbols. It referred to him as 'Christo Ferens' – like his namesake St Christopher, carrying Christ across the Atlantic; he believed he was God's chosen instrument.*

Columbus's coat of arms includes the crests of Castile and León, two of the four kingdoms that were eventually to make up Spain, plus the islands he discovered and his own personal symbol.

Columbus's childhood and young adulthood are also obscure. He may even have been notorious as a corsair in the ongoing struggle over Genoa between the French and Aragonese. What we do know is that in 1476 the 25-year-old Columbus was shipwrecked on the coast of Portugal when his convoy was attacked by French pirates. From there he ended up in England, probably first in Southampton, where the convoy had originally been heading, and then Bristol. Here he would have witnessed the great 15-m (50-ft) tides – a clue to the size of the Atlantic Ocean before him. It was at this point also that he must have made the trip to Iceland that he boasted about later, sailing tantalizingly close to Greenland and the edge of the known world. While in Iceland, he may well have heard stories about the old Norse settlements beyond in Helluland, Markland and Vinland. And in Galway on the way home, something happened that definitely gave him an idea for the future. A small boat was towed in containing a man and a woman who were still alive though they had been found after drifting for some time; both were of 'most unusual appearance'. Columbus believed they were Chinese.

Making Plans

The events that led Columbus across the Atlantic, as with so much else concerning him, have been both well documented and bitterly argued over. They include his marriage into an eminent family of Portuguese explorers, his time on the remote island of Porto Santo, and his correspondence with the Sage of Florence, Paolo del Pozzo Toscanelli, who had long since advocated the idea of sailing west if you wanted to reach the untold riches of the east. There was also his time in Lisbon – where he would have heard the gossip in the dockside bars.

This suggests another intriguing possibility. It seems likely that one of the people Columbus encountered in Lisbon was his fellow Genoese merchant John Cabot, by then a naturalized Venetian. The relationship between them remains hazy, yet the thrust of their stories implies that the enterprise of the Indies was in fact originally a joint project by Cabot and Columbus (along with Christopher's brother,

Bartholomew), which subsequently unravelled in debt and acrimony. Both were from Genoa and probably had connections to the same political party and to the coastal port of Savona. They were almost exactly the same age. Both were involved around the edges of the wool and silk trade from southern Europe to Bristol and London. Both frequented the same ports. And both ended up so heavily in debt in the mid-1480s that they had to leave their homes with their families to live elsewhere.

This joint venture – if it did emerge between them in Lisbon – involved a tentative answer to the key problem: they would need some means by which they could profit from their discoveries. One option for prospective explorers in those days was to hitch themselves to a monarch, but that gave them no personal rights over the territory they discovered: they would be rewarded and that would be the end of the matter for them. What Columbus and Cabot both developed was something different – an agreement with a monarch that, if they succeeded, they would get a cut of all the proceeds of their discovery, as well as other rights. If their plan had worked, and they had reached China, this would have made them the richest men in the world.

The Mappa Mundi *of Juan de la Cosa, the owner of the* Santa Maria *who sailed with Columbus on his first two voyages, was drawn around 1500 and contains the oldest known representation of the New World, visible to the left. It was discovered in a junk shop by the Seine, Paris, in 1831.*

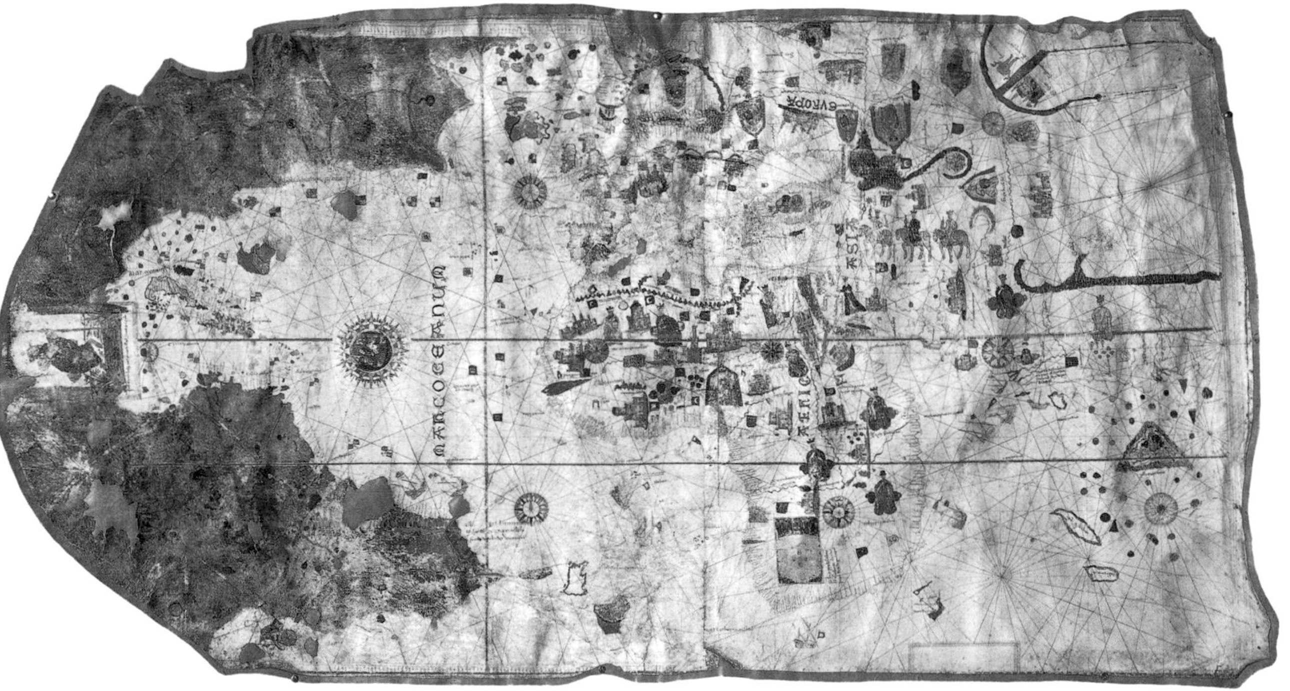

Whatever the truth of the matter, Columbus abandoned the idea of involving the Portuguese. He and his brother Bartholomew then offered the enterprise instead in turn to Castile, England and France, without success. But, thanks to the backing of the Castilian treasurer, Luis Santángel, Columbus was finally given his chance by the monarchs of Castile, Ferdinand and Isabella. So it was that the *Santa Maria*, *Nina* and *Pinta* sailed from Palos in August 1492.

The First Voyage

Once at sea, Columbus, who was congenitally over-optimistic, continually exaggerated their progress. But he kept a set of parallel charts to convince the crews that their journey into the unknown was not irreversible, and these were actually more accurate. Even so, his crews were in open revolt when, at 10 p.m. on 11 October, Columbus thought he saw something on the horizon 'like a little wax candle, rising and falling'. Then at 2 a.m. the following morning, the lookout on the *Pinta* sighted land. Columbus named the small island San Salvador, took the royal standard ashore and fell on his knees on the beach. He next turned his attention to the naked people watching him and gave them red caps and glass beads 'and many things of slight value in which they took much pleasure'.

The tragedy of Columbus's achievement, and his settlements on the island of Hispaniola – which the natives called Haiti – was that his delight at the innocence of the natives soon turned into desperate frustration at the lack of gold, followed by brutal suppression and finally genocide. It was to become the pattern of the relationship between the Old World and the New, and largely because Columbus's expedition was not so much exploration as speculation. It had to make a profit. It eventually did so, but the basic problem was that Columbus was wrong about the sea route to China. His calculations were mistaken. He had underestimated the circumference of the earth by a quarter and yet refused to believe it, even when it was clear to all his contemporaries that a vast new continent stood in the way.

On Christmas night, *Santa Maria* ran aground and sank. Its wood was rescued with the help of the locals and turned into a small settlement, where Columbus left the crew under the command of Diego de Arana, the cousin of his mistress. On the return voyage to Europe, Columbus had to rescue his crew from arrest by the Portuguese in the Azores and then lost touch with Martin Pinzón in the *Pinta* – nearly also losing the credit for his discovery as a result. He finally stumbled by mistake into Lisbon harbour and had to face a difficult and dangerous interview with the Portuguese king.

Theodor de Bry imagining Columbus's first encounter with the Tainos, the Caribbean peoples who populated the islands he discovered. This image dates from a century after the events it portrays, but some scene like this did happen. Columbus was initially charmed by the simplicity of the people he met.

ADMIRAL OF THE OCEAN SEA

Safely back in Castile, Columbus was addressed by the delighted Ferdinand and Isabella by all the titles he had demanded if he succeeded: 'Admiral of the Ocean Sea', 'Viceroy' and 'Governor of the islands that have been discovered in the Indies'. On his way to see them in Valencia he processed through the streets – proud and unsmiling, with six of his captives around him, almost naked, wearing as much gold and finery as he could find, each of them carrying a brightly coloured parrot in a cage. Among those who watched him was Cabot.

Columbus was desperate to get back, and in September 1493 he sailed from Cadiz with 17 ships, 1,300 men, including colonists, cavaliers and friars, and instructions from Isabella to convert the natives and to treat them kindly. But this was also the moment when his fortunes began to change, starting with the grim discovery the moment he arrived back on Hispaniola. His first New World settlement, La Navidad, had disappeared and its inhabitants were dead. A small faction had roamed about the island stealing gold and women, and the islanders had exacted a terrible revenge.

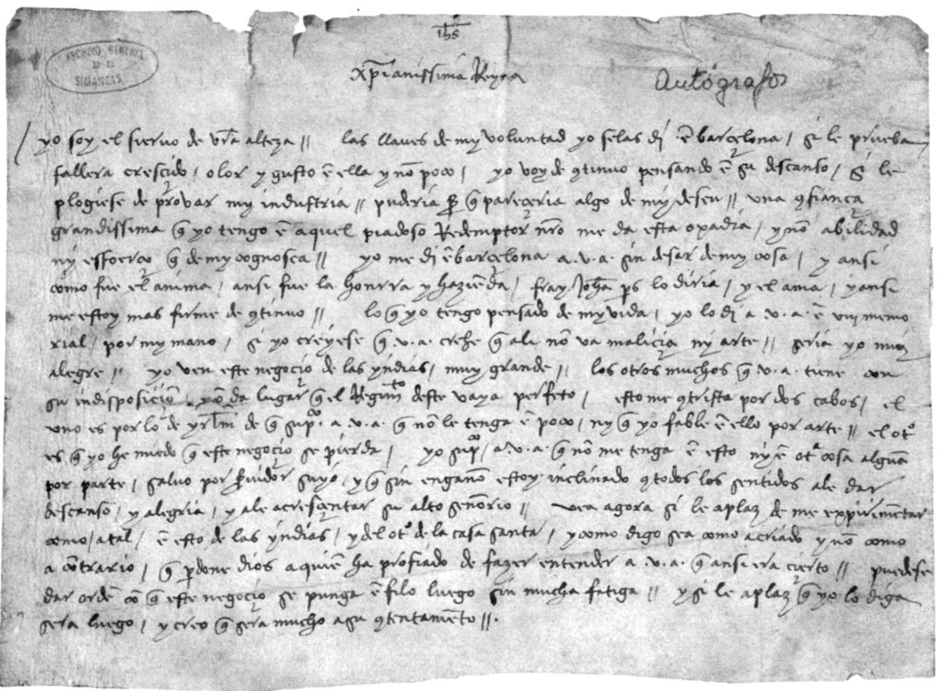
ihs
Xpianissima Reyna
Autógrafos

yo soy el siervo de vra alteza ...

Columbus felt an enormous emotional bond with Queen Isabella, and many of his letters are addressed to her, such as this one, from the Archivo General de Simancas, Spain. Her continuing belief in Columbus allowed him to rehabilitate himself for each new voyage.

In deteriorating health, and despite voyages to Cuba, Trinidad and the coast of what is now Venezuela, Columbus clung rigidly to his original theory. Nothing deflected him from the conviction that he had found the way to the Indies and his belief that he was God's chosen instrument. But his enslavement of the natives of Hispaniola, the Tainos, brought him into conflict with the one person in authority who really admired and valued him, Queen Isabella. His brutal treatment of his fellow colonists, his hangings and other cruel punishments, all of which had been expressly forbidden by her, also led to a growing political clamour for his removal. He was sent home from his third voyage in chains.

Despite his fall from grace, Columbus was allowed one last expedition. He called it the 'High Voyage' and it was intended finally to break through to the Indies and bring back enough gold to restore his lost titles. Instead, it ended with him marooned on the beach in St Ann's Bay, Jamaica, in armed conflict with half his companions and awaiting rescue from his enemies in Hispaniola.

It was at this point, when the local natives refused to supply any more food, that Columbus performed his famous trick with the eclipse. He discovered in his almanac that an eclipse of the moon was due on 29 February 1504. Bartholomew therefore summoned all the chiefs nearby to meet them that night and, when they had arrived, Columbus told them that if no more food was forthcoming, God would punish them by making the moon disappear. Right on cue, the shadow began to cover the moon and the villagers begged him for forgiveness. Timing his response carefully, he said it would only reappear if they promised to bring regular supplies of food. The supplies began again the following day.

Columbus spent his final years in increasing ill-health, complaining bitterly about his treatment by the sovereigns and his poverty. He was not actually poor. The ship carrying his own gold had been the only one which had escaped the disastrous hurricane (a Taino word) that destroyed the returning fleet of his nemesis Francisco de Bobadilla, but he felt poor.

He died in Valladolid on 20 May 1506 aged only 54, in a small house, looked after by the Franciscans whom he had long admired. There was scarcely any contemporary mention of his death. Cruel, mistaken and obsessive, he was undoubtedly a great navigator and – although he never recognized the truth about where he had been – a great pioneer.

Vasco da Gama

BY SEA TO INDIA

(1469/70–1524)

God gave the Portuguese a small country as cradle
but all the world as their grave.

17th-century Portuguese Jesuit António Vieira

The vast sweep of the Portuguese discoveries during the 15th century is generally unappreciated for its far-reaching consequences. It is not too much to say that the world as we know it, for better and for worse, came into being because of the Portuguese, and the pivotal act of the Portuguese accomplishment was Vasco da Gama's discovery of the all-sea passage to India.

The Portuguese expeditions were a part of a decades-long, systematic exploration of the unknown world. No other nation in history spread itself so widely, so fast, so utterly. It was the Portuguese who opened the way into the Atlantic and were the first to sail down the west coast of Africa. They were the first Europeans to cross the equator, to double the African continent, as well as being the first to reach India, then Asia beyond, by sea from Europe. In the Americas they 'discovered' Brazil.

In their quest to establish a sea route to India and gain access to its lucrative spice trade, the Portuguese invented, or adapted, the latest advances in navigation and modified their ships repeatedly. It was the Portuguese caravels, with the exotic lines of their hulls and triangular lateen sails, that made it all possible. The most disturbing aspect of the Age of Discovery was the introduction of black African slaves into the European economy. The Portuguese did not invent slavery, nor did they create African slavery, but they gave it a scale unknown previously and brought untold misery and suffering to countless millions through its merciless application.

The Passage to India

Neither rich nor aristocratic, the Gama family had a long and renowned history of service to the crown. Gama's father was a *cavaleiro* and was for a time the captain and *alcaide-mór* (similar to mayor) of Sines, where Gama was born in either 1469 or 1470. He grew up during the fascinating time when the accounts of the Portuguese discoveries had already become legend and continued to unfold with each new sailing season. Gama became a skilled navigator, probably among the best in Europe, and fought with distinction in Portugal's war with Castile. In 1492 he was given a delicate assignment by the then king, which he handled with uncommon dispatch and integrity.

Significantly, Vasco da Gama was not allied with any of the families in historic opposition to the king. And so when King Manuel I planned an expedition to discover a sea route to India, the honour fell to the young Vasco, since the last thing the king wanted was for his venture to bring wealth and distinction to any potential rivals.

Vasco da Gama is one of those rarest of explorers who succeeded in every mission, and who enjoyed celebrity, honour and enormous riches in his lifetime (from the Livro de Lisuarte de Abreu, 1565).

The voyage was audacious in the extreme and this first passage to India was the 15th-century equivalent of a contemporary mission to Mars. About 175 men formed the crew of the modest four-ship armada. Amid enormous fanfare and in the presence of King Manuel, the fleet set sail from Belém, just south of Lisbon, on 8 July 1497. In a manoeuvre known as the *Volta da Guine* they sailed in a great loop southwestwards, entirely out of sight of land, over an estimated 5,420 km (3,370 miles), yet anchored within 160 km (100 miles) of their target in southern Africa on 4 November. It remains one of the most remarkable sailing accomplishments in world history.

Contact with the indigenous populations was largely benign, with some exceptions, until the Portuguese encountered the region of Arab, and Muslim, dominance at Mozambique Island on 1 March. Once the local ruler determined the visitors were Christians he ordered an attack on them. The pilots Gama had obtained attempted to wreck the ships. Overcoming this treachery, he managed to get his fleet, now reduced to three vessels, to Mombasa on 7 April. Relations here were no better, and the Portuguese fought off a determined night attack. But a week later, at Malindi, Gama encountered a friendly Regent who was in competition with the ruler in Mombasa and who allowed reprovisioning, and, best of all, provided a skilled pilot. In 23 days, sailing with favourable monsoon winds, the ships crossed the Arabian Sea and arrived off the Malabar Coast in southern India on 20 May.

The Impact of Gama's Voyage

India had known conquerors, many of them far more violent and lethal than the Portuguese ever proved to be, but the coming of the Portuguese and the other Europeans who followed in their wake changed the subcontinent permanently. Just as the Muslims had blocked direct European contact with India, so they had likewise barred the Hindus in India from direct European interaction as well.

Though initial relations were friendly, the local Arab traders persuaded the ruler in Calicut to deny a trade agreement. Reluctantly accepting the inevitable, and on learning of more treachery, Gama sailed north, refitted and resupplied. Then, on 29 August, against the advice of his pilot, he set sail for Africa in the absence of the vital monsoon winds. In a deadly passage lasting just under three months, the Portuguese lost to scurvy nearly half of those who died on the entire voyage, and when the remaining two ships reached Portugal just 44 of those who had sailed remained alive.

The voyage had taken two years and Gama and his crew had sailed 23,000 nautical miles, greater than the distance around the world at the equator. They had accomplished what only decades earlier had been considered unattainable. Cast as Homeric heroes, their expedition was portrayed as a national epic of divine providence. Gama became the greatest Portuguese of all time. The Portuguese king profited immensely from the nearly insatiable demand for spices stimulated by their new abundance through regular trade with the east. Production there rose dramatically, while the price in Europe actually increased threefold. King Manuel lived in luxury such as had not been seen in Europe since the Roman emperors.

Vasco da Gama returned to India twice again. His third voyage came late in life in 1524, when he was 54 years old. There, Dom Vasco da Gama, Admiral of India and Count of Vidigueira, took ill shortly after landing and died peacefully a few months later. His final resting place is at the Mosteiro dos Jerónimos in Belém.

The epic voyage of Vasco da Gama is arguably among the most significant in human history, as it brought about the first direct meeting of men from the west with those of the east since Alexander the Great, and from it came permanent contact and interaction. The consequence was to impose European superiority in technology and weapons across the world. It spread Christianity and western culture to the most distant lands. The conflict between Christians and Muslims which it renewed has scarcely played itself out even now.

To sail the incredible distances necessary to reach India by sea from Europe, the Portuguese invented new ships and new methods of navigation, as seen in the Livro das Armadas, *a late 15th- to early 16th-century manuscript.*

No Anno de 502 – 4

Tornou aa Jndia Dom Vasq̃ da gama Almirante por capitão mór, e partio a dez de feur͠o co vinte vellas, repartidas em tres capitanias – ss – Vicente sodree tio delle dom Vasquo da gama jrmão de sua may q̃ leuaua a sucessão por capitão mór de cinq̃ vellas que avião de figar na Jndia em fauor das feytorias de cochi e cananor, e tambem pera e alguũs meses do verão jrem guardar a boca do estreyto do mar Roxo, e a capitania mór doutras cinq̃ vellas que não estauão prestes se deu a estevão da gama primo co jrmão de Vasquo da gama, que depoys partio a primeyro dabril; na qual frota hião estes capitães &

C francisq̃ da cunha D
das jlhas terceyras.

C Antonio do campo D
com temporal esgarrou e mes perdido foy Jnvernar e huã jlhas na costa de Mellinde sem saber onde estaua

Ferdinand Magellan

CIRCUMNAVIGATING THE GLOBE

(1480–1521)

Most versed in nautical charts, he knew better than any other the true art of navigation, of which it is certain proof that he knew by his genius, and his intrepidity, without anyone having given him the example, how to attempt the circuit of the globe, which he had almost completed.

Antonio Pigafetta, Journal

Ferdinand Magellan attempted the ultimate ground-truthing project. His expedition was the first actually to prove that the earth is round and that its circumference is just over 40,000 km (24,855 miles). He achieved this despite the fact that the map he was using on his voyage was 11,000 km (6,835 miles) out because it missed most of the Pacific.

Magellan was born in Portugal in 1480, and although his parents died when he was nine, the family's connections and influence meant that he was taken on as a royal page when he was 12. In 1505, aged 25, he was sent to India to help install Francisco de Almeida as the Portuguese Viceroy there, and to establish military and naval bases along the route. It is clear that Magellan was a talented seaman and a brave fighter (he took part in the battle of Diu in 1509), but his stubborn determination often led to trouble, and shortly after being promoted to captain he was sent back to Portugal in disgrace after disobeying fleet orders.

Controversy followed him after his next success too. In 1512 Magellan sailed to Morocco, where he received a severe leg wound while fighting against the Moorish stronghold in the battle of Azamor in 1513. Although he had distinguished himself in battle again, Magellan was accused of illegal trade with the Islamic Moors. Several of the accusations were unfounded, but Magellan ultimately fell out of favour with King Manuel I, who told him that he would have no further employment in his country's service. So in 1517, at the age of 37, Magellan formally turned his back on Portugal, renounced his nationality and travelled to Spain to offer his services to Charles V. On arrival there he changed his name from Fernão de Magalhães to Fernando de Magallanes.

The Route West to the East

For Spain at this time finding a route to Asia by travelling west was the ultimate strategic goal, since Portugal had the monopoly on the route east. In 1513, Vasco Núñez de Balboa had crossed the Panama isthmus and sailed along the Pacific coast – becoming first European to do so. Magellan was determined to make a passage to the Spice Islands and if he could not do it for his native country then he would lead an expedition there under Spanish colours, and this would mean going west. He convinced Charles V that he could succeed since he not only had the skills and resolve, but he had also come to Spain equipped with new information and maps about a possible route through the tip of South America. The value of a west-about route was almost literally priceless and the king gave full support for the expedition. In August 1519 Magellan set sail from Seville in command of a fleet of five ships: *Victoria, Trinidad, San Antonio, Concepción* and *Santiago*.

Though Magellan himself did not survive the expedition he led in search of a route west to the Spice Islands, it was his ruthless determination that led to its ultimate success.

Conditions were difficult from the start and Magellan learned that some of the captains were threatening mutiny. Juan de Cartagena, captain of the *San Antonio*, refused to take orders from Magellan and was relieved of his command. In addition, Antonio Salamón, captain of the *Victoria*, was condemned to death for sodomizing a cabin boy. Dissatisfaction was made worse by problems with the quality and quantity of the ships' provisions, which meant that in mid-Atlantic the crews were put on reduced rations. Such difficulties had to be resolved against the backdrop of superstitions and beliefs that interpreted the natural phenomenon of St Elmo's Fire as a divine presence. Antonio Pigafetta, a Venetian scholar and the expedition chronicler, recorded: 'During these storms the body of St Anselm appeared to us several times. And among others on a night which was very dark, at a time of bad weather, the said saint appeared in the form of a lighted torch at the height of the maintop, and remained there more than two hours and a half, to the comfort of us all.'

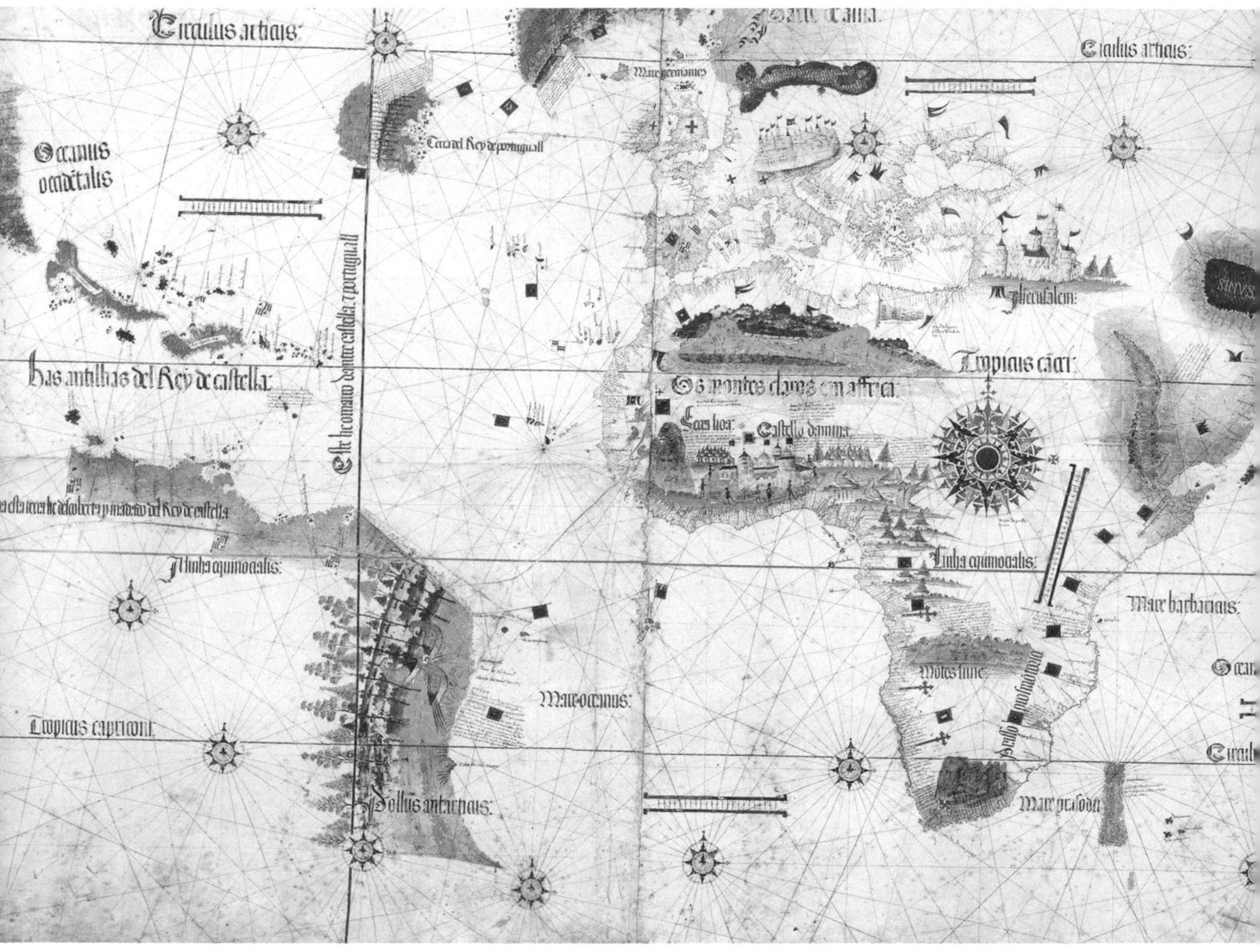

The division of the world: in 1493, by the Treaty of Tordesillas, Pope Alexander VI decided on a dividing line in the Atlantic, west of the Cape Verde Islands (at approximately 46° 30′ west) and decreed that everything to the west of this line would belong to Spain, and everything to the east to Portugal. Because the known route to the Indian Ocean at this time was by sailing east, this effectively gave all access at that time to the valuable Spice Islands to Portugal. This detail from the Cantino map of 1502 shows the Portuguese interpretation of the line's position.

In December they reached the coast of Brazil, close to present-day city of Rio de Janeiro, and Magellan then started the search for the passage through the landmass of South America. Almost every inlet, deep bay and river mouth was investigated, while all the time travelling south, towards winter and worse weather. Supplies were

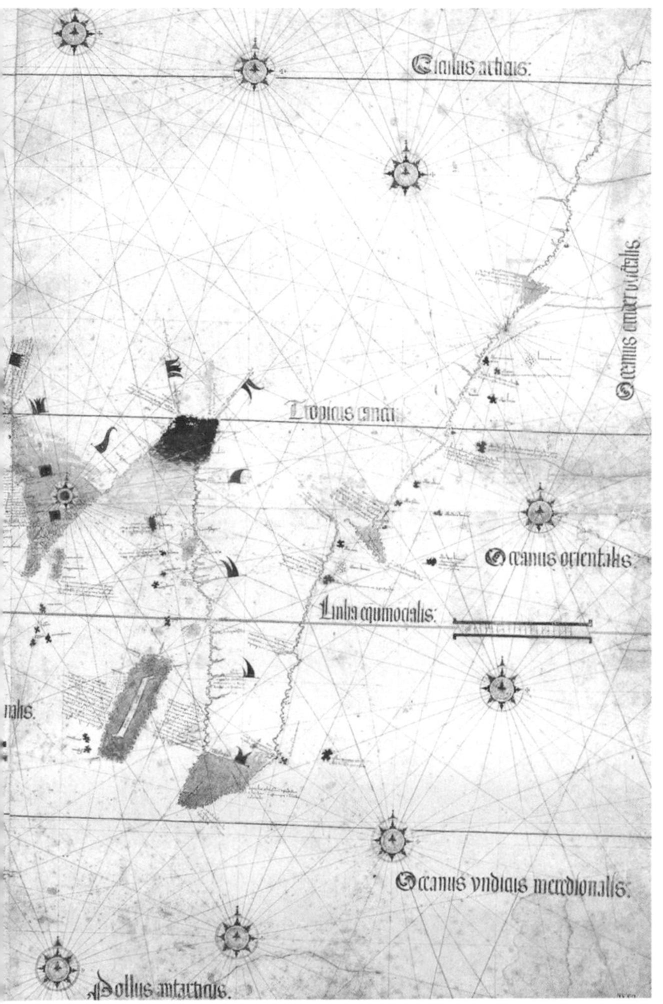

running out, and this, combined with the trials and difficulties of handling the ships through uncharted waters and the occasional running aground, led to calls from some of the captains for their leader to order the expedition home. Magellan, with his customary determination, was certain he could find the passage and insisted on continuing south.

By March the situation was so bad that it was clear they would have to winter on the South American coast, so they anchored in Puerto San Julían, at approximately 49° south. It was a good anchorage, with hardwood trees for repairing the battered ships and there were birds, seals and fish for reprovisioning. But the atrocious weather meant that repairs were slow and Magellan was anticipating a long winter – everyone was now put on survival rations.

Discontent thrived, and in April Magellan heard of another conspiracy against him. He acted quickly by sending a boat to the *Victoria* to have one of the mutinous leaders, Captain Mendoza, killed in a surprise attack. The mutineers succeeded in taking control of some of the ships, but Magellan prevented any of them from leaving by blocking the inlet. The combination of swift, ruthless action and sufficient remaining loyalty among the men meant that Magellan managed to quell the mutiny. He then issued the penalties: 40 men were sentenced to death, which was later commuted to hard labour; San Martín, an astrologer, was tortured; others, including Gaspar de Quesada, the captain of *Concepción* were executed. Cartagena and Pero Sánchez de la Reina, a priest, were later left marooned on the coast, along with the impaled bodies of those who had been executed.

Through the Strait to the Pacific

Magellan then sent the *Santiago* south to continue the search, but while exploring a likely route, which turned out to be yet another river, the ship was caught in a gale and wrecked ashore. Two of the crew made it overland back to the other ships and the rest were rescued. By October, with the remaining four ships repaired and reprovisioned, the search for the route west continued. They finally entered the passage at 52° south. In the confusion of the 480 km (300 miles) of maze-like channels they had to struggle through, the *San Antonio* took the opportunity to escape and make a run for home. But Magellan, now with three ships and about 200 men, persevered. Eventually, at the end of November 1520, they left the confines of the Strait and entered the Pacific.

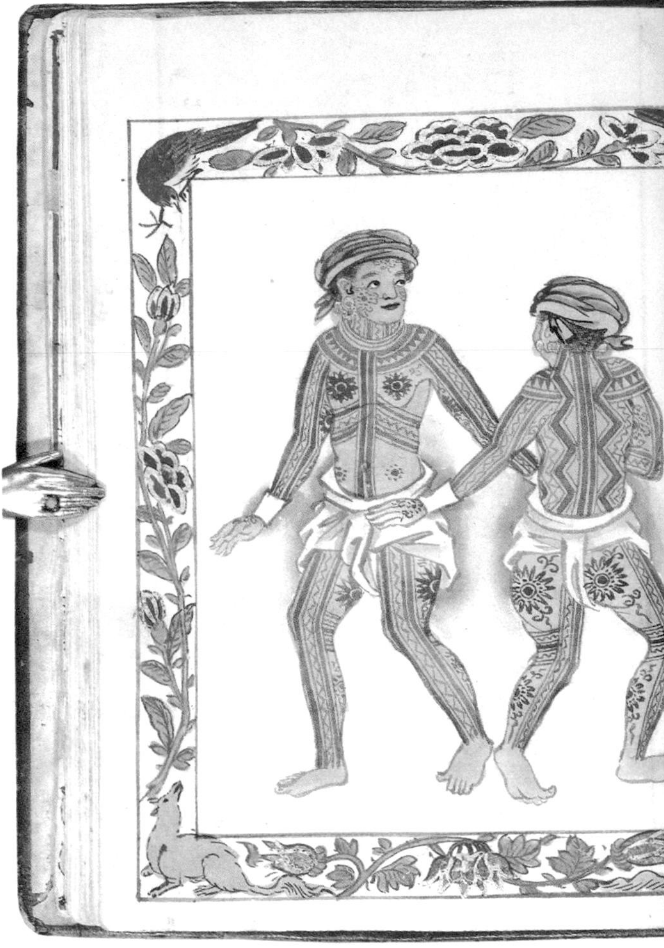

Magellan's charts were based on Ptolemy's calculations of the 2nd century AD, which underestimated the circumference of the earth by 11,000 km (6,835 miles). This meant that Magellan would have expected his Pacific passage to have been far shorter than the 96-day epic it turned out to be. Supplies of food and water ran out, scurvy became prevalent and the crew were at the utmost limits of survival. As Pigafetta recorded: 'we ate only old biscuit turned to powder, all full of worms and stinking of urine which the rats had made on it, having eaten the good.... And of the rats, which were sold for half an écu apiece, some of us could not get enough.... I believe that nevermore will any man undertake to make such a voyage.'

In early March the survivors first landed at Guam, where they found food; later that month they arrived at Homonhon Island and Magellan claimed the Philippines for Spain. The ships sailed among the island group for a month, enjoying the relatively easy trading, friendly natives, good food and an increasing intimacy with women. Magellan used this opportunity to baptize as many people as possible: converting communities to Christianity was all part of establishing a Spanish stronghold.

The Death of Magellan

Magellan followed the Portuguese approach he had grown up with, which was to befriend a local chief and help him win battles against his enemies in order to earn support in the area. On Cebú, Magellan became a close friend and then 'blood brother' of Rajah Humabon, the island's leader, who was converted to Christianity. Humabon's enemy was Lapu Lapu, on the nearby island of Mactan, and so Magellan made a promise to attack and kill the latter. Magellan felt certain of an easy victory and took only a small party of men ashore at Mactan. But for once his supreme confidence was mistaken, as he and his men found themselves facing 1,500 well-trained, fierce warriors. In the battle Magellan was killed and hacked to pieces. Eight of his men were also slaughtered and the rest fled back to the ships. As the shocked Pigafetta recorded: 'all these people threw themselves on him, and one of them with a large javelin (which is like a [scimitar], only thicker) thrust it into his left leg, whereby he fell face downward. On this all at once rushed upon him with lances of iron and of bamboo and with these javelins, so that they slew our mirror, our light, our comfort, and our true guide.'

Islanders of Cebú, in the Philippines, depicted in a 16th-century Sino-Spanish codex. Magellan set about converting the population and became a blood brother of Cebú's leader, promising to attack his enemy on the nearby island of Mactan, which led to Magellan's death.

The Spice Islands and the Voyage Home

The remaining 115 men were not sufficient to sail the three ships, so the *Concepción* had to be scuttled and the *Victoria* and *Trinidad* made for the riches of the Spice Islands. They spent six months sailing between Mindanao, Palawan and Brunei, capturing some local pilots to help find the route, fighting tribal leaders for food and supplies, taking women hostage for an onboard harem, and losing some men from desertion and a few others from the skirmishes. Eventually, in November 1521, they reached the Moluccas – the Spice Islands.

Having traded goods for the sought-after spices it became clear that the *Trinidad* was in poor condition and it was decided that it should return to Spain by going back east. But after seven months, overcome by scurvy and on the verge of sinking, the *Trinidad* sailed once more to the Moluccas to find them now in the hands of the Portuguese; the crew were imprisoned.

The *Victoria*, with Juan Sebastián Elcano as captain and 60 crew, was loaded with tons of cloves and in December 1521 headed west for the run home. The ship needed constant repairs and they laid up in Timor and Java, where some of the crew deserted. By the time they rounded the Cape of Good Hope the only supplies they had were rice and foul water. Twenty more men were lost to starvation and in July Elcano realized that he would have to risk putting into the Cape Verde islands, a Portuguese holding, to take on essential supplies. Having acquired a minimal amount they came under attack, and Elcano had to sail on, abandoning 13 men. The rest sailed north in a ship leaking so much that it required constant pumping and with virtually no rations. On 10 September 1522 the *Victoria* and her crew, now numbering just 18, arrived at Seville. The single cargo of cloves was so valuable that it paid for all the expenses of the expedition and made a profit.

Although Magellan never completed the circumnavigation himself, his ruthless, single-minded determination meant that his dream of finding a western route to the Spice Islands was realized. The voyage also helped establish the International Date Line, because the crew of the *Victoria* realized on their return trip that their calendars were out by one day. They had discovered the passage through the tip of South America and observed two of our closest galaxies, all now named after Magellan. But most significant of all, the voyage proved that our earth is round.

An illustration from a French manuscript of Pigafetta's journal, showing four of the main spice-growing islands of the Moluccas, with a stylized rendering of the coveted clove tree.

Louis-Antoine de Bougainville

FRENCH ENTERPRISE IN THE PACIFIC

(1729–1811)

But geography is a science of facts: one cannot speculate from an armchair without the risk of making mistakes which are often corrected only at the expense of the sailors.

Louis-Antoine de Bougainville, **Voyage autour du monde**, *1771*

One of the most colourful characters of Pacific exploration, Louis-Antoine de Bougainville was born in Paris on 12 November 1729. The youngest of three children in a well-to-do family, Louis-Antoine first studied law but soon realized his passion lay in mathematics, publishing a two-volume treatise on calculus at the age of 25. This not only brought him to the attention of the learned élite of Paris, where his brother, Marie-Jean, was also a respected scholar, it also won him election to the British Royal Society in 1756. The same year, Charles de Brosses published his masterly history of Pacific exploration, but neither Bougainville nor his brother could have guessed it would change the direction of Louis-Antoine's life.

Bougainville entered a military career, first as a musketeer then aide-de-camp and finally, after a spell in London as secretary to the French ambassador, captain. At the start of the Seven Years War, a struggle between Britain and France for control over North America, he made his first significant voyage when he travelled to New France (Canada) in April 1756 with the Marquis de Montcalm. The lifeline of the French colonists was along the St Lawrence River to Quebec and Montreal and Bougainville spent much of his time between sorties there, reading extensively from his library of the Classics and playing as hard as he worked.

French fortunes waned with the disastrous loss of Louisbourg Fort, which guarded the mouth of the St Lawrence, and the fall of Quebec to the British in September 1759. Ultimately forced to retreat to Montreal, Bougainville took part in the last stand against the British, which ended in the French army's final surrender in

Tahitians presenting fruits to Bougainville, attended by his officers. Philibert Commerson, the naturalist on this voyage, collected large numbers of botanical specimens in Tahiti; the Tahitians were more interested in his 'valet', Jeanne Baret, whom they outed as a woman.

September 1760. There was no option for him but to return to France, stripped of all military honours and forbidden to fight for the rest of the war.

Frustrated with life on parole, he soon found solace in womanizing (including a relationship with the famous French actress Sophie Arnauld) and gambling, as well as more high-brow trips to the salons. By the time he was allowed to take an active part in the war again it was over: the Treaty of Paris was signed in February 1763. France was left humiliated by its overseas losses, demoralized and virtually bankrupt.

Les Îles Malouines

With characteristic optimism, by early 1763 Bougainville was already planning an ambitious scheme to recover some French pride and his own fortunes. Encouraged by his brother and Charles de Brosses, he had read widely on Pacific exploration and the possibilities it presented for discovering new lands to rebuild France's empire and provide a home for those colonists displaced from Canada. And Bougainville knew just the place to start.

During the war, he had learnt about the Îles Malouines (Falkland Islands). This had planted the seed of an idea in Bougainville's mind to settle there the French Acadians dispossessed from their lands in Nova Scotia. By making these uninhabited islands French, he could secure the gateway to the Pacific and control the passage from the Atlantic into the Pacific Ocean. With little state money on offer, Bougainville set up his own company, purchasing two ships – *Aigle* and *Sphynx*. With the blessing of the king, Louis XV, the ships set sail for the Malouines in September 1763. In April 1764, France took possession of the islands, leaving 29 colonists to make a new life under the control of Bougainville's cousin.

Bougainville returned in January 1765, finding the colony in good shape. Having restocked with food, timber and saplings, he again headed home to discover that not only had Spain demanded that France give up all claims to the islands, but, worse still, the French government had agreed. Throughout the winter and spring of 1766, Bougainville tried – and failed – to argue his case, but it was too late: although he won compensation for his losses, he sailed in November to hand over the growing colony to the Spanish – and begin a much greater adventure.

A Voyage Round the World

With two ships – *Boudeuse* and *Étoile* – Bougainville now began one of the first ever scientific expeditions, re-igniting French dreams of maritime dominance. Passing through the Strait of Magellan, he finally arrived in the Pacific at the end of January

1768 and headed northwest. Three months later, he sighted, named and took possession of the Dangerous (Tuamotu) Archipelago – though without actually landing.

In April, Bougainville sailed into a paradisal series of islands he called Nouvelle Cythère (Tahiti). He claimed them for France and nine days later sailed again, having taken on board a local man, Ahu-toru (Aotourou) to convey back to France. There, Ahu-toru would more than fulfil French ideas about the 'Noble Savage' and confirm the impression of Tahiti as a Pacific utopia as described by Bougainville: 'The climate upon the whole is so healthy that, notwithstanding the hard work we have done in this island, though our men were continually ... exposed to the meridian sun, though they slept upon the bare soil and in the open air, none of them fell sick there'.

Bougainville now passed through the modern Samoan group of islands, the Hoorn Islands and then on to 'Austrialia del Espíritu Santo' (Vanuatu), which had been discovered and named by Pedro Fernández de Quirós on his expedition of 1605. Here, the French first met with the Melanesians of the Pacific, an uneasy encounter that ended in a skirmish. Anxious to push on, at the end of May Bougainville sailed west in search of New Holland (Australia). A few days later, the sound of breakers alerted the ships to a dangerous reef – an outlier to Australia's Great Barrier Reef. Though some of his men believed they could see land from the mastheads, their

An engraving of the 1820s showing Bougainville hoisting the French colours on a small rock near Cape Forward in the Strait of Magellan. After a slow start to the voyage and delays caused by weather in the Strait, Bougainville finally entered the Pacific Ocean on 16 January 1768.

captain steered away northeast towards New Guinea (leaving the exploration of Australia to James Cook: p. 46), but again they found it too unsafe to land. Having sailed on to the Solomon Islands, where there were more skirmishes with the Melanesian population, Bougainville then tracked via New Ireland back to New Guinea's northern coast and towards the Spice Islands.

Supplies were critically low and *Étoile* was in poor shape, so it was with huge relief that the ships finally arrived in Dutch-controlled Ceram in August 1768. The French were reluctantly allowed into harbour for emergency repairs and restocking, but sailed six days later for Batavia (Jakarta), where both the men and the *Boudeuse* and *Étoile* could be properly restored. From here, they sailed to Île de France (Mauritius). The naturalist Philibert Commerson and Jeanne Baret, his 'valet', discovered in fact to be a woman, elected to stay there. With *Étoile* needing further repairs, the *Boudeuse* sailed alone for Cape Town, but by April 1769 both ships had arrived back in France.

Aftermath

Bougainville became a great celebrity, feted even by the king: he had made the first successful French circumnavigation of the globe and had returned with the 'Noble Savage', Ahu-toru, and seven new 'possessions' for France. Aged 40, he was promoted and granted a life pension of 50,000 livres by the impoverished French government.

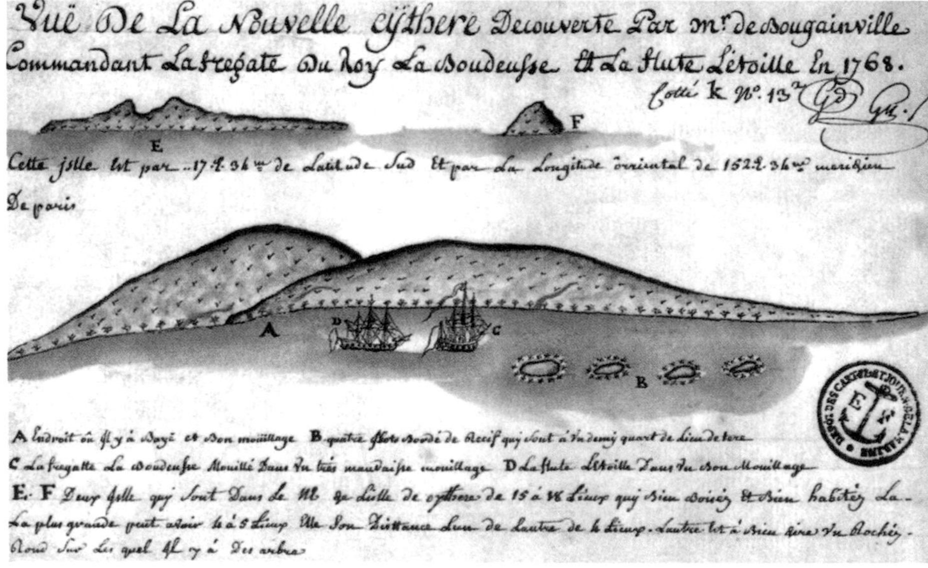

View of Tahiti, called La Nouvelle Cythère by Bougainville. Despite spending only nine days here, French reports helped create the idea of Tahiti as Utopia, inhabited by real-life 'Noble Savages'.

The first English edition of Bougainville's A Voyage Round the World, *of 1772, translated by Johann Reinhold Forster. Originally published in French in 1771, it was an instant success.*

Ahu-toru was offered transport home as far as Mauritius, but he contracted smallpox there and died before reaching Tahiti.

Bougainville's journal was published in 1771 to popular acclaim but academic frustration: not only had half the time of the expedition been eaten up by the handover of the Malouines, but Samoa, Vanuatu and Tahiti were left only partially explored. Furthermore, Commerson and the astronomer Veron had stayed in Mauritius with all their notes and collections, undermining the journal's scientific achievements.

Later, having returned from action in the American Revolutionary War, Bougainville advised both Jean-François de Galaup de la Pérouse on his own Pacific exploration and then Nicolas Baudin on his voyage to Australia in 1800. Bougainville survived several narrow escapes during the French Revolution and met and became close friends with Napoleon Bonaparte, being later elected Senator. In 1804, with the support of Napoleon, he became one of the first to receive the new *Legion d'Honneur*, and in 1808 was elevated to Compte de Bougainville.

On 30 August 1811, Louis-Antoine de Bougainville died and was given a state funeral. His ashes were placed in the Pantheon and his heart was buried next to his wife in Montmartre. France had lost one of its most flamboyant and brilliant characters – a soldier, sailor, statesman and scientist: a Renaissance man of the Enlightenment.

James Cook

SCIENTIFIC EXPLORATION OF THE SOUTH SEAS

(1728–1779)

Ambition leads me not only farther than any other man has been before me, but as far as I think it is possible for a man to go.

James Cook, Journals, 30 January 1774

In three epic voyages, Captain James Cook discovered more of the earth's surface than any other man. A prolific seaman, he was also an acclaimed cartographer, astronomer and surveyor, pioneering the new era of scientific navigation and filling in a third of the world map. As a commander, he was the seaman's seaman, winning the loyalty – even love – of his men, some of whom sailed with him time and time again. In life, his achievements left his superiors breathless; in death, he became an icon of the British empire, while his legacy spawned a generation of great navigators including William Bligh and George Vancouver. It is now widely accepted that Coleridge's *The Rime of the Ancient Mariner* was inspired by and partly based on Cook's second voyage.

Portrait of James Cook by John Webber. Cook was already internationally famous by the time of his third voyage, for which Webber was appointed artist.

When James Cook was born on 27 October 1728 in a small cottage in northern England, there was nothing to indicate that he would go on to become a national – even international – legend. Aged eight, the boy's promise was noted by a wealthy landowner, Thomas Scottowe, who paid for four years' schooling. This allowed Cook to get his first job in 1745 as shop-boy in Staithes. Here, he fell in love with the sea, and in July 1746 he signed up as an apprentice in the merchant navy to the respected Whitby

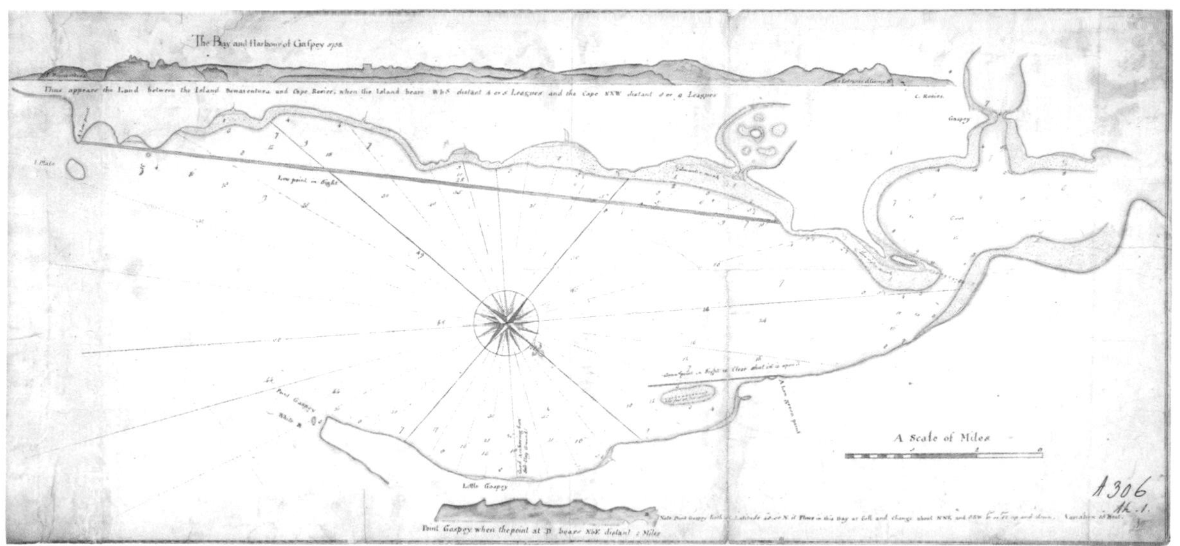

Cook's chart of the Bay of Gaspé, 1758. This was Cook's first attempt at chartmaking and reflects the political and strategic desire to understand the landscape of Canada, where the British were fighting the French for control.

ship-owners John and Henry Walker. Cook, now 18, was older than his peers, educated and with a reputation for hard work. Signing him on as a three-year servant, John Walker laid the foundations for both a legend and the deepest friendship Cook would ever have.

The North Sea was a harsh training ground. Cook's first recorded voyage was as 'servant' in the *Freelove*, a broad, flat-bottomed Whitby 'cat' or collier – the type of ship that would later take him around the globe. His three years' apprenticeship passed quickly into five more years of increasing responsibility. However, when he was offered the prized job of 'ship's master' in 1755, he turned it down to join the lowest ranks of the Royal Navy, his only explanation being that 'he had a mind to try his fortune that way'. The decision might have seemed foolhardy but it soon paid off: his first ship was the fourth-rate HMS *Eagle* with a rag-bag skeleton crew in which Cook's star shone brightly; within a month, he had regained his former merchant navy position of master's mate. Two years later, in June 1757, he became ship's master, in charge of navigation and the day-to-day running of the ship.

Early in 1758, with the Seven Years War underway, Cook set sail on HMS *Pembroke* for Halifax and then Louisbourg, Nova Scotia. Having witnessed military engineer Samuel Holland making a survey, he realized he could apply the same rudiments to transform the accuracy of naval charts. A month later Cook surveyed the Bay of

Gaspé, producing a beautiful chart. He spent that winter developing his new-found skills, which would soon help the British fleet to navigate safely the treacherous St Lawrence River – and General Wolfe to defeat the French at Quebec.

Cook continued chart-making until the close of the Seven Years War. In December 1762 he returned to England and married the 21-year old Elizabeth Batts. However, his 'genius and capacity' for surveying had attracted the attention of the admiralty, and four months later he returned to Newfoundland as the king's surveyor.

First Voyage: Around the World

Cook's life fell into a regular pattern of summers surveying in Canada and winters back home in London's Mile End, drawing up charts and writing sailing directions for the Admiralty. Meanwhile, over the winter of 1767–68, the Admiralty and the Royal Society were hard at work planning Britain's first scientific expedition to the South Seas. Its purpose was two-fold: first to observe the Transit of Venus, a rare astronomical event that would aid both science and navigation by helping to determine the distance of the earth from the sun; and then to go in search of the Great Southern Continent, a fabled land of great wealth which would make the nation that discovered it the most powerful on earth.

One of Sydney Parkinson's views of New Zealand. Parkinson's genius underscored much of the success of Cook's first voyage. This thoughtful, talented Quaker died on the way home, but left nearly 1,000 exquisite drawings and paintings, along with his journal.

The voyage's commander would need to be competent in astronomy, navigation and surveying – all skills in which James Cook excelled. Although only a ship's master, he was selected and quickly promoted to lieutenant. The ship that would take Cook on his voyage around the world was Her Majesty's Bark *Endeavour*, another Whitby cat, and joining him onboard would be the young English aristocrat and naturalist Joseph Banks, the Swedish naturalist Daniel Solander, the astronomer Charles Green, and the ship's artists Sydney Parkinson and Alexander Buchan, along with a one-armed cook, an ancient, drunken sailmaker and a lactating goat which had already circumnavigated the world on HMS *Dolphin.*

A watercolour of Banksia serrata *by John Frederick Miller, from a drawing by Parkinson. Parkinson's drawings were engraved for Joseph Banks's monumental* Florilegium, *finally published in 1988.*

On 25 August 1768, with some 94 men and enough provisions to last 18 months, *Endeavour* left Plymouth destined for the South Seas. Taking a route down through the Atlantic to Rio, then round Cape Horn to the Pacific, they arrived in Matavai Bay, Tahiti, in April 1769. Here at 'Fort Venus' they set up camp in preparation for the transit some six weeks later. During that time, Banks and his party went botanizing, while Cook and his men explored the island. Although relations with the Tahitians were generally good, thieving was rife – and not just on the part of the locals: the sailors soon discovered they could buy sex with a Tahitian woman for the price of a single iron nail and Cook had to maintain strict discipline to prevent the ship from being pulled apart.

Transit day on 3 June 1769 was frustrated by an optical illusion that gave the men differing results, and the matter was laid aside. Cook now opened his second, secret set of Admiralty instructions: to go in search of the Great Southern Continent. His chosen track took him due south, but there was no sign of the fabled land until 2 October, when the east coast of an unknown country came into view. Banks was confident this was the Continent; Cook knew it was more likely to be the place

discovered by Abel Tasman in 1642, now called New Zealand. Over the next six months, *Endeavour* meticulously charted both the North and South Islands, proving they were not part of the infamous Southern Continent. Cook grew to admire and respect the Maori who had made this land their home.

His orders now fulfilled, Cook selected a route back to England via the unknown eastern coast of New Holland (Australia) to discover whether Van Diemen's Land (Tasmania) and New Guinea were attached to the mainland. Driven north by bad weather, the first land sighted on 19 April was Point Hicks in modern Victoria. Just over a week later, *Endeavour* anchored in Botany Bay, named in honour of the collecting fervour of Joseph Banks and his 'Gentlemen Philosophers', who seized the opportunity to explore. From there Cook pushed further up the coast, little knowing he was sailing into the deadly funnel of the Great Barrier Reef.

On 11 June 1770 *Endeavour* smashed into the coral and stuck fast. It took 24 desperate hours, throwing all non-essentials overboard, before she was floated off by the rising tide. Somehow managing to reach modern Cooktown in Queensland, *Endeavour* underwent seven weeks of makeshift repairs. The enforced stay at least meant the men could finally forge a relationship with the local Aborigines and learn from them their name for the curious deer-like creature they saw – the 'kanguru'.

Cook sailed a patched-up *Endeavour* back out to sea on 4 August. With brilliant seamanship, he escaped the reef and rounded the northernmost tip of New Holland's eastern coast, naming it New South Wales and taking possession for the King. Cook was now sailing back on to the known map of the world. He passed through the conjectured strait between New Holland and New Guinea, finally arriving in Batavia (Jakarta), where *Endeavour* was properly repaired – but at a cost. Having up to now lost not a single man to sickness, by the time Cook arrived back home in July 1771, a third of his crew had died of dysentery and other diseases.

The Second Voyage: To the Far South

Despite the loss of life, Britain's first scientific voyage of discovery was hailed as an unparalleled success, though most of the credit went to Banks. Cook was promoted to captain, and plans were soon afoot for another, more audacious voyage to the South Seas. Having found no Continent at 40° south, Cook convinced the Admiralty to let him go further – to 60° south – in search of land.

'The head of a chief of New Zealand, the face curiously tataoud or marked according to their manner' from Parkinson's A Journal of a Voyage to the South Seas. *Cook developed enormous respect for the Maori, and New Zealand became his base in the Southern Ocean.*

After barely a year at home with his wife and family, Cook sailed from Plymouth in July 1772 for what was to become an astonishing voyage. The plan was to make giant sweeps of the Pacific Ocean, methodically charting any new found lands and erasing the ghosts of rumoured sightings from the map. This time with two ships, *Resolution* and *Adventure*, Cook headed via the Cape of Good Hope southwards into an 'immense field of ice'.

In January 1773, Cook and his men became the first known people ever to cross the Antarctic Circle and unwittingly sailed within 120 km (75 miles) of Antarctica until driven back by fog and ice – but still the fabled Continent was nowhere to be seen. Cook finally arrived in New Zealand after 17,700 km (11,000 miles) and 122 days at sea without sighting land. Here, to the shock of his exhausted crew at last enjoying fresh food and rest, Cook soon gave the order to make ready to sail once more. At the start of June 1773, the two ships began a giant anticlockwise loop that would take them halfway to Cape Horn, north to Pitcairn Island, westwards to Tahiti and the Society Islands, through the Cook Islands to Tonga then, in early October, back south to New Zealand – accurately adding and deducting lands on his emerging chart of the Pacific Ocean. This alone would have been an amazing feat of navigation, but he was to go further: after a month resupplying in Queen Charlotte Sound's Ship Cove, and having been separated from *Adventure*, he yet again headed south to the ice.

In late December Cook crossed the Antarctic Circle a second time, making a third crossing in January 1774, this time reaching an astounding 71°10' south – a record that would only be beaten by James Weddell in 1823. But even Cook had now reached his limits, heading north then west for a second giant sweep of the Pacific via Easter Island, the Marquesas, Tahiti, New Hebrides, New Caledonia and Norfolk Island before returning to New Zealand once again some eight months later. Yet still there was more: even on the way home, with Cook sailing east to Cape Horn, he once again turned south into the icy seas to chart South Georgia and the South Sandwich Islands before sailing northeast to the Cape of Good Hope and then finally on to Britain. In July 1775, *Resolution* anchored at Spithead after 'three years and eighteen days' and the greatest piece of exploration in the history of navigation.

The Final Voyage

Cook returned home to glory. He was elected a Fellow of the Royal Society, promoted to full Post Captain and granted an audience with King George III, along with a pension of £230 per annum. At nearly 47, with two growing boys and a newly pregnant wife, many men would have retired – but not James Cook. Despite his

*A watercolour by Georg Forster of a grey-headed kingfisher (*Halcyon leucocephala*) from Cook's second voyage. Georg and his brilliant but difficult father, Johann, were the naturalists on the two giant ocean sweeps, replacing Banks who had stormed off in a temper over his accommodation.*

View of part of the island of Ulietea (Raiatea) by William Hodges, artist on Cook's second voyage. After Tahiti, Raiatea is the second largest of what Cook named the Society Islands. In 1769, Cook became the first European to discover the island and took on board the Polynesian priest and brilliant navigator, Tupaia, who helped guide him around the Pacific. On this voyage Captain Furneaux of HMS Adventure *took on board Omai (Mai), who became a celebrity in England.*

failing health and temper on the second voyage, he agreed to lead one final voyage: to return home 'Mai' (Omai), a Tahitian famously brought to England by the captain of *Adventure,* and also to go in search of the Northwest Passage linking the Atlantic and Pacific oceans.

Cook sailed from England for the last time in July 1776, with two ships, *Resolution* and *Discovery.* Hopelessly behind schedule and with *Resolution* leaking badly, he rounded the Cape of Good Hope then headed east to Van Diemen's Land and New Zealand. Here Cook learned the details of the earlier massacre of a party of men from *Adventure,* but knew nothing would be gained by revenge. Instead, he restocked and got underway by late February 1777 for Tahiti. Battling against time, poor winds and with bad feeling between the decks, the two ships diverted to the Friendly Islands (Tonga) where the great commander threw tantrums one moment and parties the next: a confused crew realized all was not well with Captain James Cook.

In August 1777 the ships finally arrived in Tahiti, with Mai setting up home on nearby Huahine. The first part of his mission completed, Cook briefly stopped at Raiatea and Borabora before beginning his long trek up north to the Arctic. After passing the shark-infested waters of Christmas (Kiritimati) Atoll on 24 December 1777, Cook did not expect to see any more land until he reached the coast of North America. Instead, less than a month later, he spotted a series of volcanic islands which he named the Sandwich Islands – modern-day Hawaii. He knew he had stumbled across a major discovery though he could not have guessed it would soon achieve fame for a darker reason. Meanwhile, the crew took advantage of the bountiful food, water and women before the ships headed north in search of the Northwest Passage.

Almost two months later, in late March 1778, the ships finally made landfall at King George's (Nootka) Sound on Vancouver Island before pushing north again to look for the Passage. Frustrated by poor weather, they crossed the Bering Sea to Siberia's Chukotskiy Peninsula and up into the Arctic Ocean, but progress was short-lived: in mid-August, at 70° north, Cook ran into a wall of ice. There was no option but to retreat south for the winter then try again the following year.

In January 1779 *Resolution* and *Discovery* anchored in Hawaii's Kealakekua Bay, where Cook was greeted with almost surreal reverence as the Hawaiians showered the men with their bountiful hospitality: it seemed as though their luck was finally turning. A fortnight later, restocked and rested, Cook gave the order to sail north once more, but *Resolution* sprung her mast a few days out and they were forced to return. However, this time there was no welcome party, just disgruntled locals who turned to thieving – and a furious Cook demanded retribution.

The climax came at daybreak on 14 February. One of *Discovery*'s boats had been stolen overnight and so, with his men blockading the bay, Cook went ashore with a party of marines, their muskets loaded with ball. Having taken a local chief hostage, he was heading back to his boat when the watching crowd exploded into violence. With rocks, daggers and bullets flying, Cook ordered his men to withdraw to the boats, but it was too late: moments later, he disappeared face-down in the surf.

After one final attempt to find the elusive Passage, Cook's ships returned home in September 1780. By then, news of Cook's death had already reached the newspapers. In a public outpouring of grief, Cook was elevated from hero to legend – a position he has rightfully maintained ever since.

THE LAND

Once the oceans of the world had mostly been navigated and only isolated islands remained to be discovered, the majority of explorations took place on land. In the Americas, the fresh prospects opened up to the newly arrived Europeans offered unlimited scope to those motivated to seek, in James Elroy Flecker's words, 'always a little further … beyond the last blue mountain barred with snow'. Sadly, the incentive of the conquistadors was an insane lust for gold, which drove them to extreme acts of cruelty. In the process, bolstered by their absolute faith in the superiority of their way of life and their religion, they destroyed innumerable cultures, whose values are now seen to have been at least the equal of theirs. One of the most ruthlessly efficient of these Spaniards was Hernando de Soto. He and his 650 men (reduced, over time, to 311 survivors) opened up vast tracts of the south of what is now the United States of America, but left devastation behind them.

Meriwether Lewis and William Clark, the joint leaders of a full-scale expedition in 1804–05 to explore the unknown west of the North American continent, had a very different approach. They lost only one man, from appendicitis, of the 48 who set out and, significantly, were joined on the way by a Shoshone woman, Sacagawea. She is the real heroine of that story, as without her interpretation and intercession they might well have been annihilated by unfriendly tribes en route.

The fame of the artist-explorer Thomas Baines rests on his ability to record meticulously all he saw, while travelling through hostile country under conditions of considerable discomfort and danger. His contribution through his art to a botanical, anthropological and cultural awareness of what the landscapes of southern Africa and Australia looked like at that time is without equal. Richard Burton achieved celebrity, or even notoriety, for different reasons. His 'mania' for discovery led him to places, often alone and in disguise, where no European had been before.

Thomas Baines made this painting in Mozambique in 1859, while he was travelling with Livingstone. Baines's evocative and sensitive paintings of the remarkable places he travelled through were also extremely accurate, allowing species of plants and local geology to be identified.

During the later 19th century, the Great Game provided an opportunity for many extraordinary feats of exploration in Central and eastern Asia. The Russians were consolidating their hegemony over their far-flung territories, which made the British nervous about the unknown country to the north of their Indian empire, through which, it was feared, invaders might arrive. It was important for both sides to glean first-hand information as to what the local rulers were up to and what was the state of the terrain. These preoccupations threw up a new sort of explorer, a cross between geographer and spy. The distances some of them travelled in their quests for information were astonishing.

Nikolai Przhevalsky, Russia's leading exponent, was a tough soldier, whose passion was shooting and who travelled fast and hard, often living off the land, but also killing, for sport, far more than he needed. The British-born Ney Elias, by contrast, was modest and self-effacing to the point of invisibility, a useful trait in a spy, but he was considered by his peers to be the greatest traveller of them all.

When it came to mapping the most substantial unknown and inaccessible zone left on earth, the mysterious country of Tibet lying in and beyond the Himalayas, Europeans simply could not become invisible enough. It was embarrassing for the

A 'Grandee's litter' from Personal Narrative of a Pilgrimage to Al-Madinah and Meccah *(1855–56) by Richard Burton. Although Burton was not the first European to reach Mecca, his was the first colourful description of the pilgrims, as well as of the drama of the journey.*

A Kirghiz camp below the Merki Pass, Mustagh Ata Range, south of Kashgar, in a photograph taken by Aurel Stein. He was the first European to pass this way and would have stayed in these felt tents of nomadic herdsmen.

British Empire to have a neighbouring area almost as large as India itself as a 'geographical enigma'. Thomas Montgomerie of the Survey of India came up with the answer: train Indians to survey and send them into these hostile regions disguised as pilgrims. Some of the most dangerous, arduous and valuable journeys in the history of exploration were undertaken by these men, the first of whom was Nain Singh, often for little or no reward. Francis Younghusband was lucky enough to be born at a time which suited admirably his burning desire to excel in just this field. After pulling off one of the longest solo journeys ever, from Peking to Srinagar, he went on to become a legend in his own lifetime, culminating in his leadership of the ill-considered British invasion of Tibet.

Aurel Stein was a towering academic, whose arduous explorations led him to discover more about the history of past civilizations between the Mediterranean and China than anyone else before or since. His archaeological excavations uncovered innumerable artifacts, many of which are now housed in the British Museum, most notably the huge cache of early Buddhist manuscripts that he discovered in the Cave of a Thousand Buddhas at Dunhuang in the Gobi Desert.

Hernando de Soto

THE QUEST FOR GOLD

(*c.* 1500–1542)

... at the distance of two days' journey, there is another town, called Ocale ... They say there are many trades among that people, and much intercourse, an abundance of gold and silver, and many pearls. May it please God that this be so; for of what these Indians say I believe nothing but what I see ... although they know, and have it for a saying, that if they lie to me it will cost them their lives.

Hernando de Soto, letter from Tampa Bay, La Florida, to the Justice and Board of Magistrates in Santiago de Cuba, 8 November 1539

On 8 May 1541, the Spanish conquistador Hernando de Soto and his army of 500 men reached the shore of the Mississippi River, which he is credited with discovering. Fanciful paintings from the US Capitol in Washington, DC, to courthouses and museums across the southeastern United States depict Soto on the banks of the great river wearing glittering armour and beaming in triumph.

The truth is less spectacular. Not only did Hernando de Soto not discover the Mississippi – explorers and sailors had known about it for 30 years – but he also was more desperate than resplendent. For two years Soto had been searching in the interior of this unexplored continent for an empire to rival those of the Aztecs and Incas. But by the time his army had reached the Mississippi, the men had lost most of their magnificent clothing, tents, armour, swords, crossbows, pikes, arquebuses and other equipment. One in five of Soto's original party of 650 had died – some killed by native warriors, while others had succumbed to starvation, exhaustion and disease. Thousands more natives had died after being impressed as slaves and driven to exhaustion from carrying the expedition's equipment. And when the 311 survivors finally staggered back to Mexico in September 1543, the expedition had covered over 6,440 km (4,000 miles), twice the distance travelled by Lewis and Clark 265 years later (p. 64).

The gradual degradation of this *entrada* ('entrance' in Spanish) was in stark contrast to the earlier exploits of this 41-year-old master of the *conquista.* Aged 14, he had left a life in rural Spain of near poverty as the son of a minor noble to become a well-known captain in the early Spanish colony in Panama. Trained in the brutal tactics of that era, in which marauding bands of conquerors combed the settled areas of Central America in search of gold and slaves, Soto was a leader in the seizure of Nicaragua and its prosperous cities.

Soto was second-in-command under Francisco Pizarro in the conquest of the Incas in South America, where he was renowned for being the captain of the vanguard that swept into the middle of Inca armies and towns on horses – then unknown in the Americas – so fast and with such fierceness that a few hundred Spaniards often defeated armies of seasoned Inca fighters. He also participated in the brazen kidnapping and ransom of the Inca emperor Atahualpa, when 168 men in the midst of 80,000 Inca soldiers demanded a room full of gold and two of silver in exchange for setting the ruler free. Soto famously opposed Pizarro's decision to execute the Inca anyway, although he did not refuse his sizeable share of the ransom.

In 1536, Soto needed nine ships to carry 13,000 pounds of gold and silver back to Spain, where he bought great palaces, threw sumptuous parties and married into the high nobility. But he shared the weakness of all conquistadors, from Alexander the Great to Napoleon – he was not satisfied with what he had accomplished. Wanting an achievement to match that of Hernan Cortés's conquest of the Aztecs in Mexico and Pizarro in Peru, Soto set sail for North America in 1538, convinced by rumours and legends that a third great empire of gold existed in the country the Spaniards called 'La Florida'.

La Florida

Soto spent lavishly to outfit his army with the latest in Renaissance weaponry. He took 250 horses, and 'more abundant provisions than could be gotten out of Spain for an armada', as he boasted in a letter. Landing in the Tampa Bay region in the spring of 1539, Soto soon

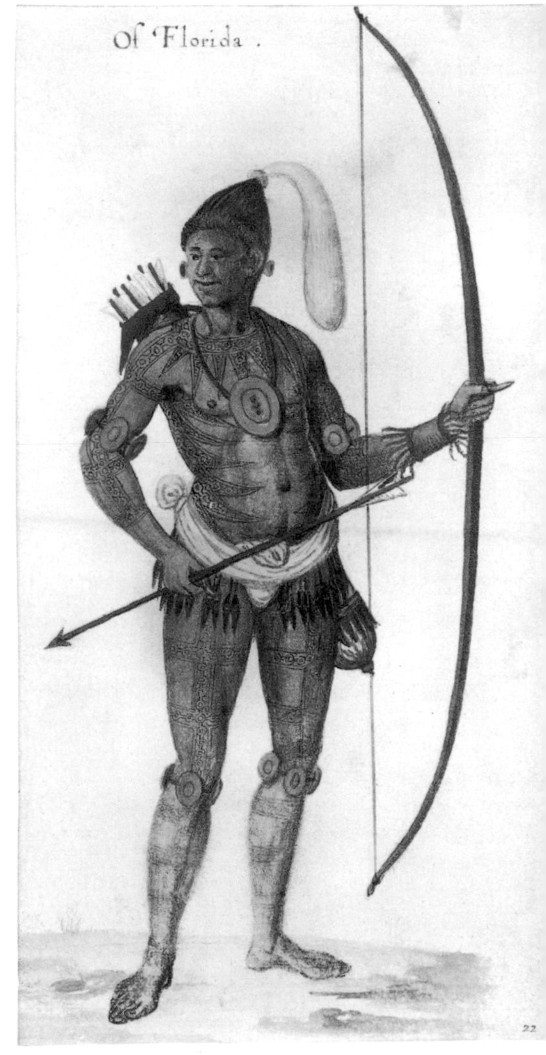

A Timucuan chief wearing gold or copper ornaments, drawn by John White after Jacques Le Moyne, 1564. The Timucuan Indians lived in the St John's River area of northeast Florida.

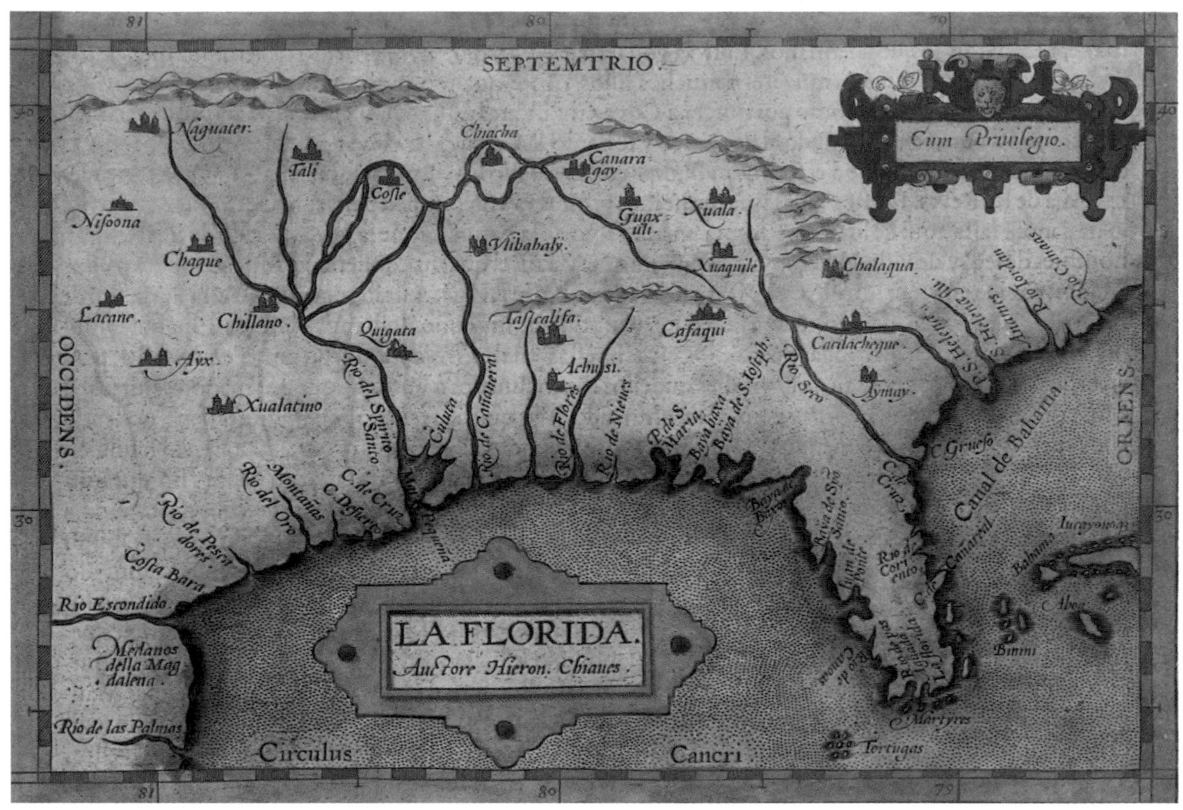

Map of La Florida from the Theatrum Orbis Terrarum *of Abraham Ortelius, Antwerp, 1584. The first separate printed map of Florida, it includes a vast area from Virginia to New Mexico and was based in part on information derived from Soto's exploration of the region.*

confronted a civilization in the interior that would be extinct by the time the next major wave of explorers arrived from France and Britain more than a century later. Called the Mississippians, these people were ruled by chieftain-kings and had sophisticated religions, rituals, games and armies. They lived in settlements that in a few cases approached the size of major European cities at the time, about 30,000 people, with populations supported by vast fields of maize, beans, squash and other vegetables. Today, all that is left are massive earthen mounds that mysteriously appear across the southeastern US and as far north as Illinois. The Mississippians also had enough pearls and traces of metals such as copper to convince the gold-gullible Soto that even greater riches lay in the next town.

Few conquistadors were as brutally efficient as Hernando de Soto. He would come sweeping into a new Mississippian kingdom and quickly overwhelm it, asking for food and men to carry his equipment to the next town. Those who refused were subjugated, their leaders killed and their people enslaved. Several times coalitions of native chiefdoms threatened by the sudden appearance of this alien *entrada* tried unsuccessfully to stop him. The first efforts failed, but one attack in central Alabama proved disastrous to the Spaniards. Ironically for the kidnapper of the Inca emperor, the chieftain Tascalusa tricked Soto into entering a fortified town for a feast with a small guard and then attacked – the same ruse Soto used to capture Atahualpa. Eventually, Soto's men prevailed, killing Tascalusa and routing the Indians, but not before dozens of Spaniards were cut down and much of their equipment was destroyed.

Hernando de Soto, conquistador and explorer. Although he became extremely wealthy from his part in the Spanish conquest of the Inca empire in Peru, he was not satisfied and went in search of the rumoured gold of La Florida.

After this attack, and facing the prospect of going back to Spain empty-handed, Soto stunned his rag-tag men by refusing even to contact a fleet waiting for him in Mobile Bay to the south. For another year he chased rumours of gold in Arkansas in a desperate search for riches that culminated in Soto's death from fever on 21 May 1542. He had led his increasingly mutinous army back to the Mississippi, where he succumbed shortly after claiming to be a god to the powerful local chieftain, who haughtily replied that if he was able to 'dry up the great river he would believe him', according to one of Soto's men who kept a journal.

Soto's surviving men took over a year to escape La Florida. They first tried to march through Texas to Mexico, but had to turn back because of a lack of food and water. Eventually, they built rafts and floated down the Mississippi, harassed by natives until they reached the Gulf of Mexico. On 10 September 1543 they astonished a band of Spaniards in an outpost of the empire, which had long ago given up the splendid company of Hernando de Soto's men for dead.

CAROLYN GILMAN

Lewis and Clark

INTO AMERICA'S UNKNOWN WEST

(1774–1809 & 1770–1838)

We were now about to penetrate a country at least two thousand miles in width, on which the foot of civillized man had never trodden; the good or evil it had in store for us was for experiment yet to determine, and these little vessells contained every article by which we were to expect to subsist or defend ourselves.

***Meriwether Lewis, Journal,* 7 *April* 1805**

In 1803, the western half of North America was still a mystery to residents of the continent's east coast. In that year, when President Thomas Jefferson asked United States government mapmaker Nicholas King to compile all the plausible information on the West, King left the area mostly blank, except for the word 'Conjectural'. 'Who can tell how far it extends?', wrote journalist Hector St John de Crèvecoeur as he looked westwards: 'For no European foot has as yet travelled half the extent of this mighty continent!'

There were theories, of course. They tended to reflect the dreams of Americans at the time: not cities of rubies or gold, but useful things like lead mines, salt and land – miles and miles of green, inviting farmland. And then there was the old dream of a water route across the continent. The idea of a Northwest Passage had dwindled by now from a sea route to a river route. Armchair geographers reasoned that there must be two rivers – one flowing east, the other west – that interlocked near their sources, so that only a short portage would be necessary to cross the continent by boat.

Jefferson was one of those great explorers who never set foot in a wilderness. His travels lay entirely within the covers of books and his inventive mind. He had been interested in the American West for years; but his reasons went beyond just scientific curiosity. To Jefferson, the West was the solution to the central dilemma of democracy – the need for a virtuous and vigilant citizenry to guard against the constant pull towards despotism and corruption. Provided with a proper environment, Jefferson believed, a new type of citizenry would emerge, with the self-reliance essential for democracy. The West was that proper environment, fresh and uncorrupted by history, where Nature could be counted on to infuse humanity with sturdy virtues.

The journals kept by Lewis and Clark cover every day of their two-and-a-half-year journey. When first published 100 years after the expedition, they filled eight volumes.

As Jefferson saw it, the main obstacles to his vision were the Spanish and the Indians. While the United States had inherited the land east of the Mississippi River from Britain in 1783, Spain still claimed everything west of that. But, unknown to most of the world, Spain had transferred the northern slice of its holdings, known as Louisiana, to France; and in 1803 Jefferson had ambassadors in Paris negotiating with Napoleon for its purchase. The Indians were a more intractable problem. Regardless of which European power claimed the West, the Indian nations still controlled it. The United States had just been through a bloody war with the tribes east of the Mississippi, in which the Indians had won most of the battles. Jefferson's solution was the same: send ambassadors – not to purchase the land just yet, but to open trade and diplomatic relations. And so was hatched his scheme for a western expedition.

The Corps of Discovery

When Jefferson needed someone to lead what came to be called his Corps of Discovery, he simply looked across the table at his 29-year-old personal secretary, Meriwether Lewis. A former army officer, Lewis was also a self-taught polymath

Thirty years after Lewis and Clark, when artist Karl Bodmer retraced their steps, the upper Missouri River still teemed with the buffalo and elk that they had described.

like Jefferson. Together, the President and his protégé set out to plan an expedition that would show the world that Americans were capable of state-of-the-art exploration. Their gold standard was the Enlightenment model of the British Royal Navy, particularly the expeditions of Captain James Cook (p. 46). Lewis's expedition would have multiple goals – commercial, imperial and scientific. It was to be a comprehensive inventory of the land and its resources – including botany, zoology, mineralogy, ethnology and geography corrected by astronomical observation. The budget of $2,500 that Jefferson was able to extract from Congress was too small to send along any scientists, so all these assignments were to rest solely on Lewis's shoulders.

Fortunately, before setting out Lewis wrote a crucial letter to his old army friend, William Clark. In it, he offered Clark the co-captaincy of the expedition, with rank and responsibilities 'in all respects [to] be precisely such as my own'. It was an extraordinary offer, but equally extraordinary, it worked. Over the three years in which they shared command, there is no record of anything but the most perfect friendship between the two men. Lewis and Clark had sharply contrasting personalities. Clark was tall and red-headed, a natural commander from a large family of Revolutionary War heroes. His letters are forthright and enthusiastic, his journals full of pragmatic (albeit misspelled) detail. Lewis was more complex – moody and introspective, as solitary as Clark was gregarious. His journals, where they are not full of rapturous botanical description, are far more insightful and literate than Clark's; but he was also capable of impetuous, even imprudent, action.

They spent the winter of 1803–04 camped on the Mississippi River, delayed by Spanish refusal to let them enter Louisiana until the transfer to US sovereignty became official, in March of 1804. Two months later, the Corps of Discovery set out up the Missouri River in a 17-m (55-ft) keelboat and two large pirogues, manned by some 48 men – an assortment of French boatmen, Kentucky frontiersmen, US army soldiers, one African-American slave and Lewis's dog, Seaman. The keelboat soon proved too large for safe travel on the rapid, snag-infested Missouri; they ended up poling and dragging it by ropes most of the first thousand miles upstream before replacing it with canoes.

After two months they entered a landscape unlike any they had seen – the Great Plains. An uninterrupted sea of grass stretched to the distant horizon on every side, populated by immense herds of antelope, elk and buffalo. The explorers diligently documented the new species, boiling down carcasses and preserving hides for naturalists to study. They even managed to capture a live 'barking squirrel' (a prairie dog). Carefully tended by the boatmen, the animal survived to arrive back in Washington the next year, where the delighted Jefferson kept it in the White House reception room.

Peoples of the Plains

Their diplomatic mission did not go as well as the scientific one, however. The greatest military power of the Plains was the Sioux nation, equestrians who followed the buffalo herds and lived in skin tipis. Lewis and Clark's meeting with the Teton Sioux nearly erupted in violence when the captains refused to pay a tribute for permission to pass, and instead informed the well-armed warriors that there was a new 'father' in Washington to whom the Sioux must be obedient 'children'. Only the intercession of an elderly chief saved them to travel on.

Snow was flying by the time they reached the spot in present-day North Dakota where the allied Mandan and Hidatsa tribes lived in villages of dome-shaped lodges constructed of logs and earth. These tribes farmed the fertile river valley and did a booming business with Canadian fur traders who had flocked there since the 1750s. The explorers built a log fort nearby, where they could trade for food and information with their hospitable neighbours.

Over the frigid winter – their only unbroken thermometer registered –40° C (–40° F) – they quizzed the Indians about geography and learnt that the Shoshone nation controlled the mountain pass they would have to cross to reach Pacific waters. Luckily, a Shoshone-speaking war captive lived in the village – a pregnant teenage girl named Sacagawea (inexplicably spelled 'Sacajawea' by the editor of their journals). They hired her rather disreputable husband, Toussaint Charbonneau, in order to get the girl as a translator, and so when they set out again in spring, their slimmed-down party of 31 men also included one woman and her two-month-old baby. Clark, who was given to nicknames, called her 'Janey' and the little boy 'Pomp'.

The Missouri now led them westwards through a rugged, arid land where distant mountains often hung on the horizon. The river banks were infested with ferocious grizzly bears that towered over 2.4 m (8 ft tall); but of people they saw nothing. By August, they were beyond the limits of their information, following a shallowing, pebbly stream southwards between pine-clad mountains. With no idea how to locate the pass that would take them across the Continental Divide, they desperately needed to find the Shoshone to guide them. Lewis went ahead on foot with three companions to look for the elusive tribe. In fact, the Shoshones were in hiding. They had just suffered a devastating attack by the enemy Blackfeet tribe and were in no mood for visitors. When a scout brought news of four strangers advancing on their mountain camp, 60 mounted warriors set out, led by their chief Cameahwait, to intercept the party. They came charging down upon Lewis at full speed.

In 1807 Meriwether Lewis posed for artist Charles B. J. F. de St-Mémin in the regalia given him by the Shoshone chief Cameahwait.

Luckily, Lewis had come across three Shoshone women shortly before and convinced them of his friendly intentions. Persuaded by the women, Cameahwait decided to welcome the strangers instead of annihilating them. With gestures, Lewis convinced the chief to return with him to meet the rest of the expedition. On

The figure third from the right is thought to be Sacagawea's husband, Toussaint Charbonneau, who was still interpreting for the Hidatsa tribe when artist Karl Bodmer met him in 1833. The Hidatsa were then at the peak of their prosperity; four years later, smallpox struck them.

his arrival, the exhausted travellers welcomed the chief with all the ceremony they could muster, and called in their translator – whereupon Sacagawea recognized Cameahwait as her brother. 'She instantly jumped up, and ran and embraced him, throwing over him her blanket, and weeping profusely', Clark later said.

Finally able to converse, the captains discovered how much trouble they were in. Lewis already had an inkling of it. Over the next ridge, he knew, lay a panoramic view – not of gentle slopes leading down to the Pacific, but 'immence ranges of high mountains still to the West of us with their tops partially covered with snow'. They had barely arrived at the start of the mountains, and summer was almost gone. Moreover, to reach the only viable pass, they would have to retrace their steps over 240 km (150 miles) northwards. And, Cameahwait warned them, 'the road was a very bad one'.

Crossing the Divide

What followed was a hellish ordeal. Having obtained pack horses and a Shoshone guide, they set out to cross the mountains. The trail led up nearly perpendicular slopes littered with fallen timber. They woke covered with snow and grew so hungry they started to kill their horses for food. Lacking socks, the men wrapped their feet in rags. It was a starving and frozen troop that stumbled out of the mountains and into the camp of a Nez Perce Indian band on 20 September. Once again, a woman advised the startled native people not to attack the expedition. Her name was Watkuweis, and unlike any of her tribe she had seen white people before. So the Nez Perce welcomed the novel strangers, fed them and helped them construct canoes to travel down the Clearwater River out of the mountains.

Going downstream for the first time, the Corps soon came to the Columbia River, lying in a grassy valley densely populated by tribes that lived on the colossal salmon runs. The Chinookan peoples dealt with the trading ships from England and the US that plied the Pacific coast, and had acquired beads, teakettles and expressions such as 'son of a bitch'. The more familiar the Indians were with Europeans, the unfriendlier they became. 'We are at all times & places on our guard', Clark recorded. The Cascade Mountains still lay in their way, but the Columbia flowed through them in a dramatic gorge, then spread out into a wide estuary. On 7 November the travellers finally heard the roaring of waves. '*Ocian in view*', Clark wrote. 'O! the joy'.

They had hoped to meet a trading ship from Boston and catch a ride back by sea. But over the rainy winter that followed, no ship appeared. They built a fort and waited in waterlogged misery on the Oregon coast till the Rocky Mountain snows had a chance to melt, then turned around to retrace their steps back across the continent.

The Return

On 23 September 1806 the canoes of the Corps of Discovery hove into sight of the levee of St Louis, and the townsfolk gathered to give three cheers and marvel at their homecoming. It had been a year and a half since any word of them had trickled east, and the United States had long since given them up for lost. Now the news of their return raced ahead of them, and they were greeted by delirious welcomes wherever they went.

By some measures, it had been an astonishingly successful expedition. Of the men who set out with Lewis and Clark, only one died, of appendicitis, a few months into the journey. They returned laden with specimens, seeds, artifacts and voluminous journals. But their great geographic mission – to find a water route to the Pacific – had failed, because there wasn't one. Their arduous mountain crossing finally drove a stake through the heart of the Northwest Passage myth.

More disappointments would follow. Lewis, tasked with writing up the journals for publication, dismayed everyone by failing to do so. Then, three years after return-

*Many of the plants collected by Lewis and Clark were species new to science. This type specimen of dull Oregon grape (*Berberis nervosa*) is one of over 200 specimens that still survive.*

ing to a hero's welcome, he took his own life on a remote trail in Tennessee. As a result, the expedition's scientific findings were not published for a century. With their collections scattered, their discoveries lapsed into obscurity. But as an adventure, Lewis and Clark's story took on a fresh life. The news they brought of a boundless West ignited the imagination of the nation. In countless retellings, their journey became an emblem of America's journey: an optimistic story about leaving behind the past and setting out in search of new lands and ways of life. The Northwest Passage might be illusory; peace and commerce with the Indians might prove a cruel hoax; scientific discovery might be frustrated – but in creating a unifying national narrative, Lewis and Clark succeeded beyond their grandest expectations.

JOHN McALEER

Thomas Baines

PAINTER OF DISTANT CONTINENTS

(1820–1875)

I am simply an artist telling …
what I have seen as truthfully as I know how.

Thomas Baines, **Journal of Residence in Africa,** *1842–53*

In his presidential address to the Royal Geographical Society in 1876, Sir Henry Rawlinson remarked that Thomas Baines was 'a born artist and explorer, a lover of wildlife, and skilled in all the shifts and resources of an explorer's career'. As both an explorer and an artist, Baines irrevocably changed Victorian perceptions of distant continents. His travels, in southern Africa and Australia, yielded scientific data, natural history specimens and fresh perspectives on the people who lived in the lands through which he passed. In place of *terrae incognitae* and blank maps, Baines flooded his canvases with the rich profusion of life and the glorious panoply of colour that he found there. Instead of the weighty tomes of other explorers, Baines's response to the landscapes that he encountered was crystallized in his art and journals, which bristle with the excitement of discovery, exploration and awestruck wonder in the face of the natural world.

A Spirit of Adventure

Thomas Baines was born in the Norfolk town of King's Lynn on 27 November 1820. At the age of 16 he was apprenticed to William Carr, an 'ornamental painter' in the town. In 1842, Baines set sail for South Africa, where he spent three years working for a carriage painter in Cape Town. On the advice of a friend who knew his work, he set up as a professional artist, trying his luck as a 'marine and portrait painter'. He relied on selling the 'never-failing "Cape Town with Table Bay and Mountain"' to the constant stream of sailors, soldiers and merchants who passed this tavern of the seas. Throughout his career, Baines continued to rely on this European interest in Africa to support his explorations. When he wasn't painting popular tourist scenes of the city or the adjacent coastline, Baines spent his time researching the history of European exploration there. Inspired by these tales and following a visit by another artist-explorer, George French Angas, in 1846–47, Baines admitted that 'the spirit of adventure that … for some time had slumbered within me' revived, and he and Angas agreed to plunge into the interior to seek out the 'great lake' that was reported to exist there.

It was when he sailed to Algoa Bay in 1848, however, that Baines's career as an artist-explorer began in earnest. Between June 1848 and August 1849, he accompanied William and George Liddle on hunting and trading trips into the interior of the eastern Cape, travelling to the Orange River. Baines filled sketchbooks with everything he saw, recording the flora, fauna and geology of the region. He made detailed pencil sketches and watercolours of interesting scenes, noting the time, date and place (sometimes even the latitude and longitude), which were later worked up into finished oil paintings. In February 1850, with Joseph McCabe, he charted Lake Ngami, in present-day Botswana. This was his first journey with definite scientific objectives, and Baines had prepared by taking instruction in computing distances, making observations and taking bearings. The following year, Baines met Colonel Henry Somerset, who employed him to sketch the events of the Eighth Frontier War (1850–53), one in a long series of conflicts between European settlers and the amaXhosa people on the eastern border of the Cape Colony. Despite his status as official war artist, and the fact that some of his sketches appeared in the *Illustrated London News*, Baines left after only a year. Following a stay in Grahamstown, he returned to Britain in May 1853 and spent two years writing, painting and lecturing on his African experiences.

Baines's sketch of a branch of buffalo pear tree (1849) highlights his interest in capturing the precise botanical details of the plants he encountered.

In 1855 Baines was appointed artist and storekeeper on the expedition to northern Australia led by Augustus Gregory, and in March he sailed for Brisbane. He fulfilled his duties so successfully that on his return to Britain in 1857 Baines was elected a Fellow of the Royal Geographical Society for services to geography. He was then introduced to David Livingstone (p. 142), who was preparing for an expedition to the River Zambezi, which he believed would herald the introduction of commerce and Christianity into central African areas still blighted by the slave trade. Parliament allocated £5,000 to investigate the possibility of establishing trading posts in the

Zambezi region. Baines was appointed in January 1858 to a role similar to the one he held on the Australian expedition, and he set about following the instructions laid down for the expedition artist, which were exhaustive and demanding. He was to give 'faithful representations of the general features of the country, make drawings of wild animals and birds and delineate for the general collection … useful and rare plants, and fossils'. Baines's work captures the power of the natural phenomena, such as the Kebrabassa Rapids, that the party encountered as it made its way up the river. He was also charged with making 'portraits of the natives for the purposes of ethnology', but his work goes beyond mere scientific studies and preserves the individuality, dignity and grace of his models. Tensions among the various personnel on the trip proved calamitous, however, and disaster struck when Baines was accused, probably unjustly, of purloining official expedition materials to make sketches for sale to Portuguese officials. Despite his dismissal in July 1859, and suffering from fever and eye problems, Baines stayed until the end of the year, anxious to make the most of the sketching and exploring opportunities.

'Humphreys and myself killing an alligator on the Horseshoe Shoal between Curiosity Peak and Broken Hill, Victoria River' (1856). Attacks from crocodiles (which Baines called alligators) were a real danger to the explorers on the North Australia expedition.

Commercial Expeditions

After his experience with Livingstone, Baines avoided government-sponsored ventures and kept to commercial undertakings. In April 1860, he met James Chapman, an ivory and cattle trader. Chapman wanted to traverse the continent, from Walvis Bay on the west coast to the mouth of the Zambezi on the east, establishing a line of commercial stations across southern Africa from sea to sea. Baines decided to join him – the costs were to be defrayed by his painting. They left Walvis Bay in July 1861, reached Lake Ngami in December, and spent three weeks at the Victoria Falls in July and August 1862. Ultimately, they found their way blocked by rapids and had to return by the route they had come.

Baines's account of this journey was published in 1864 as *Explorations in South West Africa,* and was followed in 1865 by the publication of a portfolio of lithographs derived from his oil paintings. As an artist he was deeply influenced by the aesthetic notions of the sublime and the awe-inspiring power of nature so much in evidence at the Victoria Falls. For him, the panorama presented 'the most lovely *coup d'oeuil* the soul of the artist could imagine'. His album is one of the most extraordinary records in the history of European exploration of Africa and had a significant impact on subsequent representations of the Falls.

Following this expedition Baines spent time in Namibia and was back in Britain by 1865, co-writing (with W. B. Lord) a practical manual on travelling, published as *Shifts and Expedients of Camp Life.* In 1868, Baines was approached by the South African Gold Fields Exploration Company who sought to acquire mineral extraction rights in Matabeleland (in present-day Zimbabwe). From 1869 to 1872 he led two expeditions from Durban, locating promising sites and negotiating mining concessions with the Ndebele king, Lobengula. His map of the region, his paintings and diaries were all published posthumously. Thomas Baines died of dysentery in Durban on 8 May 1875, while preparing for a third journey to Matabeleland.

'I Am Simply an Artist'

Baines once assured the recently appointed governor of the Cape Colony, Sir George Cathcart, that his 'principal object would be to obtain sketches as characteristic and well finished as possible of the country, its inhabitants, its animals and plants'. Despite such modesty, throughout his career Baines's explorations provided valuable scientific insights. For example, in the field of zoology his work illustrates the distinguishing features of species, placing them in the context of their natural surroundings. References to animals form an integral part of his descriptions and observations.

He also alluded to 'my small skill in botany', but his landscapes are characterized by recognizable portraits of trees or flowering plants that are both factual and evocative. He engaged in correspondence with some of the most eminent botanists of his day, such as William and Joseph Hooker at Kew, and made two important botanical discoveries on the Chapman trip by identifying and recording *Welwitschia mirabilis* and *Aloe dichotoma*. As Dr John Kirk, a member of the Livingstone expedition to the Zambezi, confirmed: 'Mr Baines has given actual views, and has so scrupulously adhered to nature, that any one familiar with the vegetation may name the very plants represented in his paintings'.

Baines also took advantage of new technologies to assist him in conveying the beauty of African nature and life to audiences in Europe. For example, he used photographs taken by Chapman to ensure the correct depiction of 'native weapons or ornaments' in his paintings. Through astronomical observations and systematic mapping of the landscape, Baines brought European concepts of scientific surveying

ABOVE *Baines's painting of a herd of buffalo, opposite Garden Island, Victoria Falls (1862) captures the sublime quality of the waterfalls in the background. Baines made at least three versions of this oil painting, and also selected it for reproduction as a lithograph.*

OPPOSITE *In his paintings of people, Baines managed to convey the personality and dignity of the individuals he met on his travels – here 'Conde, a native of Tete' (1859).*

In this painting 'Welwitschia mirabilis' *(1867), Baines is sketching a specimen of the strange plant. By including himself in the picture, as an 'eye witness', he guaranteed the accuracy of the scene and his recording of this plant is one of his greatest contributions to botanical science.*

to bear on Africa, and his artistic skill in evoking texture and relief assisted in depicting the geological features he encountered. His love of nature shines through in his work. In *Explorations in South West Africa*, he excused his interest in the ecology of the unexplored environment through which he was passing: 'I confess I can never quite get over the feeling that the wonderful products of nature are objects to be admired rather than destroyed'. Baines's paintings frequently include images of himself as a guarantor of truthfulness, authenticating the scene laid out before his viewers. He cultivated an image as a mere journalistic recorder – the only merit that he claimed for his sketches was 'that of being as faithful to the character of the country as my ability will permit'.

In 1867, 20 of Baines's paintings were selected to appear at the Paris World Exposition. His work appeared at many other exhibitions in Britain and Europe and it was also published in popular journals and travel books, thereby broadening the reach and impact of his explorations. Baines's contribution to the dissemination of information was not limited to art: he also lectured extensively when he was back in Britain. Sir Roderick Murchison believed that the real benefit of Baines's work was to those in Britain who were 'destined never to penetrate into the southern part of Africa', and who 'may quite realize to our mind's eye the true character of that grand continent'.

Although Baines subscribed to Victorian values of imperialism and the consequent taming and organizing of the land, he also revelled in its beauty and uniqueness. His sketchbooks are copiously annotated and full of the vibrancy of nature. They confirm his belief that 'nothing whatever is too insignificant to be recorded'. He travelled in the most unprepossessing circumstances, painting as bullets whizzed overhead and as flies ate the pigment off the canvas as he applied it. Yet he produced enduring testaments to his own fascination with these wonders of nature as well as their awe-inspiring grandeur. Baines regarded travelling, collecting data and presenting that information to the British public as an end in itself, claiming that he would consider himself 'sufficiently rewarded if through my efforts any extent of country hitherto unexplored may be made known to the British Public and a portion, however small, subtracted from the blank that still occupies the central region of the map of Africa'.

As well as presenting informative and accurate images of the people, animals and landscapes he encountered, Baines's paintings, here hippopotami near the mouth of the Luabo River (1859), also convey the beauty and magnificence of these places.

Richard Burton

A MANIA FOR DISCOVERY

(1821–1890)

Do what thy manhood bids thee do from none but self expect applause; He noblest lives and noblest dies who makes and keeps his self-made laws.

Richard Burton, The Kasidah, *1880*

In a quiet churchyard in Mortlake, in suburban southwest London, stands a strange tomb, stone built, in the form of an oriental tent. A short ladder up one side allows a view through a window of the coffins of Sir Richard and Lady Burton lying side by side, at peace. Above them is a device that looks like a rusty telephone bell. It is in fact an old solenoid designed to ring a camel's bell inside the tomb. A Victorian folly? Not really. The tinkling of the camel's bell is the refrain of Burton's long poem *The Kasidah.* In it he reveals, in the persona of a Persian mystical author he calls Haji Abdu El-Yezdi, his extraordinary beliefs, motivations and ideals:

Pluck the old woman from thy breast:
Be stout in woe, be stark in weal;
Do good for Good is good to do:
Spurn bribe of Heav'en and threat of Hell.

This was the man of whom H. M. Stanley said, 'Could have been the greatest except for his damned cynicism'. This was also the man who terrorized drawing rooms with his tales of murdering men casually and eating human flesh – though there is little evidence that he did either. With Burton, outlandish tales and bizarre reality merge.

Born in Torquay on 19 March 1821, Richard Francis Burton was raised peripatetically, mainly in France and Italy, including Pau, a town in southwest France then, as now, much favoured by the English. Several times he wrote blaming his parents for not having sent him to a 'first rate school', yet there is every evidence that Burton would not have stood the discipline of a conventional boarding school for long. In 1840 he returned to England to attend Trinity College, Oxford, and on his first day

Portrait of Burton as 'The Pilgrim', which formed the frontispiece to volume 2 of his Personal Narrative of a Pilgrimage to Al-Madinah and Meccah *(1855–56). His mastery of languages and love of disguise enabled Burton to reach dangerous or forbidden places undetected.*

Burton arrived in India in 1842 and spent seven years there in the army, much of it in Sindh. In addition to his military duties he acted as an intelligence officer, travelling in disguise and collecting information. Having suffered from cholera, he returned from India ill: this plate, 'Toda family and village', is from Goa and the Blue Mountains; or Six Months of Sick Leave *(1851).*

challenged a fellow student to a duel for laughing at his large moustache. The student declined the offer. Burton was, in his early years, driven by an oft-stated desire to emulate Lord Byron; he was more studious than Byron though less gifted at versifying. Burton was a shapeshifter of a man, as out of place in the starchy era of the Victorians as he was at Oxford, where he got himself rusticated for going to the races during term time. In fact he almost certainly had done no work and simply wanted to leave with a bang not a whimper.

In India and Arabia

Burton joined the 18th Regiment of the Bombay Native Infantry at Baroda in October 1842, and achieved astonishingly quick success at learning the vernacular tongues of Marathi, Gujarati and Hindustani, as well as Persian and Arabic. Burton is an enigma – yet the key to his development lies in these early years in the Indian army where he studied Hindustani for 11 hours a day in order to be able pass himself off as a local. Dark hair and sallow skin helped, but he was also a master of disguise. It was in

India that he encountered the Sufism he wrote of in *The Kasidah*, in the form of real exemplars and in the Persian and Arabic authors he devoured – having set himself the task of perfecting his then weak knowledge of those tongues. He developed his own method of language learning that involved studying grammar for a week and then launching straight into translating the St John Gospel out of the new tongue. It worked: by the time he died in 1890, he could speak over 27 different languages.

His years in India, however, he later claimed 'broke my health'. Returning to Europe for five years he fenced regularly and wrote a manual on bayonet exercises (still well regarded) as well as four travel books. But the influence of his Sufi studies continued. Sufi exemplars tend, in the east, to be high achievers. It is a brand of Islamic mysticism that encourages its followers both to take life lightly yet also to be 'extraordinary' in what they do. Burton was eager to make his mark – first in the army, then by writing, finally by his explorations. But having failed to succeed to his satisfaction in soldiering or writing, he set out in 1853 to enter Mecca, and though he was not the first European to do so, he was the first to play up the drama of his subterfuge. 'Discovery is mostly my mania', he wrote, and his insatiable curiosity, as well as a desire to achieve fame drove him to penetrate that most secret of Arabian cities disguised as a Pathan merchant.

A spear wound received in Somalia left Burton with a dramatic scar on his cheek, which featured in photographs and portraits of him.

Personal Narrative of a Pilgrimage to Al-Madinah and Meccah was the result, which, along with *First Footsteps in East Africa*, is his most readable book. The paradox being that Burton, though an incredible storyteller and mimic, was not a very engaging author – there is fabulous material in his works but it is encrusted in layers of learning, languages, strange facts and stranger opinions. It was Burton who conjectured there was a 'sotadic zone' that stretched mainly around the Mediterranean where 'the French vice' was practised by men. Sodomy in other words. Burton's sexuality was another mystery. He claimed he was sidelined in the Indian army for obeying an order to write a report on the male brothels of Karachi – the report has never been found. He almost certainly was exaggerating secret trips he made to male brothels, probably just to satisfy a voyeuristic urge.

Controversy in Africa

In 1854 Burton did something even more hazardous: accompanied by J. H Speke (p. 136) and two other officers he set out to explore the interior of Somalia. Being Burton, the hardest part he did alone – becoming the first European to enter the forbidden city of Harar, where he even engaged the king in conversation. A pattern was beginning to emerge. It was in Somalia that Burton received a spear through his jaw that left him with the frightening visage of his later years, not helped by the 'basilisk stare' he liked to cultivate. (Though children reportedly found him extremely amusing and unperturbing.) The following year, Burton begged to be sent to the front during the Crimean war. But he never was to achieve any kind of military glory; almost certainly viewed as a troublemaker, he served out 'his war' on the staff of General Beatson's Bashi-bazouks in the Dardanelles.

Burton returned to Africa in 1856 for the exploit that would pioneer the great phase of African exploration. What Shackleton's endeavours in 1909 were to later southern polar triumphs, Burton was to the African exploits of others, including Speke, Stanley and Livingstone. He was the first to discover the great lakes of Central Africa, when, again accompanied by Speke (whom Burton genially despised for his

Burton became determined to find the source of the White Nile and set out with an expedition of 100 bearers and accompanied by John Speke in 1857. Both men became ill, and although they reached Lake Tanganyika their achievement later became clouded by controversy.

'View in Usagara' from The Lake Regions of Central Africa, *Burton's account of the expedition, published in 1860. Speke had returned to London before Burton, claiming to have discovered the source of the Nile; Burton used his book to dispute this and attack Speke.*

inability at languages and love of hunting), he walked from Zanzibar to Lake Tanganyika. Suffering from fever Burton rested while Speke made his own journey and found Lake Victoria and one probable source of the Nile. And therein lay the making of a controversy that only ended when Speke shot himself (which may or may not have been suicide) the day before he was due to confront Burton in a debate about the source of the Nile. Far from feeling triumphant over Speke's demise, Burton cancelled his own speech, ultimately feeling a tremendous sorrow for his old protégé, despite their falling out.

Marriage and Diplomacy

Not surprisingly, Lord Derby wrote that Burton in half his life had already compressed 'more of study, more of hardship and more of successful enterprise and adventure than would have sufficed to fill up the existence of half a dozen ordinary men'. But then, in 1861, he got married. Isabel Arundell is just one more enigma in Burton's life. He chose (or rather she chose him from her account) to marry someone of a conventional upbringing and religious background who burnt many of his private papers on his death to 'preserve his reputation'. In other words, she disapproved of the salacious stuff. Despite this, she was a passionate supporter of Burton, learning languages and fencing in an attempt to emulate her hero. Burton's ways were not easy. He preferred to leave her behind when they moved with the curt instructions 'pay, pack and follow'. Perhaps her revenge was burning the manuscript of the Arabic sex manual *The Perfumed Garden* (though this failed in intent as another copy survived). Their relationship baffled those who knew them. They had no children, but, in the times they were together, seemed devoted. It was Lady Burton who ordered the construction of the Mortlake tomb.

As a married man Burton acquired a sense of duty lacking in his ruffian explorer days. He obtained a consular post in the remote island of Fernando Po, a place he deemed far to unhealthy for his wife to share with him. In 1865 he shifted to Santos in Brazil for four years and then to Damascus in 1869 and Trieste in 1871, where he stayed until his death on 20 October 1890. He was never going to get anywhere in the diplomatic corps – he had offended too many people. Given his chance to advise Lord Salisbury on British policy in Morocco he scribbled one word 'annexe'. When asked to elaborate he wrote several sides of foolscap saying the same thing in as many different and convoluted ways as possible. It did not go down well.

During his consular years Burton still managed to travel a great deal. He visited almost every state in America and interviewed the head of the Mormon church in Utah, Brigham Young. When he asked to be initiated into that church Young replied dryly, 'I think you have done that sort of thing before'. In 1863 he published *Wanderings in West Africa*, which detailed his exploratory journeys in Dahomey, Benin and the Gold Coast. *The Highlands of Brazil* was the result of his four years in Santos. He also went to Iceland and managed to fit in covering a war in Paraguay while on a journey to Peru.

His last great venture was the translation of the *Thousand and One Nights* complete with all the obscenities and near-pornographic stories of the original. The book (ultimately published in 16 volumes) was far in advance of its time, though it sold well and is still in great demand as a collector's item. As Burton said, 'Now that I know the tastes of England, we need never be without money'. He ended the final verse of his *The Kasidah* with:

Wend now thy way with brow serene,
Fear not thy humble tale to tell:-
The whispers of the Desert-wind;
The tinkling of the camel's bell.

Nain Singh

MAPPING THE FORBIDDEN LAND

(1830?–1882)

For the first time the great plateau of Tibet has been traversed by an educated traveller, who was able to take observations and describe what he saw. Thus a great increase has been made to our scanty knowledge of Tibet.

Sir Clements Markham,
Secretary of State for India and President of the Royal Geographical Society, 1871

In the mid-19th century Russian troops were marching on the great mountain range that separated British India from its trans-Himalayan neighbours to the north. Britain had completed its annexation of the Punjab and the North-West Frontier, pushing the borders of imperial India almost to within firing range of Cossack troops. Alarm bells were ringing in London, for no one knew who or what lay beyond the Empire's newly conquered territory.

Nain Singh, whose code-name was No. 1.

What were the likely invasion routes? How close were the Russian encampments and their rapidly advancing railway lines? Were the rivers navigable, could the mountains be crossed? And where were the maps? To this final question the Government of India feebly replied that there weren't any. The Great Trigonometrical Survey of India had but the vaguest notion of where major cities such as Lhasa were located. The important strategic issue of whether the Tsangpo and Brahmaputra rivers joined was a mystery. Gilgit, Chilas and Chitral, key outposts of the North-West Frontier, remained unexplored. Yarkand was a hundred miles out of position on the Survey's map. The entire landmass of Central Tibet was a geographical enigma.

Enter Captain Thomas George Montgomerie of the Royal Engineers. Montgomerie sailed to Bombay at the age of 21 and joined the Survey a year later. He quickly identified the problem and set about rectifying it. By the early 1860s the Survey possessed a fairly reliable set of data on some 103,600 sq. km (40,000 sq. miles)

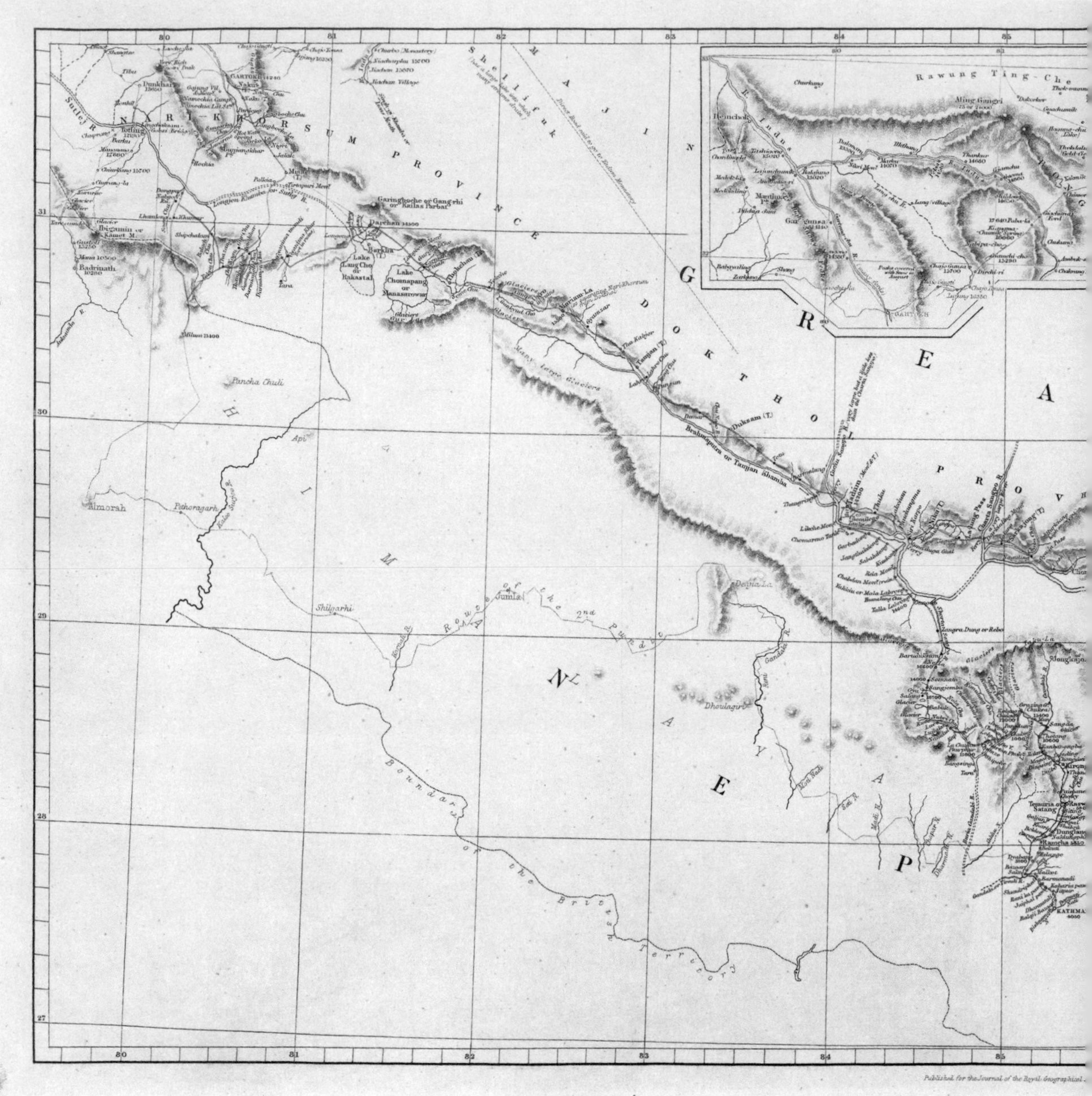

Map showing the route survey made by a Pundit from Nepal to Lhasa, published by Captain Montgomerie in the Journal of the Geographical Society *in 1868. Although the Pundit was not named, the map's publication would seem to have compromised the secrecy and safety of these dangerous missions, which were still being carried out.*

of trans-Himalayan territory. But this still left a blank on the map the size of India. Montgomerie estimated that roughly 3.6 million sq. km (1.4 million sq. miles) of unexplored land north of the Himalayan and Karakoram ranges could be penetrated from India. Conversely, this same vast territory was a potential gateway to British territory.

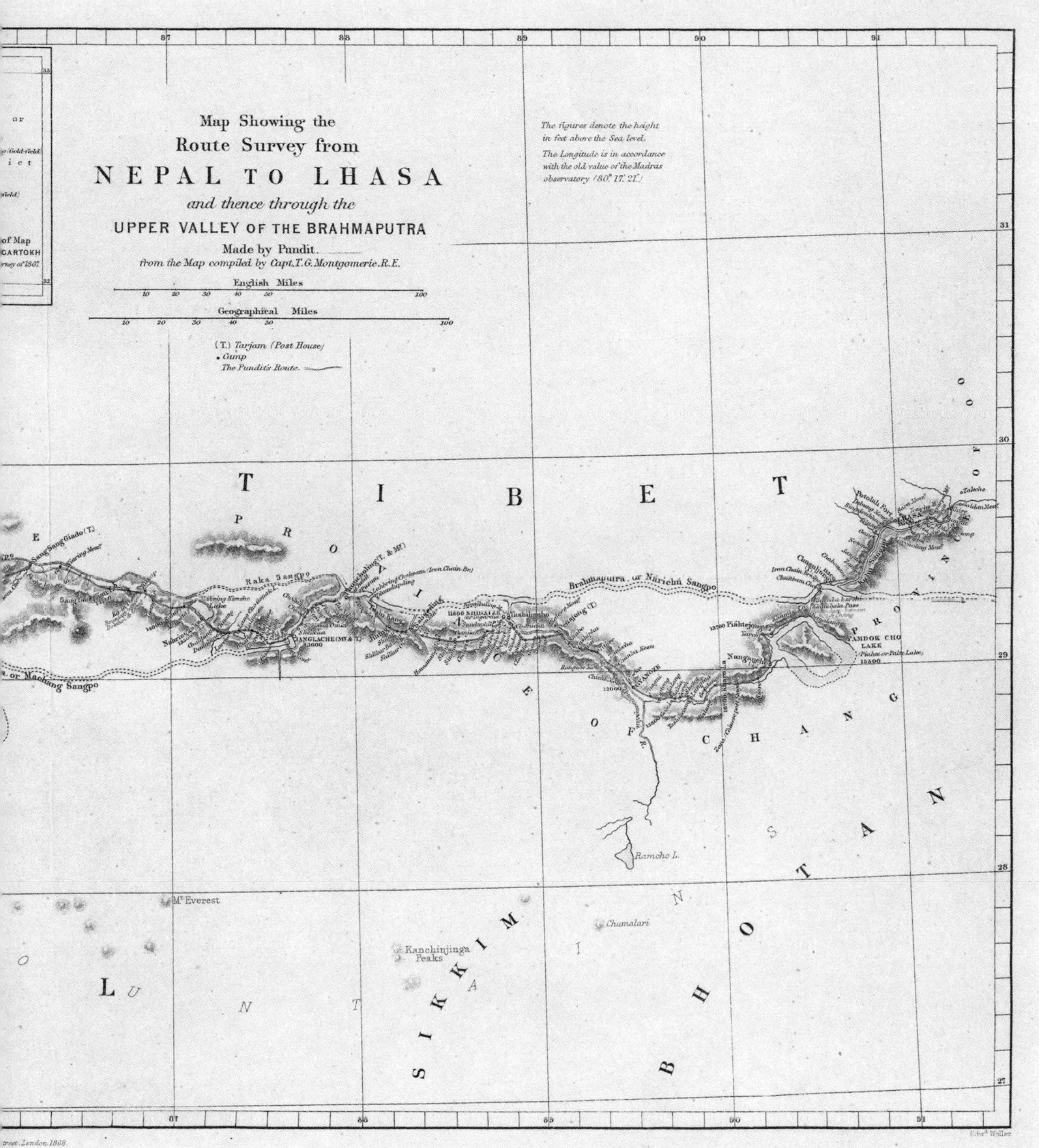

Enter the Pundits

Europeans had been travelling to Central Asia in general and to Tibet in particular since the 17th century, even though it was a very risky region and foreigners were forbidden to enter the country. Many had met an unpleasant fate. The Portuguese Jesuit Bento de Goes, the British veterinary surgeon William Moorcroft, the German explorer Adolf Schlagintweit and others had perished in dubious circumstances. Montgomerie's plan was simple: send Indians, not Europeans. As he later told the

Royal Geographical Society: 'In carrying out my plan for exploring beyond the frontiers of British India … I have always endeavoured to secure the services of men who were either actually natives of the countries to be explored, or who had at any rate the same religion as the people, and who had been in the habit of travelling or trading in the said countries.'

Nain Singh was a Bhotia of Tibetan stock, a schoolmaster in Kumaon who spoke Hindi, Persian, English and Tibetan. He was made an offer to become the first in Montgomerie's corps of native surveyors known as 'Pundits', and take on a secret mission for the Survey in Tibet. It was an offer he could not easily refuse, for here was a chance to extricate himself from debts incurred by certain of his father's 'social misdeeds', with a bit of adventure thrown in. Nain Singh was placed in the hands of Captain Montgomerie, who devised what must stand as one of history's cleverest pieces of spycraft.

At the Survey's headquarters at Dehra Dun, Nain was put through a rigorous training course lasting nearly two years. He learnt to use the sextant to determine latitudes, the compass for taking bearings, the basics of astronomy for night navigation and the use of a thermometer for measuring altitude. Recording the distance covered each day was achieved by one of the most ingenious contrivances in Montgomerie's bag of tricks. Tibetans carry a rosary of 108 prayer beads which they turn while

This almost topographical view of Lhasa, with the Potala palace, was drawn by a Tibetan lama around 1859, not long before Nain Singh set out on his first secret journey. At this time Europeans were forbidden to enter Tibet and the country was virtually unknown beyond its borders.

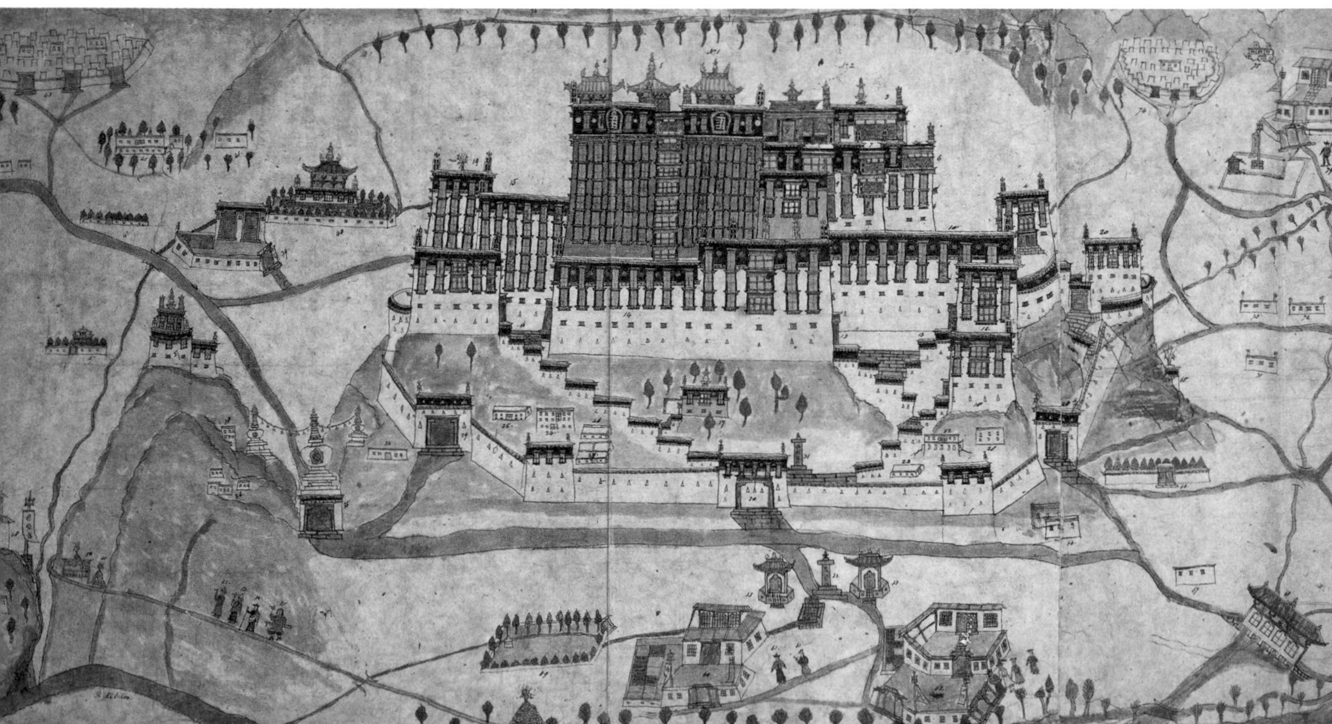

chanting a holy mantra. Montgomerie had eight beads removed to leave a mathematically convenient 100. Nain Singh was instructed to slip one bead every 100 paces, so that each circuit of the rosary signalled 10,000 paces. To ensure a high degree of accuracy when measuring distance, Nain Singh and subsequent Pundits spent months learning to take a pace of the same length, regardless of the terrain they crossed. Montgomerie bound their feet with a cord measuring what he deemed the ideal stride for each Pundit. In the case of Nain Singh, this worked out at 33 inches, and so 1,920 paces would equal 1 mile.The Pundit would also need somewhere to stash his daily route notes – the copper cylinder of a typical prayer wheel would serve nicely, and later the Dehra Dun spy workshop began assembling prayer wheels that could hold the Pundit's compass as well. Sextants and other large pieces of equipment were concealed in the false bottoms of travelling cases.

Into Tibet

By 1865 Nain Singh, known to the Survey under the *nom de guerre* of No. 1, was ready to begin his first secret exploration of Tibet. His mission was to travel through Nepal and carry out a route survey from Tibet's holy Lake Mansarowar, following an easterly course along the road between the great commercial centre of Gartok and the Tibetan capital, Lhasa. After completing his survey work, the Pundit was to trace an arc westward back to Mansarowar, and make his way home. In all, a journey, as it turned out for Nain Singh, of 2.5 million paces on his rosary, or 1,500 miles (2,400 km). Montgomerie hoped the mission would define the unknown course of the Tsangpo, which was erroneously believed to flow from Mansarowar, to beyond Lhasa.

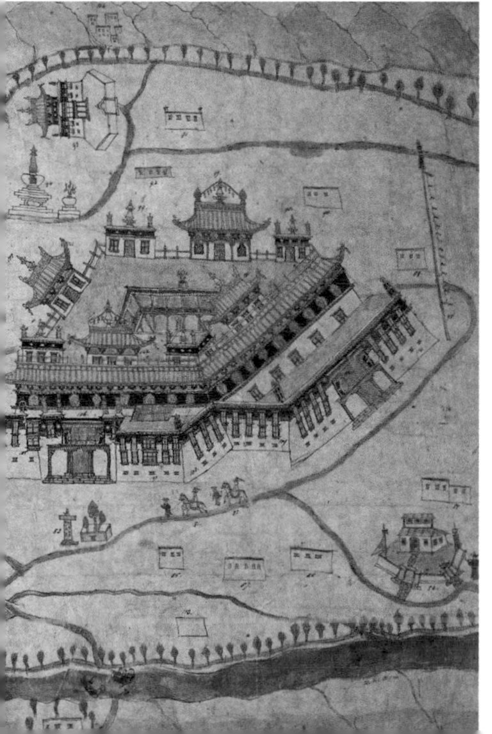

After an abortive start, Nain Singh journeyed north to Kathmandu to attempt to enter Tibet from Nepal. It was midwinter and the journey took three months – over snowbound passes 4,875 m (16,000 ft) high and with narrow escapes from Chinese border guards. He eventually reached Lhasa, where he stayed for three months; the observations he made while there allowed the latitude and altitude of the city, both unknown at the time, to be calculated with an amazing degree of accuracy. However, having witnessed the beheading of a Chinese man, a sobering reminder of the fate in store for foreign gate-crashers, he lost little time in signing on to a caravan travelling to Mansarowar. When he eventually returned to Dehra Dun, Nain Singh delivered an elaborate route survey defining the road from Kathmandu to Tandum and the whole of the Tibetan road from Lhasa to Gartok. He had also fixed the course of the Brahmaputra from its source near Mansarowar to Lhasa, and determined the height of 33 previously uncharted peaks and passes.

While in Lhasa, Nain Singh had overheard some intriguing tales of gold mines in a remote area of Tibet, and when Montgomerie learnt of these gold fields he immediately began putting together a second expedition. After setting out in 1867, Nain Singh and two other Pundits returned months later with confirmation of the mines and also with far more impressive results. In all, some 30,000 km (18,000 miles) of explored territory were added to the Survey's maps, along with route surveys of 80 summits. The course of the Sutlej was traced through Tibet to the border of British India, and the position of Gartok was finally fixed on the map.

Nain Singh's later adventures confirmed him as the most celebrated of the Pundits. He was called back into service in 1873, aged nearly 50 and travel weary. Montgomerie instructed the Pundit to accompany a mission to Yarkand. This was to be his final bow, earning the praise of such establishment luminaries as Sir Clements Markham, who served as Secretary of State for India and President of the Royal Geographical Society. 'The journey performed between July 1874 and March 1875 by the Pundit Nain Singh, of the Great Trigonometrical Department, is the most important, as regards geographical discovery, that has been made by any native explorer', said Markham. In recognition of his achievements, the Pundit was awarded the Royal Geographic Society's Patron's Medal to 'the man who has added a greater amount of positive knowledge to the map of Asia than any individual of our time'.

A drawing by the Pundit Sarat Chandra Das of 1879 of a traditional Tibetan prayer wheel. Cleverly adapted, this was the ideal device for secreting field notes from the prying eyes of border guards.

JOHN URE

Nikolai Przhevalsky

GEOGRAPHY, POLITICS AND HUNTING IN CENTRAL ASIA (1839–1888)

You can't walk here if you don't carry a Nagaya whip … this Russian weapon is the only way of putting sense into the exceedingly persistent impudent fellows.

Nikolai Przhevalsky on travelling in Central Asia

Nikolai Przhevalsky was a paradoxical character in many ways. His lifelong ambition as an explorer was to reach the forbidden city of Lhasa in Tibet; in this he failed, but his reputation and achievements in exploration were much celebrated in his lifetime and much commemorated afterwards. His chosen career was the Tsarist army of Russia, and he rose to the rank of major-general; but he never commanded troops and his views on strategy were too aggressive even for the most territorially ambitious of Tsars. He made contact with remote peoples on the fringes of Russia and China and with virtually unknown rulers such as Yakub Beg in Kashgar; but he never could bring himself to respect them and some of his opinions do not bear repeating. He is credited with having discovered the Przhevalsky wild horse (*Equus przewalskii*); but it is forgotten that the first specimen he encountered only survived for classification because it was out of range of his rifle at the time, and his disrespect for local inhabitants was matched by his disrespect for the wildlife he so voraciously slaughtered. Here was an explorer who was far from being a role model.

Some explanation – or at least excuse – for his difficult personality may be found in his upbringing. Born in 1839, his genes were a strange cocktail of Russian Cossack and Polish nobility. He was encouraged to fend for himself from an early age, hunting in the forests around Smolensk and surviving childhood encounters with wolves, bears and other predators. He was a misfit at school and a bully to his younger brother at home. The army seemed the only hope for him, and even here he was frustrated by arriving too late for action in both the Crimean war and the Polish uprisings.

A Zest for Exploration

Moving on from regular soldiering to exploration, his first major expedition was to take him to eastern Siberia – to the banks of the Amur River and the Ussuri region bordering China. The Imperial Geographical Society in St Petersburg specifically commissioned him to correct existing maps and make new ones. He rode for over a week from Lake Baikal to a tributary of the Amur, where gold-panning and fur-trapping were virtually the only occupations of the inhabitants. He then proceeded into Korea, where he undertook some unauthorized diplomacy with the local authorities, and supported his small team by shooting wild duck and gambling with the natives. He returned to a mixed reception in St Petersburg, but he had acquired a lasting zest for exploration.

Four more major expeditions were to follow. On the first of these he penetrated to the region where the Yangtze River rises. He shot or otherwise recorded new specimens of wildlife, particularly numerous specimens of birds as wells as plants, which he sent back to the Academy of Sciences in St Petersburg and for which he was awarded the Imperial Geographical Society's medal. His next mission was a more political one: to establish relations with Yakub Beg, the new Muslim ruler of Kashgaria. On this he was accompanied by some nine companions, a staff of bearers, two dozen

Николай Михайловичъ
ПРЖЕВАЛЬСКІЙ.

БІОГРАФИЧЕСКІЙ ОЧЕРКЪ.
составилъ
Н. Ѳ. Дубровинъ.

съ 4 портретами Н. М., 3 автографами, 2 фототипіями и отчетною картою четырехъ его путешествій.

Цѣна 5 руб.

С.-ПЕТЕРБУРГЪ
Военная Типографія (въ зданіи Главнаго Штаба).
1890.

ABOVE *Title page from the biography of Przhevalsky by I. F. Dubrovin: Przhevalsky's likeness to Stalin has been the subject of comment and speculation.* OPPOSITE *Although Przhevalsky did shoot much of the wildlife he encountered, he also recorded and published it in in his books.*

(3/4)

*The Tibetan gazelle, or goa (*Procapra picticauda*), from Przhevalsky's* Mongolia, the Tangut Country *(1875). This species is now threatened with extinction.*

camels and a sizeable baggage train. They made an arduous crossing of the Tien Shan Mountains and established contact with Yakub Beg; but there was little follow up to the expedition from the Russian side, and the Muslim leader's domain was soon to be reoccupied by the Chinese. So Przhevalsky's political achievements did not match his topographical and scientific ones.

A series of expeditions followed, in 1877, 1879 and 1883, specifically aimed at reaching Lhasa. Although the ultimate goal was to elude Przhevalsky, a great deal was discovered in the process of making the attempts. He mapped the Humboldt

Mountains; he surveyed the Lop Nor region for the first time; he visited the Caves of the Thousand Buddhas in Dunhuang; he filled in the blank regions on the map of Saltyn Tagh and Tsaidam in western China; and he penetrated the Gobi Desert in Mongolia, the fringes of the Taklamakan Desert and entered Tibet itself. All these regions had hitherto been an unknown wilderness, and it was Przhevalsky who brought them within the compass of western knowledge.

Conditions on all these expeditions were challengingly tough: food was so scarce that his camels tore open their saddles to eat the straw stuffing; water was so short that on occasions he had to drink from wells where dead bodies had been found; again and again his small party had to rely for their rations on the produce of Przhevalsky's shooting forays. He would stalk elk holding his rifle tripod above his head, in the hope that his prey would mistake the spikes for the antlers of a fellow animal. But he had no sense of preserving the wildlife of the steppes, and would often continue shooting long after the requirements of the cooking pot were fulfilled; he thought nothing of expending nearly 10,000 cartridges on a single expedition and leaving tons of rotting animal meat and dead birds behind him on the hillside to feed the wolves; vultures and other pariahs followed his every excursion.

Personal Life

Przhevalsky was feted for his exploratory prowess during his brief spells in St Petersburg between expeditions. The Tsar even invited him to tutor his son (the future, and last Tsar, Nicholas II) about Central Asia; but this was not entirely on account of his geographical and scientific achievements – the Russian Court saw him as an instrument of territorial expansion into the disputed heart of Central Asia.

Przhevalsky never married, and his emotional life was centred around his companions on his expeditions. These included a succession of handsome young men, and many of his contemporaries and later biographers have assumed that his interests were homosexual. His home in the forests of Russia was also important to him, and he preferred to spend his time between expeditions as a recluse rather than being lionized in St Petersburg society. For all his eccentricity and lack of sensitivity in so many directions, Przhevalsky left a real legacy of exploration behind him: he pushed out the frontiers of European knowledge of Asia in a manner which led to comparison – in the opinion of the Royal Geographical Society in London – with Marco Polo, and despite his penchant for indiscriminate slaughter, he sent back a steady stream of specimens of animal, bird and plant life which were in no way limited to the discovery of his namesake horse.

Ney Elias

SOLITARY PLAYER IN THE GREAT GAME

(1844–1897)

Few of the Queens' servants in Asia have done so much and talked so little of what they have done.

Obituary,* Times of India, *1897

In 1873 two men were chosen to stand in front of the gathered Fellows of the Royal Geographical Society to receive its prestigious gold medals. Recognized as the greatest explorers of their time, the two were equally illustrious. One, Henry Morton Stanley, remains a hero in the history of exploration (p. 158); the other, Ney Elias, is almost completely forgotten. Stanley's good fortune was that he travelled in areas of Africa where British interests were focused for the next century; Elias, however, travelled in China and Central Asia – far more important politically and economically in the mid-19th century than Africa, but later to become comparatively disregarded and mainly closed to foreigners.

Members of the Anglo-Siamese Boundary Commission, 1889–90, with Ney Elias standing at the right; this was his last major expedition.

But there is another reason for Elias's relative obscurity today: he did almost nothing to court fame as an explorer. The more typical Asian travellers, such as Alexander 'Bokhara' Burnes, would seek trophy destinations and then speed back to London to trumpet their achievements. Elias eschewed personal publicity. The public knew almost nothing about him, particularly his private life. He was one of those many 19th-century and later travellers who journeyed partly because they felt safer away from social expectations. He had no known relationships with women, having this in common with his Russian contemporary,

The compass that Elias used on his travels. Together with all his papers and notebooks, it is now held in the archives of the Royal Geographical Society.

Nikolai Przhevalsky (p. 93). Both men also shared an apparently fearless determination to proceed whatever the odds against them. Each was their country's outstanding Central Asian explorer.

Elias was born in 1844 into a Jewish merchant family in Bristol and was sent to school in Dresden. He was expected to join the family firm, and this took him to their Shanghai office. It quickly became clear, however, that his bent was for discovery rather than commerce. He started in 1868, exploring in three journeys the Yellow River, which had just gone through one of its periodic gyrations and altered course to flow northeast instead of southeast and emerge in a different sea altogether. But Elias's mind was already elsewhere and his ambition was to reach 'the civilization surrounded by deserts', or Chinese Turkestan and Kashgaria, the Muslim-dominated areas in the shadow of the Tien Shan Mountains.

His second expedition – the one which made his name – was a Herculean journey. Leaving Peking (Beijing) in July 1872, he travelled alone, picking up guides as best he could along the way. He went north to Mongolia, across the Gobi, north of the Western deserts, ran into local fighting and eventually crossed the Russian border over the Altai Mountains. He had covered 4,345 km (2,700 miles) at about 24–32 km (15–20 miles) a day, mainly walking, sometimes on horse or camel, but he was still only half way to his final destination. This was the start of the trans-Russia railway at Nizhniy Novgorod (Gorky) at the other end of Siberia, which he crossed in what was by then midwinter. All the way he continued to take his observations and positional readings, which were eventually delivered to Kew Observatory. Sir Henry Rawlinson, President of the RGS, described this expedition as 'one of the most extraordinary feats of modern times, that would live in the memory long after other [journeys] are forgotten'.

The Great Game

Elias had by now either run out of money or exhausted the patience of his family and needed income. He was appointed Extra Attaché of the Foreign Department of the Government of India, beginning the major phase of his career as in effect a government agent or spy. He held a number of appointments, but all disguised his real function – intelligence gatherer. Over the next 15 years Elias undertook six major and many minor expeditions, often ostensibly as a private citizen but always in fact pursuing the interests of the British Empire in Asia. The expeditions were sometimes his own initiative, but more often the government needed information. The alternatives were either to send a fully equipped and publicly appointed mission or to waive formalities and leave it to Elias. Britain's greatest fear was the possibility of Russian designs on India, and the stand-off between the two empires became known as the Great Game – a phoney war fought by gentleman explorers on both sides with hardly a shot fired. Elias was the archetype and most experienced of all Britain's Great Gamers.

His first two missions were into Chinese Turkestan, travelling across the forbidding Karakoram Mountains to Kashgar, then as now the centre of power, information and politics in Central Asia. The next was the Pamir, or Roof of the World, expedition, in 1885, where he sought to discover the source of the Oxus. Crossing into Afghanistan from Chitral, he became the first Briton to explore the Pamirs north of Lake Syr Kul. He claimed Rang Kul as the legendary Dragon Lake of Chinese Buddhist pilgrims and spent months investigating and mapping, reporting back on the considerable difficulties any potential invading force would encounter. There was an aura of impenetrability and mystery about the Pamirs, so this journey further enhanced Ney's reputation as a fearless, clandestine adventurer, particularly as once again he was alone and was also now sick, probably with amoebic dysentery. Despite ill health, he was soon recruited to go to Sikkim to help the Indian government in a political dispute, while his final major expedition, in 1889, took him to Burma to negotiate borders with Siam. He returned to England because of his illness, and died there in 1897.

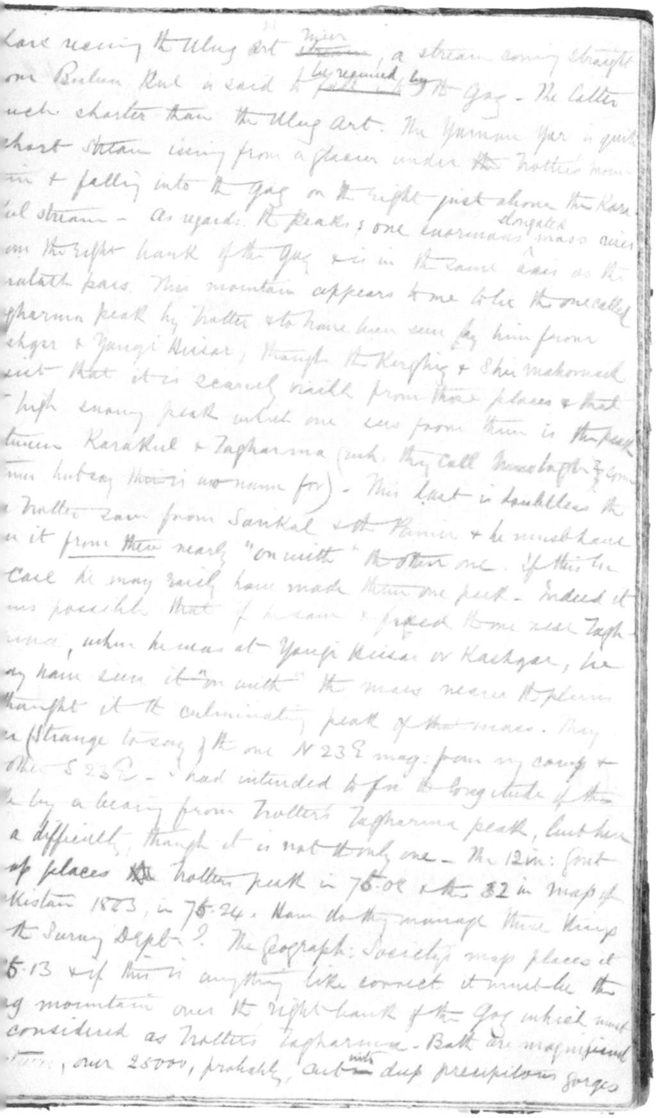

Even the other great names of Central Asian exploration looked up to Elias, partly because of his indisputable breadth of knowledge and experience, but also partly because of his refusal ever to be competitive about his career and impressive achievements.

Pages from one of Elias's notebooks, with his copious observations, drawn and written, of mountains seen from Karakol (in Kyrgyzstan). On all his expeditions Elias made thorough records, including survey measurements and meteorological and geological data, which provided valuable information about the topography and the political situation of the regions he passed through.

Francis Younghusband

SOLDIER-MYSTIC IN TIBET

(1863–1942)

We had brought with us every scrap of rope that could be spared from the ponies' gear, and we tied these and all the men's turbans and waist-clothes together into one long rope, by which we let a man down the ice-slope on to the first projecting rock ... when he had reached the rock we tied the upper end of the rope ... and one by one we came down the slope, hanging on to the rope.

Francis Younghusband,* The Heart of a Continent, *1896

Francis Younghusband was inspired to travel by his uncle, Robert Shaw, a tea planter, who was the first European to enter Kashgar and received a Royal Geographical Society Patron's Medal for the achievement. A serious young man with an ingrained morality rare even in Victorian days, Younghusband sailed for the first time to India, aged 19, in July 1882. He joined his regiment, the 1st Dragoon Guards, at Meerut, the town where the Mutiny had broken out, and soon made himself unpopular with his fellow officers. Prudish to a degree and very conscious of his stature, being only 1.65 m (5 ft 5 in) tall, he did his best to wean his companions from the sins of the flesh. He dreamt of proving himself in some dramatic way and settled on Manchuria as being the key location in the Great Game; after careful research he managed to persuade his colonel to allow him to go there.

In 1886 he sailed to Shanghai, making his way then by mule cart to Mukden, Manchuria's capital. Heading north, things became much tougher and Younghusband showed for the first time his extraordinary fortitude and courage. His two British companions were much older and more experienced, but they were amazed by his reckless daring, combined with a Spartan dedication to conducting and writing up their research. Conditions deteriorated as winter set in and they approached the Siberian border. There they were well received by the Russians guarding the frontier and allowed to cross over to visit the garrison port on the Amur River, where they gathered much useful strategic information.

Back in Peking, staying at the embassy, Younghusband wrote a substantial report, which he was just finishing when his colonel arrived. Astonishingly, after a telegram from the British ambassador to the Viceroy of India, the 23-year-old cavalry officer was given permission to set out alone to travel some 4,000 km (2,500 miles) west through country virtually unknown to outsiders. He crossed the Gobi Desert by camel, struggled through the foothills of the Altai Mountains, then across the dreaded desert of Dzungaria, up into the Tien Shan or Celestial Mountains and, at last, to Kashgar and civilization of a sort.

His subsequent journey south to India over the Himalayas was, typically, by a route never before tried by a European: the fabled Mustagh Pass. His description of the way he and his companions descended thousands of sheer feet using turbans, reins and cloths for ropes has become legendary in the annals of exploration. Sven Hedin described it as 'the most difficult and dangerous achievement in these

Probably taken in 1891, this group portrait shows Younghusband (second from right), who had been sent to Kashgar on an unsuccessful diplomatic mission, with other Great Gamers, Sir George Macartney, Henry A. Lennard and Richard Beech. He had arrived there from China after achieving the first part of the remarkable overland journey which made his name.

mountains so far'. On arrival in Srinagar on 30 October 1887, after being unheard of for seven months, he was hailed as having made one of the most remarkable journeys ever.

Mission to Tibet

With his fame as an explorer established, Younghusband made several more political, scientific and adventurous expeditions over the Himalayas. In 1890 he was awarded the Patron's Medal of the Royal Geographical Society and soon after he set off for Kashgar again, where he spent seven depressing months in rather unsuccessful diplomacy with the Russians. Ten unsatisfactory years followed, during which his military career stagnated and he searched for meaning in life, becoming increasingly obsessed with a mystical search for God. Then, in 1899, his close friend Lord Curzon took over as Viceroy of India. Both men were firm believers in the threat the Russians posed to British interests in India and the need to defeat them at every turn. As a result, Younghusband was invited in 1903 to lead an extraordinary punitive military expedition to Lhasa, the capital of Tibet. It was, perhaps, the last undertaking of its kind. In addition to 1,200 troops and 16,000 pack animals, 10,000 coolies carried the massive amounts of equipment thought necessary to establish in the eyes of supposedly ignorant natives the power and the glory of the British Raj. Younghusband alone packed, among much else, 67 shirts, ranging from twill to dress, and at least seven suits, including full dress for audiences.

Tibet was still a relatively unknown land the size of western Europe and surrounded by myths and legends. With the two Maxim guns and four artillery pieces they dragged over the mountains the British had complete military superiority, but they were still lucky the whole affair did not end in disaster. The ignorance of Tibetan ways was profound and the country hostile in the extreme (around 700 Tibetans were massacred at one village en route). When, eventually, they reached Lhasa in August 1904 and marched behind a Gurkha band through the streets in full dress uniforms, all the Tibetans watching clapped. The British thought they were making a fine show and were being appreciated, little knowing that Tibetans clap to drive out evil spirits. Moreover, his government had never really wanted Younghusband to reach Lhasa and he had exceeded his authority in doing so. As a result, in spite of the added fame it gave him, the eventual outcome for Tibet was disastrous. Instead of retaining British influence there, which might, perhaps, have led to independence, as with India, responsibility for Tibet was ceded to China, whose interests have predominated ever since.

In 1904, at the head of a massive force, Younghusband marches into Lhasa. He was exceeding his authority and, while this adventure gained him great fame, it also ruined his military career. A punitive expedition, the like of which was never again to be mounted under the British Empire, it sealed the fate of Tibet and arguably led to its domination by China.

A Remarkable Life

Younghusband's life was remarkable in the extreme. He was outstandingly fit and strong (as a young man he held the World Record for the 300-yard dash); he discovered a new overland route from China to India; as President of the RGS, of which he had once been the youngest Fellow, he organized – in fact he practically invented – expeditions to climb Mount Everest; and he invaded Tibet. On one of his expeditions his presumed death as a spy in the Pamirs almost sparked off a war between British India and Tsarist Russia. Pompous and repressed, he spent his declining years leading the way in developing outlandish mystical philosophy and advanced sexual thinking.

Marc Aurel Stein

SCHOLAR ON THE SILK ROAD

(1862–1943)

The most prodigious combination of scholar, explorer, archaeologist and geographer of his generation.

Owen Lattimore on Marc Aurel Stein

For Stein the explorer, the landscape was his guide but the past was his destination. He deserves a place among the great because of his unparalleled ability to read a landscape and visualize its historical role. Coupled with his scholarship, organizational skills, extraordinary stamina and a doggedness which proved exasperating to many but ensured results, he was able to carry out archaeological explorations over a vast swathe of Eurasia during five decades and return not only with over 100,000 excavated artifacts, but also over 10,000 photographs, extensive and accurate maps, and a store of knowledge which continues to inform scholarship today.

Marc Aurel Stein was born to Jewish parents in Budapest in 1862 but baptized into the Lutheran Church for practical reasons. He showed little signs of faith during his life and was only confronted with his background when asked to help family fleeing the Nazi regime and Jewish colleagues in Mussolini's Italy; by this time he had taken British nationality. His interests were formed early: as a boy he was captivated by Alexander the Great's travels and this fascination continued for the rest of his life. Other explorers soon also excited his attention, among them Marco Polo and Xuanzang, the 7th-century Chinese monk who made a pilgrimage to India.

Educated in Budapest, Dresden, Vienna, Leipzig and Tübingen, Stein completed his doctoral work on Old Persian and Indology in 1883 and then studied Punjabi in England. Military service in Hungary equipped him with surveying skills. On his return to London he impressed members of the Indian Council and was offered the joint position of Principal of the Oriental College in Lahore and Registrar of Punjab University. He sailed to India in 1888, intending to return to an academic post in Europe within a few years. But archaeological forays to the Punjabi Salt Mountains – where he learnt the rudiments of photography – and to the Swat Valley in the North-West Frontier with the British army awakened a passion that determined the course of his life. The research and writing that sandwiched his explorations was not done in cloistered university libraries, but on a folding table in an alpine meadow 3,350 m

(11,000 ft) above sea level in the mountains of Kashmir near Srinagar – at a place called Mohand Marg – with flowers on the table and his dog at his feet. And although in his early years he gave academic papers, these were soon replaced by public lectures intended to promote his work and aid fundraising for his next expedition. Exploration became an addiction that was never satisfied.

Without private means, Stein had to work for a living and to cultivate patrons. Apart from a brief posting in Calcutta, he remained in Lahore for his whole life. He had to secure extended leave both for the explorations themselves and for preparing his reports and publications. His employers praised his efficiency, zeal and tact while despairing at his constant demands for leave and better conditions. As the secretary of the Royal Geographical Society remarked over a minor financial matter: 'As usual I found that in spite my best efforts I had been defeated by Stein'. Without this resolute determination his major expeditions would have been impossible.

Treasures of the Taklamakan

Stein's name as an archaeological explorer was made on his first major expedition – to the Taklamakan Desert in what is now Xinjiang in western China. The first tantalizing glimpses of archaeological treasures began to appear in the 1890s. These included manuscripts on paper written in Indian script but in an unknown, possibly Iranian,

Stein's desk at his summer camp at Mohand Marg in Kashmir, taken in 1905. The dog beneath the chair is the second in the line of Stein's fox terriers, Dash II, also known as 'Dash the Great' for his expedition exploits.

language. As an Indo-Iranian scholar, Stein was intrigued and he determined to explore Khotan, a thriving Silk Road kingdom in the 1st millennium, noted in Chinese histories and by Xuanzang. Stein went to the highest levels, gaining the patronage of the Viceroy, Lord Curzon, but it still took him two years to secure permission and the necessary funds. He was 37 when he set out in May 1900.

This arena – the sand-buried towns and temples of the Taklamakan – was to engage him for three decades and four expeditions, during which he covered over 16,000 km (10,000 miles) on pony and foot. He considered the Sahara and the Arabian and Iranian deserts 'tame' compared to the Taklamakan, whose interior held no water and no life. Stein always prepared meticulously, never underestimating the dangers of the terrain (although downplaying them in his accounts). Uncompromising in his concern for the safety of both men and animals, he was more distraught at the death of his favourite pony in the arid Kunlun – sacrificing his last bottle of brandy in a vain attempt to revive him – than at the loss of two of his own toes to frostbite.

This last mishap occurred when he was photographing the surrounding ranges with his newly acquired photo-theodolite camera. Stein loved technology and was always keen to test the latest gadgets, camping equipment and clothing. But the lapse of concentration which resulted in the injury was uncharacteristic: his goal was not the adrenaline rush of testing the limits of his endurance to the point of danger, but to ensure the safe return of his discoveries and record them for future generations of scholars. And the finds from this, his second expedition, included the manuscripts and paintings for which he is best remembered. They were acquired on a foray further east to Dunhuang in the Gobi Desert.

Dunhuang

Almost a thousand years before Stein, monks at the site of the Mogao Buddhist cave temples, also known as Caves of the Thousand Buddhas, had reused a small cave, originally excavated as a memorial to the local abbot, as a store for tens of thousands of paper manuscripts in Chinese, Tibetan and other Silk Road languages – the earliest dated printed documents in the world – as well as hundreds of fine silk paintings. The cave was sealed in about 1000 and its treasures remained protected in the dark, dry atmosphere until 1900, when the self-appointed guardian of the cave temples stumbled upon the hidden doorway. He presented some objects to local officials, but Stein persuaded him to part with far more, which were sent to London. The rest of

Detail of an early 8th-century painting on silk of the Buddha preaching the law, found in the Library Cave at Dunhuang. The detail shows a bodhisattva and monks attendant on the Buddha.

the library was then dispersed to Paris, Beijing, St Petersburg and Kyoto, and Stein is held responsible for its breakup and either praised for his 'discovery' or vilified for his 'theft'. But Dunhuang forms only part of his achievements: his books, maps, photographs, desert excavations and other finds remain just as significant for our understanding of the history of the eastern Silk Road kingdoms, their imperial neighbours and world history.

Themes Old and New

The arena of Stein's interest was vast, from the Mediterranean Sea to the Pamir Mountains and northern India, and from China to India. It was not restricted to one landscape – desert and mountains each had their seductions. The Taklamakan remained the major theme in the first stage of his explorations, but minor themes also crowded in, including a passion for identifying the ancient battle sites of Alexander the Great in northern India and Pakistan, uncovering the westernmost examples of Buddhist temples in eastern Iran and mapping the desolate peaks of the Kunlun.

After his unsuccessful and frustrating fourth Taklamakan expedition of 1930, it was clear that China was closed to him and he moved his attention elsewhere – the western Silk Road of Iran. He completed four archaeological expeditions in the 1930s. His young Iranian companion on the last of these wrote that 'It would be useless to repeat all the sufferings and unheard of hardships which we endured on this dangerous and unbearable journey'. The 75-year-old Stein described this same journey as 'delightful marches'.

In between these major trips he added new themes: Iraq and the Middle East, including aerial surveying of ancient fortifications in Syria and Jordan, as well as continuing in the tracks of Alexander. In his 79th year he completed a three-month tour in the Indus Kohistan, most of it on foot over glacial moraines leading to snow-covered passes at 4,750 m (15,000 ft).

Stein was single-minded but not solitary. Although he did not marry, he had a large circle of devoted friends, family he supported throughout his life and colleagues who held him in the highest respect. His efficiency at his work and his explorations was matched in his friendships: even in the middle of the Taklamakan after a long day of digging, he would settle down to ensure he completed his Christmas cards. His death was appropriate. Having vainly attempted for four decades to explore sites in Afghanistan – constantly thwarted by politics – in his 81st year he finally received an invitation from the American Consul. Making plans for a year-long tour of places he had dreamed of since reading of Alexander's travels in

The frontispiece of a popular Buddhist text, 'The Diamond Sutra', found in Dunhuang and printed using woodblocks in May 868, making it the earliest dated printed book in the world. It was commissioned by a man called Wang Jie in memory of his parents: disseminating images and words of the Buddha was an act of merit and the Buddhist community took full advantage of this new technology.

childhood he reached Kabul in October 1943. He promptly caught a cold and, on realizing he would die, spoke of his funeral and expressed his happiness at having reached Kabul at last. He was buried there with Christian rites and his grave, still well tended, lies in the British Cemetery.

Although Stein did not start his explorations until relatively late in life and had a full-time job, he spent years in the field, climbing mountains, traversing deserts and, above all, excavating at over 1,000 archaeological sites, uncovering groundbreaking finds. His maps and photographs are still used today. He recorded the sites and their objects in amazing detail, with a care not found among his contemporaries. And unlike most of these, he did not generally travel with a team of experts and assistants. He was never seriously injured nor did he flirt with death. His explorations were driven by a love of landscape and history, and the desire to make new scholarly discoveries for others to use.

No account of Stein as an explorer should fail to mention his constant canine companions, a succession of fox terriers all called Dash. The second among them earned the soubriquet 'Dash the Great' and was lauded by the *Daily Mail* for having 'true British terrier blood in his veins'.

RIVERS

A disproportionate amount of exploratory effort has been devoted to rivers. Their existence, pouring out of unknown lands, challenged men to discover their source and find out whether they might provide routes to undiscovered places or ways around *terra incognita*. This was especially the case in North America, where the compulsion to find a quick route to the Indies obsessed explorers for nearly 500 years. Samuel de Champlain was the man who opened up much of the territory that was to become Canada to colonization. Unlike most of his contemporaries, he recognized the skills of the indigenous tribes already living there and strove to learn from them and to emulate them. As a result, he was successful in achieving much settlement peacefully and without the usual bloodshed associated with the conquest of Amerindians. Two hundred years after Champlain, in 1793, a young Scotsman, Alexander Mackenzie, finally achieved the first crossing of the North American continent, while seeking a commercial route to trade with Russia. With a short portage over the watershed at the Rockies, he proved that there was a virtually continuous river route to the west, but it was never to be of any use commercially.

In Africa, two of the mysteries that preoccupied the gentlemen in London who sent explorers out into the world were where the fabled gold of Timbuktu came from and which way the River Niger flowed. Mungo Park attempted to find answers to these questions, but perished on his second expedition. However, most attention in Africa was devoted to seeking the source of the Nile. The first European to achieve this in 1770, although it was that of the Blue rather than the White Nile, was James Bruce, a formidable traveller blessed with great size and huge charm. These ensured his survival when most would have expired. Eighty years later, one of the most significant and oldest mysteries of geography remained unsolved and the search became frantic. Finding the true source of the Nile, for no other purpose than to establish its

A detail from a watercolour of the Mackenzie River by J. Linton Palmer, 1868. Almost a hundred years earlier, Alexander Mackenzie made the first crossing of the North American continent, by birch bark canoe. Although he did find a river route, it proved unsuitable for trade.

A boat in the rapids of the Mekong River from Garnier's Voyage d'exploration en Indo-Chine *(1885). The realities of the Mekong's turbulent waters soon shattered all Garnier's dreams of a navigable river that would open up vast areas to French influence and trade with China.*

existence, became as important in its day as reaching the summit of Everest or sending a man to the moon. Richard Burton (p. 80), among his many adventures, was determined the glory would be his, but it was John Hanning Speke who found and named Lake Victoria and claimed, without actually proving it, that this was the fabled source, and one of the epic – and tragic – feuds of exploration was born.

David Livingstone is the epitome of African missionary explorers and the journeys he made in pursuit of his zeal, especially following the course of the Zambezi, equal or surpass any who came before or after him to the 'dark continent'. Henry Morton Stanley is best known for his encounter with the missing Dr Livingstone. But he went on to undertake a series of major journeys and military exploits throughout the continent, many of which were by river, including the Congo, which he effectively opened up for commercial exploitation. His transformation from childhood in a Welsh workhouse to becoming a famous American newspaper reporter, then a legendary explorer and military leader and finally a Member of Parliament and a knight of the realm, is one of the most remarkable in the history of exploration.

In the Far East there were riverine mysteries to solve, as well. The Mekong, which flows down from the Himalayas through Indo-China was, in the 19th century, seen as a possible gateway to China for the French. Francis Garnier was obsessed by the possibilities this offered for French influence in the region and was the man who, although technically second-in-command, led the expedition which eventually ascended the river as far as China and then descended the Yangtze to the coast. Less recognized in his native France than in Britain, the RGS described him as 'the century's most gallant and talented explorer'.

Discovering the source of the Nile was one of the greatest challenges and quests of 18th- and 19th-century explorers. James Bruce, accompanied by the artist Luigi Balugani, who drew this watercolour of a hammer-headed shark, succeeded in finding the source of the Blue Nile.

Samuel de Champlain

OPENING UP CANADA'S WILDERNESS

(mid-1570s–1635)

All men are not suited to run risks; the toil and fatigue are great, but nothing is to be had without toil. That is what one must think in these affairs [exploration]; it will be when it pleases God. As for me, I will always prepare the way for those who will wish, after me, to carry it on.

Samuel de Champlain, 1632

Champlain was the first explorer in North America to conclude that exploration away from the Atlantic seaboard depended entirely on establishing good relations with the native peoples, and learning from them about the geography of the land and how to live off it. He was born during the mid-1570s at Brouage, on the Atlantic coast of France, where his father, Antoine Champlain, was a naval captain and pilot. Two uncles, George Camaret and Guillaume Allene, were also naval captains, and the latter was particularly influential on Champlain's life. The Champlain family had the status and respectability that comes from such occupations in a small town where the harbour dominated the economy. In view of his maritime background it is no wonder that Champlain once wrote that he had been drawn to the sea from early youth.

It is probable that Champlain attended an academy for young men of respectable families known to have existed in Brouage. Graduates were suitable for careers in the army or service with a lord. His strengths in surveying and cartography, and his lack of polish and absence of classicisms in his written French are reflections of the academy's curriculum. The first documentary evidence relating to Champlain comes from the pay records of Henri IV's Brittany army during the 'Wars of Religion'. In late February 1595 he arrived at the Quimper garrison as a *fourrier* and *aide* to Jean Hardy, *maréchal de logis* of the army. As a *fourrier* he was responsible for seeking accommodation for the royal retinue and officers, and as aide to the *maréchal* he would have worked on the sketches and surveys that were compiled for Hardy's map *Duche de Bretaigne.* Although a *fourrier* was a low-ranking position, Champlain's pay was that of a lieutenant: he received extra pay for delivering confidential memos between the king and his senior officers. In 1598, when he was demobilized, Champlain was an ensign.

After leaving the army, Champlain met his uncle Guillaume Allene in Blavet (now Port-Louis) on the south coast of Brittany, where the Spanish troops, allies of the Catholic League against Henri IV, were being evacuated. Allene had been hired to take the 500-tun ship *Saint-Julian* with Spanish troops and armaments to Cadiz. Champlain joined the ship and stayed with it for a tour of the Spanish Caribbean for two and a half years. It was during that time that he learned the basic principles of navigation. Upon his return to France, Champlain gave a full report of his knowledge of the Spanish West Indies to Henri IV.

To Canada

Late in 1602 Champlain met Aymar de Chaste, Governor of Dieppe, who asked him if he would join his fact-finding expedition to Canada. Champlain was eager to go but thought it necessary first to get permission from the king, who had given him a pension and to whom he felt obligated 'by birth'. Henri IV was determined to colonize Canada and sent an order through his Secretary of State that Champlain was to

Champlain surveyed the Grand Sault St-Louis (Lachine Rapids) in 1611; after having seen them in July 1603, he correctly deduced that exploration with European technology was impossible and could only by carried out with native help and their canoes.

accompany the expedition to determine if the banks of the St Lawrence could be settled and whether it was possible to explore westwards across the Lachine Rapids. Champlain arrived at Tadoussac on the St Lawrence in May 1603, where he witnessed a treaty between the resident Montagnais and the court of Henri IV permitting French settlement in Canada in return for French help against their Iroquois enemies.

During the summer Champlain made a resource survey of the river from the Gaspé to Montreal Island and obtained three accounts, with maps, from Algonquin and Montagnais informants of the water routes westwards. His conclusions had a profound effect on the future exploration of Canada, which Champlain maintained was only possible with Native help, because of both their geographical knowledge and ability to live off the land, and their canoes. To explore and live in Canada meant that peaceful relations had to be developed between the Native inhabitants and the French, involving reciprocal obligations such as mutual aid in war and trade.

Champlain's manuscript map of his survey along the Atlantic coast from the La Have River, Nova Scotia, to Cape Cod, Massachusetts, made between 1604 and 1607. This map shows Champlain's cartography at its best.

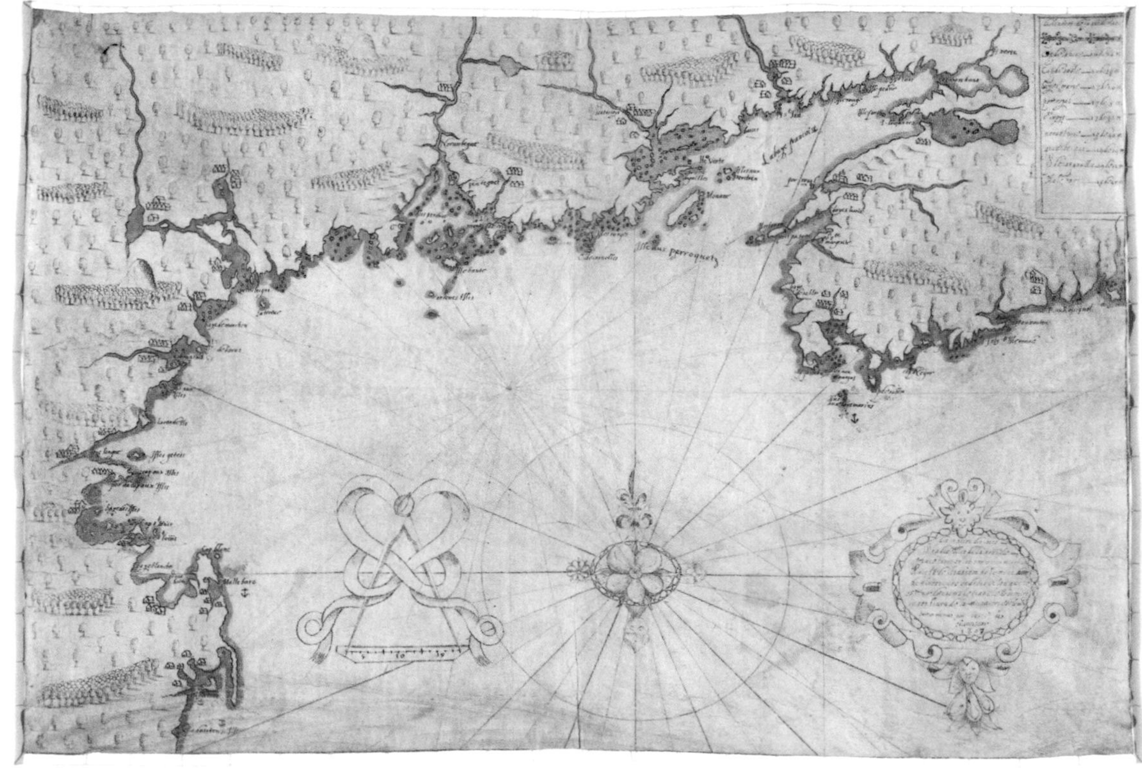

An engraving depicting the first shot fired on the Iroquois in the raid Champlain joined against them. Although historians have pilloried him for this action, they have overlooked the fact that he was ordered to fulfil France's obligations to their new allies.

Champlain again gave a full report, with a map, to Henri IV on his return late in the year, and published his first book *Des Sauvages.*

Between 1604 and 1607, Champlain was charged with a similar resource survey and detailed mapping of the Atlantic coast of North America, from Cape Breton Island to Cape Cod, and once more he dutifully reported to the king. In 1608 he was back on the St Lawrence, having been ordered to build a settlement at Quebec and initiate exploration westwards. In 1609, to fulfil France's treaty obligations, he joined his Native allies on a raid against the Iroquois on Lake Champlain (named after him). This resulted in a last report to Henri IV, who was assassinated in 1610. In 1613 Champlain attempted to explore the Ottawa River without Native guides and was turned back by the Algonquin. Finally, in 1615 he made it to lakes Huron and Ontario by joining a Huron-Algonquin war party into Iroquois country, where he was severely wounded.

On his return to Quebec in 1616 Champlain ceased exploration and devoted himself to the settlement of Canada. In 1629 he was appointed lieutenant-governor of Canada by Cardinal Richelieu, the most powerful man in France after the king. During his lifetime he published four substantial books and a number of documents,

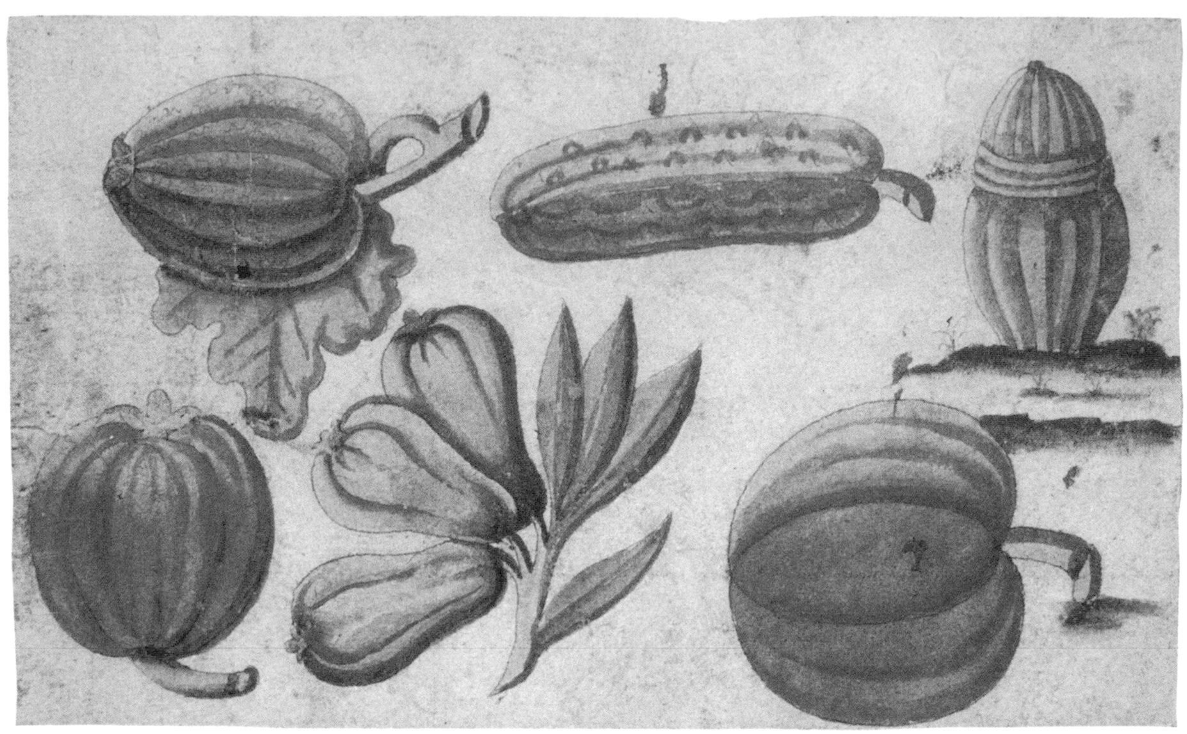

Illustration of squash from Brief Discours*: this manuscript journal, with its illustrations, exists in three varying copies, each in a different hand, none of them Champlain's, although it has been attributed to him.*

comprising some 1,300 printed pages, five folding maps, 22 small maps and 14 illustrations. Champlain died at Quebec of a stroke on 25 December 1635.

Champlain's Legacy

Champlain's appointments and successes were due not only to his personal qualities and abilities – an uncomplaining nature, tenacity, honesty, a capacity for hard work, a desire to improve himself, skill in surveying and description of observable facts – but also to his complete loyalty to his superiors and the trusting, active support of his monarch. Fundamental to Champlain as an explorer was his ability to free himself from European views of technological and social superiority. He was the first to see that only the adoption of many Native customs would make it possible to live in and explore the formidable physical environment of Canada. Supported by the Jesuits, he came to the conclusion that it was desirable to promote intermarriage between the Huron and the French: 'that we be one people'. So successful were his policies that by 1685, when the first English-Dutch expedition reached Lake Ontario, the French had already explored and mapped the entire Great Lakes system, the Mississippi River to the Gulf of Mexico and two of the major river systems to James Bay.

James Bruce

CHARM AND COURAGE IN ABYSSINIA

(1730–1794)

All who had attempted the same journey hitherto had met with disappointment, disgrace or death; for my part, although I underwent every sort of toil, danger, and all manner of hardship, yet these were not confined to myself. I suffered always honourably, and in common with the rest of the state; and when sun-shiny days happened (for sun-shiny days there were, and very brilliant ones too), of these I was permitted freely to partake.

James Bruce*, Travels to Discover the Source of the Nile, *1790

James Bruce was a true explorer. He did his exploring for the love of it, discovering things of value and recording them accurately. His great achievement was to solve one of the great conundrums of his age: the source of the Nile. The fact that it was the Blue Nile rather than the longer, but weaker, White one, and that very few believed him, brought out all the worst traits in his character when Bruce returned to Britain in 1774. It is the Bruce of the 'sun-shiny days' – when he was living in Africa, expanding the knowledge of humankind and having a glorious time – whom we should admire and be thankful for.

Bruce was considered notably handsome in his day; miniature by John Smart (1776).

Today there are no remaining terrestrial records with which to compare finding the source of the Nile – even the wrong one. In Bruce's own day, the fact that it was yet to be discovered was seen as an embarrassment and a failure – to such an extent that it was known as the 'opprobrium of geographers'. In what historian Richard Holmes writes about as the Age of Wonder, intellectual discovery was of immense importance – voyages to the far side of the world and the finding of new planets and creatures were all followed with keen interest. Bruce not only discovered the source of the Blue Nile, he also charted the Red Sea, recovered the lost Book of Enoch and learnt a huge amount about Ethiopia and Sudan, their history, flora and fauna. He combined intellectual rigour with great physical stamina and raw courage. It is tragic that it was a hundred years before his discoveries were acknowledged.

Early Years

Born in 1730, the son of a Scottish laird, Bruce was raised an English gentleman at a time when being Scottish was politically rash. Brilliant at school, he later taught himself languages, astronomy, cartography and much else; he became a wine merchant and married, but sadly his wife died on their honeymoon. A late developer, he was 32 before he persuaded Lord Halifax, King George III's Prime Minister, to appoint him consul to Algiers. He then set off to Africa with the avowed intent to discover the source of the Nile.

Bruce's landholdings provided the coal which powered the improved steam engine of James Watt, one of the first industrial revolutionaries, and the profits allowed Bruce to outfit his expedition from his own pocket. He bought the best of everything – from chronometers and telescopes to horses and weapons. And when he lost most of his equipment in a shipwreck off Libya, his quadrant was replaced by the French King Louis XV, at the behest of the great naturalist the Comte de Buffon. Given that Britain and France were at war at the time, this showed quite how charming Bruce was.

In Abyssinia

This charm also helped him in Abyssinia (Ethiopia), when after many travails and adventures he eventually arrived in that country, having been replaced as consul in Algiers. Abyssinia was in a state of near anarchy, with the young emperor on the throne being controlled by his chancellor, a wily old general, Ras Michael, from the northern province of Tigray. The Oromo people of the south were fighting their way up into the Christian highlands in an expansion that continues to this day. At court, Bruce won over the emperor and Ras Michael, as well as the dowager empress and Michael's wife, Esther. Throughout his travels, he made friends with men with similar characteristics to his own, while those with less bold temperaments disliked him. Women fell at his feet.

Assailed by Muslim and animist invaders, the Christian highlands of Abyssinia were unknown to the modern world and through a sort of national paranoia the state had cut itself off from the rest of Christendom. Allies on its borders were ordered not to let travellers enter the country and those few that managed to get in were killed or detained. By a combination of charm, bombast and healing (like so many who followed in his footsteps, Bruce had learnt the rudiments of medicine), Bruce managed to be accepted wherever he went. He often pretended to be a relative of King George or to be on some special mission to give himself higher status.

Cruikshank was one of many 'chicken-hearted critics', cartoonists and writers who mocked the irascible explorer, both on his return to Britain and following the publication of his Travels.

Being accepted at court was not enough, however; he still needed to find the Nile's source, a quest that was made particularly perilous by a civil war that got in his way. It took many months of intrigue, failed attempts and a good few love affairs, before he managed to reach the source: 'It is easier to guess than to describe the situation of my mind at that moment – standing in that spot which had baffled the genius, industry and inquiry, of both ancients and moderns, for the course of near three thousand years.' But it was, of course, disappointing – sources of rivers are almost invariably puddles: 'I found a despondency gaining ground fast upon me, and blasting the crown of laurels I had too rashly woven for myself.'

Bruce's great genius was manifested in then being allowed to leave. This was achieved with yet more charm, bluff and the fact that he paid his debts of honour. He commanded the emperor's heavy cavalry at the battle of Serbraxos and, at great risk, he guarded a murdered pretender's corpse when civil war further tore the country asunder. His many noble deeds were noticed and earnt him safe passage from Abyssinia, first to Khartoum and eventually to Aswan on the Nile and home. During

A canja under sail, from Bruce's Travels *(1790). Bruce suffered badly from sea-sickness, yet he sailed up the Nile and charted the Red Sea.*

an eventful journey through the Fung kingdom of Sennaar and across the Nubian Desert, he dodged death from thirst, attack, illness and the executioner's sword before returning, with numerous specimens, finds, notes and observations, to Europe, where he was feted in France and disbelieved in his native Britain.

A Flawed Character

This description somewhat ignores Bruce's faults – and faults he certainly had. Bruce took the artist Luigi Balugani to Abyssinia with him. Balugani died there and Bruce failed to give him credit for accompanying him to the source, or helping to paint his pictures. He also attacked the assertions of two missionaries who had reached the source before him, but whose claims were not accepted by the world either. When Bruce returned to Europe, where he had been presumed dead for many years, he discovered that his fiancée had married an Italian marquis. He immediately challenged the Italian to a duel. In London he made enemies of Samuel Johnson (who had translated one of the missionary accounts), Horace Walpole and James Boswell, all men of a very different type, who sniped about him behind his back. Bruce stormed off to Scotland in a childish huff.

Sick after his escape through the Nubian Desert, he retired to his Scottish estate at Kinnaird, lashing out at anyone who doubted his word and suing his neighbours over trifles. Eventually he discovered what he had been searching for all along: someone to love who didn't immediately die. After many years of uncommon philandering, he settled down to married life with Mary Dundas. In Ethiopia he is thought to have had a child with Esther, Ras Michael's wife; at the source he had seduced the daughter of a local chief. In Italy during his return home he had inspired letters addressed to 'mio Brus' and in England Fanny Burney had fallen for him.

It took the death of his wife in 1785 and the encouragement of his few steadfast friends to force Bruce to write down the history of his travels, which were eventually published in 1790. The book started with an attack on his 'chicken-hearted critics' and rambled on for five volumes quarto. Nonetheless, there was gold inside it – gold that became more apparent in the second edition published after his death. It went on to inspire Mungo Park (p. 130) to track the Niger, Samuel Taylor Coleridge to populate Xanadu with Abyssinian maids and Wilfred Thesiger – who bought his copy with his first year's pocket money at Eton – to spend a lifetime exploring (p. 225). And he had at last discovered the source of the Nile – although the White Nile is longer, most of Egypt's water comes from the Blue.

David Livingstone (p. 142) credited Bruce with being 'a greater traveller than any of us'. And the painter Zoffany, who met Bruce when he was in his pomp, caught the man exactly: 'This great man; the wonder of his age, the terror of married men, and a constant lover'. What better epitaph could a man ask for?

TRAVELS
TO DISCOVER THE
SOURCE OF THE NILE,
In the Years 1768, 1769, 1770, 1771, 1772, and 1773.
IN FIVE VOLUMES.
BY JAMES BRUCE OF KINNAIRD, ESQ. F.R.S.

VOL. I.

EDINBURGH:
PRINTED BY J. RUTHVEN,
FOR G. G. J. AND J. ROBINSON, PATERNOSTER-ROW,
LONDON.
M.DCC.XC.

Bruce went to great lengths to ensure that his account of his travels (1790) was as similar as possible to Captain Cook's Voyage of the Pacific Ocean, *which was published six years previously.*

Alexander Mackenzie

CROSSING AMERICA BY CANOE

(1762–1820)

Without Indians I have very little hope of succeeding.

Alexander Mackenzie in a letter, 1790

The encounter or mentor that sets an explorer on his path remains hidden in many cases, but not with Alexander Mackenzie, the Scotsman who arguably made the most significant journey in the whole of 18th-century exploration by traversing the North American landmass for the first time. The occasion when he metamorphosed from an apprentice trader to a would-be explorer was the winter he spent cooped up in a hut in the far north of what is now Alberta, Canada, in the company of a notorious trader, unconvicted killer and adventurer, the American Peter Pond. It was Pond who drew the first tentative map of the land west of the Rocky Mountains 'from local knowledge' and who fired Mackenzie with a desire to find a trade route to the Pacific Ocean from the inland lake of Athabasca.

Mackenzie was born in 1762, in Stornaway, in the Hebrides, the son of respectable military folk made poor by new rent laws; his first language was Gaelic. In 1775, his father, and several relatives, emigrated first to the United States and then to Canada with the boy Mackenzie, apparently well educated though only 12. He started work at 15 as a clerk in a fur warehouse in Montreal. At 17 he joined the firm of John Gregory and had to serve another five years in the counting house before he got his chance to travel. In 1784 he headed first to Detroit, and then, offered a partnership by Gregory, he went north to get closer to the source of the lucrative beaver fur. It was money, not glory, that was always a major motive for Mackenzie.

For three years he learnt how to trade with Indians, living at a trading post on the English River, known to the Indians as the Missinipi or 'Great river'. Meanwhile, rumours of just how big a territory existed further west drew Mackenzie to winter with Pond at his trading post on the Athabasca River in 1787, some 64 km (40 miles) south of Lake Athabasca. Here, the young lad who thought he could make his fortune by simply trading with natives was instead inspired by Pond's dream of presenting furs to the Empress of Russia. Pond believed that it would be possible to travel from Lake Athabasca all the way to Europe, thus cutting out the vast trading firms that controlled the Indian and Pacific oceans.

A romantic portrait of Mackenzie by Thomas Lawrence (c. 1800). Mackenzie explored the northwest parts of Canada, then largely unknown, hoping to find a river trade route. In 1793, travelling by birchbark canoe, he became the first European to cross the Rocky Mountains and reach the Pacific coast.

But Pond had enemies and left to deal with accusations of murder, which meant that Mackenzie would be the one to explore further west. After establishing a fort on the banks of Lake Athabasca, the first site of the modern town of Fort Chipewyan, Mackenzie questioned local tribal chiefs and concluded a route to the Pacific could be found by travelling north up the Slave River. In 1789, in two large canoes, accompanied by his 'great friend' the Chipewyan chief Nestabeck, he passed through the Great Slave Lake and then down what was later named the Mackenzie River. Six weeks later he found himself not at the Pacific, but at the Arctic, facing 2,415 km

North Shore of the Great Slave Lake, by Sir George Back, 1833. On his first attempt to reach the Pacific, Mackenzie passed through the lake and discovered the river named after him.

(1,500 miles) of upstream paddling to reach home before winter set in. After 102 days out he made it back just as the ice was forming on the lakes in September.

Mackenzie had made a major discovery – a route to the Arctic – and many men would have stopped there. But he had not achieved that dream ignited by Peter Pond – the full journey west. As Mackenzie's notes were criticized for their poor grasp of navigation, he decided to spend a year back in Britain learning the skill he lacked. This meant travelling 4,800 km (3,000 miles) along Canadian waterways to the coast before embarking on a ship for Britain. In London he bought a new sextant and several chronometers, learnt how to use them and returned to Canada, which at that time meant only what we now know as eastern Canada.

The following summer, in 1792, he set off due west up the Peace River. He wrote that he went 'to traffick with the Russians' – an indication that Pond's dream was still alive. He reached what is now known as Peace River town, a distance of about 640 km (400 miles), where, with a contingent of 20 men, he built a fort and overwintered. The next year, as soon as the ice had melted, he set out with nine men and a dog in a single 8-m (25-ft) canoe, alternately paddling, towing and even sailing against the current of the increasingly powerful and unpeaceful Peace River.

After portaging the mile that separates the Arctic watershed from the Pacific watershed the going was all downhill – but the rapids grew worse and worse. Fearing for his canoe, Mackenzie followed local Nuxalk 'carrier' Indian information and walked a single-track path 320 km (200 miles) overland to the Pacific Ocean at Bella Coola. Here he pressed on some 48 km (30 miles) up a coastal fjord to reach a spot where he wrote in red paint on a rock the terse message: 'Alexander Mackenzie from Canada by land 1793'. Meeting fierce opposition from local tribes, Mackenzie was forced to beat a hasty retreat, offering steel axes and other trade goods to bargain his way out of tricky situations. In only eight days he and his party returned to their canoe on the Fraser, and in an incredible six weeks made their way the 2,575 km (1,600 miles) back to the Fort at Peace River. While he had achieved his ambition of discovering a route to the Pacific, it could never be of commercial use.

Mackenzie's health was permanently affected by his exertions. He complained of a 'bad stitch in my left breast' when forced to make a portage on the way back to Montreal. He stayed on in Canada, though, amassing a trading fortune before returning to Scotland in 1805. At 50, stooped and ill but still with business projects and a conquering energy, he married 14-year-old Geddes Margaret Mackenzie and had three children. He died eight years later at Mulnain, near Dunkeld, on 11 March 1820.

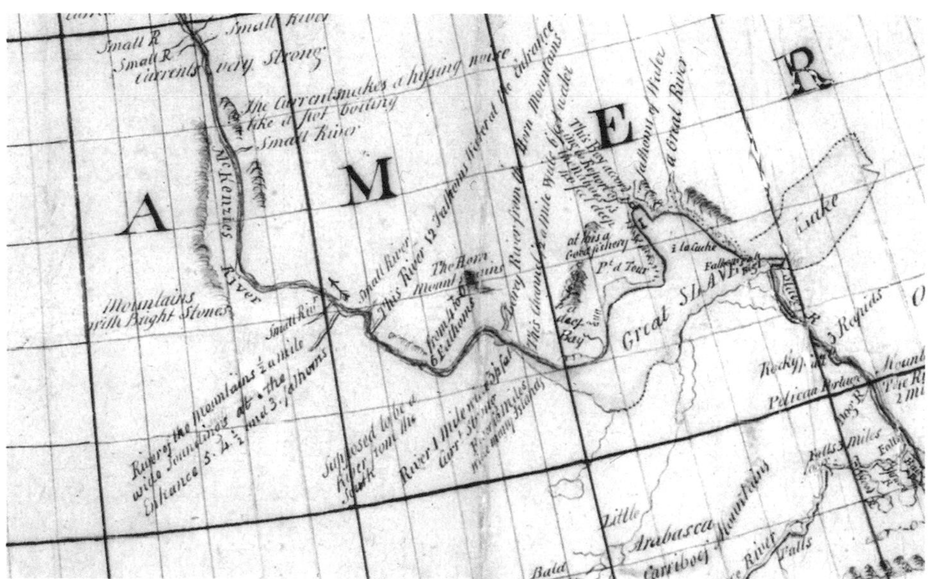

Detail from a map that is probably a copy of one made by Mackenzie during his voyage to the Arctic, with contemporary annotations describing features along the route; this section shows the Great Slave Lake and the Mackenzie River (here labelled McKenzie's River).

Mungo Park

SOLVING THE MYSTERY OF THE NIGER

(1771–1806)

He [the King of Bondo] thought it impossible that any man in his senses would undertake so dangerous a journey, merely to look at the country and its inhabitants.

Mungo Park,* Travels in the Interior Districts of Africa, *1799

Timing was everything in Mungo Park's life. A fortuitous meeting early on opened the door to exploration; a return to Britain at a moment of national crisis made him a celebrity; and bad timing on his last expedition led to his undoing in Africa. By then he had become one of the most famous explorers of the age and written a classic narrative that has remained in print ever since.

In the summer of 1792, Mungo Park, child of the Scottish borderlands, graduated in medicine at Edinburgh University. The first piece of good timing occurred that summer, when his brother-in-law, James Dickson, a seedsman at London's Covent Garden market, asked him to join him on a journey through the Scottish highlands. The young man obviously impressed the botanist, because he introduced Park to his patron in London, Sir Joseph Banks.

Banks was one of the wealthiest and most influential people in Britain. A great facilitator – scientific advisor to the British government, President of the Royal Society, founder of the Linnaean Society, inspiration behind the Royal Botanic Gardens in Kew – he recognized the young man's talents and by February 1793, Park was serving as assistant surgeon on an East India Company ship bound for Sumatra.

THE LURE OF AFRICA

Banks had travelled around the world with Captain Cook (p. 46) and seen some of the African coast. In 1788, he and some friends had founded the Association for Promoting the Discovery of the Interior Parts of Africa – the African Association in short. Acknowledging that it was a slur on the Age of Enlightenment that so little was known about the African interior, they agreed to sponsor 'geographical missionaries' to fill in the blanks on the map. The Association was created at a turning point in British history. Banks argued that overseas colonies cost time, money and manpower. And, as American colonists had shown a decade earlier, if they became successful, they

Timbuktu as it appeared in the 1820s. A Scottish explorer, Major Alexander Gordon Laing, finally reached it in August 1826, but was murdered on his way back to the coast. The Frenchman René Caillié was the first European to see the city and survive: in 1828 he revealed that it was nothing more than a 'mass of mud houses'.

tended to want independence. So Banks suggested that the British government curb its desire for colonies and look instead for trading partners. He was hoping his explorers would find one in Africa. Legend had long described sub-Saharan Africa as an eldorado, while Africans in London in the 18th century talked of kings so rich that even their slaves wore gold. Banks and his friends had heard other stories of scientific and social advances, and dreamed of finding the descendants of the ancient Egyptians or Phoenicians. Wealth and learning seemed to be centred along the River Niger – in particular at a place called Timbuktu. It was there that the African Association should send its explorers, not to colonize, but to enquire. As the Association's secretary, Henry Beaufoy, put it, 'Much, undoubtedly, we shall have to communicate [to people in Africa], and something we may have to learn.'

'A View of Ali's Tent at the Camp of Benown' (a plate from Travels in the Interior Districts of Africa, *1799), where Park was held captive for several months in 1796, an experience that appears to have affected his judgment on his second journey to Africa.*

The First Expedition

Park was commissioned to sail up the Gambia River, travel overland to the Niger and then continue to Timbuktu – in the process discovering in which direction the river flowed. His instructions made it sound simple, but he knew it was not; the Association had already sent out several travellers and the last one, following the route Park was to take, had starved to death at an oasis. And it was hoped Park would do better than the Association's first traveller, the American John Ledyard, who had died trying to cure himself of dysentery in Cairo, though he had managed to walk from Paris to Siberia. Park at least had medical training. Having caught malaria as soon as he reached the Gambia River, he taught himself some Mandingo language while recovering. He then set off into the interior, with a servant and interpreter, and sacks of beads, amber and tobacco that he planned to trade for food and to give as gifts to local rulers. He also had a sextant, magnetic compass and thermometer, and a long list of questions from the Association that needed answering: who lived in the places he was passing through? What did they grow and trade? How were they governed, what punishments did they suffer and what did they teach their children? They even wanted to know what they slept on at night.

Park made good progress, until local conflicts forced him north, into Ludamar, the scrubland between the desert and the sown and the domain of a semi-nomadic Moor named Ali. Park asked permission to enter Ali's lands, but instead was taken captive and had his goods confiscated, all except for the compass, which Ali thought was white man's magic. He was held for more than three months and abused for much of the time, physically and verbally. The only reason given for his captivity was that Ali's wife had never seen a European. Park thought he was held because he was suspected of being a Christian spy. And in a way he was. The Moors controlled the lucrative trade between the Niger and the Europeans at the mouth of the Gambia River and along the Mediterranean coast. They knew that Europeans were hungry for trade and recognized that Park was an outrider of a commercial empire. As such, he was a threat.

In the summer, the fighting moved north and, in the confusion, Park slipped away. Heading southeast, he walked towards the Niger, becoming the first European to

A view of Kamalia, where Park was the guest of a slave trader on his way out of Africa during his first journey. His friendship with and dependancy on the trader scandalized some of the African Association's anti-slavery campaigners.

report on the river 'as broad as the Thames at Westminster', and on the direction of its flow – eastwards, apparently into Africa. He was in Ségou, just days from Timbuktu, when the local ruler spelled out the reality of his situation: if the Moors didn't kill him in Ségou, they would in Timbuktu. Park knew he could get to the fabled city, but was not so certain of getting out. Better, he thought, to return home with the information he had already collected.

Again his timing was perfect. Park's journey out of Africa was as difficult and extraordinary as his journey in, but 17 months later, at Christmas 1797, he arrived back in London and was hailed by Banks, who sensed an opportunity. The war against France was going badly, the nation was in need of a lift: Park was celebrated as a hero for answering one of the riddles of African geography. Although he was lionized by London society and his account of his travels quickly sold out, he longed to return to Scotland. With the proceeds of his travels and book, he married and set himself up as a country doctor in Peebleshire. Soon, however, the dull grind of his work and the dour northern weather began to pall: he told his friend the novelist Sir Walter Scott that he 'would rather brave Africa and all its horrors than wear out his life in long and toilsome rides over cold and lonely heaths and gloomy hills'. In 1805, his wish came true.

While being feted by London Society, Park had a song composed in his honour by Georgiana, Duchess of Devonshire, with this accompanying illustration by Lady Elizabeth Foster depicting Park the night after reaching the River Niger.

THE FATAL NIGER

Banks's attitude towards Africa had changed in the 17 years since the founding of the African Association. Growing French influence along the Senegal River convinced him that if Britain didn't control the Niger and the still-elusive goldfields, France would. He persuaded the government to send Park back to Timbuktu with a detachment of soldiers who would establish British trading posts along the Niger.

On this occasion the timing could not have been worse. The plan was for Park and his force of 43 men to be afloat on the Niger by July 1805, but there were delays and, in the event, progress was slow and they didn't reach the Niger until mid-August. By then, three-quarters of the men had died from disease, including the carpenters who were to build the boats. By the time he left Ségou, the furthest point of his first journey, 39 men had died, and yet he still felt able to write to London that 'this journey plainly demonstrates that with common prudence any quantity of merchandise may be transported from the Gambia to the Niger'. Confident he had completed the first part of his commission, to test the viability of the Gambia-Niger route, Park then set out to complete the second: to settle the question of the Niger's course.

Park as the dashing explorer. This miniature (c. 1797), after a portrait by Henry Edridge, shows him at the height of his fame, having just returned from West Africa.

Opinion was divided as to where the river would end. James Rennell, the Association's geographer, was sure Park would be stranded in what we now know as Lake Chad. Others thought the Niger might flow into the Nile or the Congo rivers. Wherever he thought he was going, Park loaded food and weapons into a boat and, with the other four survivors, determined not to stop until the river's end. He passed the port of Timbuktu, turned the Niger bend and then failed to heed warnings not to pass the Bussa Falls. Whether he jumped overboard or was shot at from the banks of the river is unclear, but either way, Mungo Park died in the river whose mysteries he had done more than anyone else to uncover.

John Hanning Speke

DISCOVERING THE SOURCE OF THE NILE

(1827–1864)

I no longer felt any doubt that the lake at my feet gave birth to that interesting river, the source of which has been the subject of so much speculation, and the object of so many explorers.

J. H. Speke, **Journal of the Discovery of the Source of the Nile,** *1863*

John Hanning Speke remains one of the most controversial and enigmatic of Africa's greatest explorers. The controversy surrounding him has focused mainly on his intuitive discovery of the source of the White Nile, and whether or not he died by accident in 1864, shooting partridge on his cousin's Wiltshire estate. As for the enigma: relatively little is known about Speke's private life. His books and surviving letters give occasional insight into his feelings. His Himalayan correspondence and other papers were destroyed, apparently, some time after his death. Only the last ten of Speke's 37 years – the decade devoted to his expeditions – were documented in any detail.

Speke was born on 4 May 1827 at Orleigh Court, Bideford in Devon, and spent his childhood at Jordans, the family estate near Ilminster in Somerset. As a boy, he suffered from chronic ophthalmia and found reading painful and difficult. He nevertheless learnt to shoot well and became an enthusiastic and successful hunter. In 1844, aged 17, Speke joined the 46th Regiment of Bengal Native Infantry and served in the Punjab War. He was decorated for bravery in 1849 during the Multan campaign and promoted to lieutenant. Encouraged by his senior officers, he hunted and travelled in the Himalayas and mapped areas of Tibet. In 1854 he arrived at Aden, on his way to Central Africa to shoot big game.

Rivalry with Burton in Africa

Speke was advised to join Richard Burton (p. 80) on his Zanzibar expedition, based on the coast of Somaliland. From there he explored the Wadi Nogal in eastern Somaliland, recording his journey in a diary, mapping and collecting specimens of birds, mammals and reptiles. When Issa warriors attacked the camp at Berbera, Speke was wounded 11 times. He felt bitterly resentful when Burton not only appropriated his

Oil painting of Speke in 1859 by James Watney Wilson. It includes Speke's surveying instruments, his rifle and a background of Lake Victoria.

collections, but also added an abridged version of Speke's diary to his book, *First Footsteps in East Africa* (1856). In addition, Speke forfeited the money he had contributed to Burton's expedition. As compensation, Burton invited Speke in 1856 to join the Royal Geographical Society's expedition to explore the Ukerewe, a vast lake rumoured to exist in Central Africa – mapped by two German missionaries, Jakob Erhardt and Johannes Rebmann – and, if possible, to discover the source of the White Nile.

Following the Arab trade route from Bagamoyo, the huge caravan took five months to reach Tabora (in Tanzania). The leader of its African porters, Sidi Mubarak Bombay, a freed slave, became Speke's faithful companion. Progress was hampered by desertions, illness and wrangling with suspicious tribal chiefs. Speke suffered from trachoma and recurring attacks of fever, fainting fits and violent spasms.

Burton and Speke reached Ujiji, on Lake Tanganyika, in February 1858. But contrary to their information, Tanganyika was not a source of the White Nile. On Kivera island, during a rainstorm, a beetle crawled into Speke's ear. Attempting to extract it with a knife, he perforated his eardrum, which left him permanently deaf. Back at Tabora, Speke decided to investigate reports of a much larger lake to the north, and urged Burton to come with him. Burton, however, preferred to stay at Tabora, recovering from malaria, to gather information from the local Arab traders.

Speke returned six weeks later. He not only announced that he had discovered and named Lake Victoria, but he astonished Burton by claiming that it was the principal source of the White Nile. Despite heated arguments, Speke and Burton ended the journey as friends, although their relationship deteriorated from then on.

On the voyage back to England Burton stopped to convalesce at Aden; Speke continued alone, having promised that he would not visit the Royal Geographical Society until Burton joined him. According to an unpublished addendum to Speke's book, *What Led to the Discovery of the Source of the Nile*, Burton had intended to visit Jerusalem. Perhaps Speke feared that Burton's proposed diversion was a trick; or else he was persuaded to ignore his promise. Whatever the reason, Speke lost no time in reporting his discovery of Lake Victoria as the source of the Nile and canvassing support for a Royal Geographical Society expedition to verify his claim.

Return to the Lake Regions

In 1860 Speke returned once more to Africa, this time with James Augustus Grant, whom he had met in 1847 in India. Grant proved an ideal companion. Unlike Burton, he shared Speke's passion for hunting. He was a keen botanist and a talented draughtsman. Grant never complained; indeed he deferred to Speke in everything. In England Burton disparaged Speke's geographical claims, his patronizing attitude to Africans and Arabs, and his apparent incompetence in everything except hunting or recording details of unfamiliar terrain. Speke, to his annoyance, had left for Africa before Burton's account of their expedition, *The Lake Regions of Central Africa*, was published. The tone of Burton's letters to Speke chilled from 'Dear Jack' to 'Sir'. Burton rejected Speke's final effort to repair their friendship; this he lived to regret.

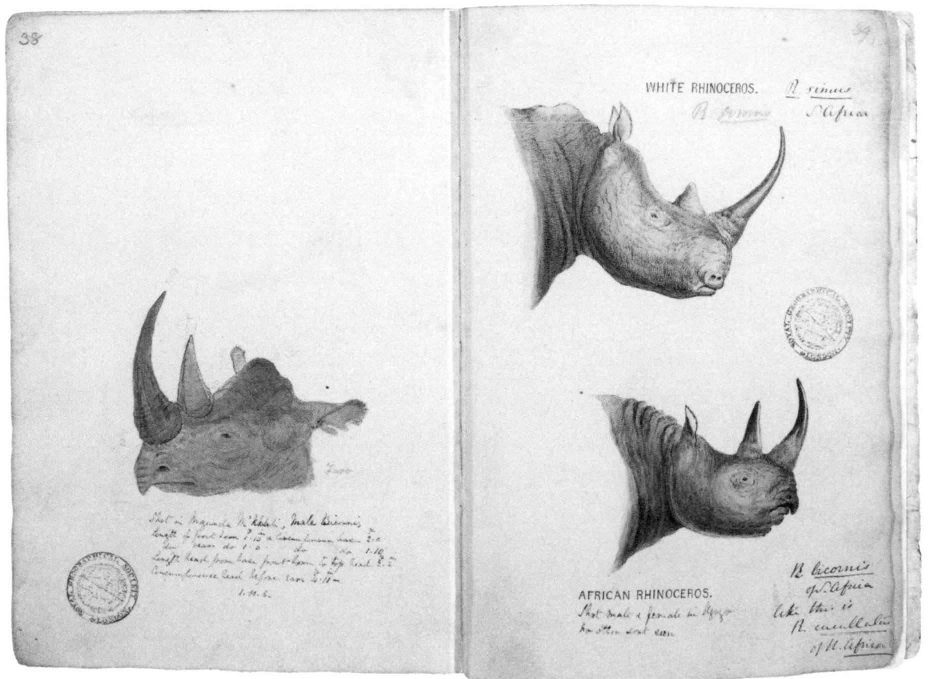

Printed illustrations of White (top right) and Black (lower right) Rhinoceros heads. Speke's own drawing of a Black Rhinoceros head, on the facing page, shows the animal's distinctive prehensile lip.

While Speke and Grant trekked inland, two other expeditions headed for Gondokoro in the southern Sudan. John Petherick, British Vice-Consul at Khartoum, aimed to rendezvous with Speke and Grant, bringing boats and supplies. Samuel White Baker, a wealthy adventurer, independent of government and the Royal Geographical Society, started from Egypt to explore the source of the Nile. Speke and Grant were delayed for months at Tabora by incessant rain, which flooded rivers and prevented them obtaining grain to feed the porters. Speke suffered a paralysed arm, and had difficulty breathing due to congestion in his lungs. At the court of Rumanika in Karagwe, Speke measured the king's enormously fat sister-in-law – an episode that was corrupted by Burton's supporters when published in Speke's *Journal*. Rumanika gave Speke skins of Sitatunga, a new species of antelope. In November 1861 Speke glimpsed the Mfumbiro volcanoes, south of Ruwenzori, the fabled Mountains of the Moon.

Speke then travelled to the court of Mutesa, ruler of Buganda, where his important, but notorious, five-month sojourn was later fastened upon by his critics, in part because of his naive and uninhibited descriptions. Speke recounted his physical examinations of Mutesa's mother, and her drunken orgies. He flirted openly at the palace and gave piggy-back rides to Mutesa's wives. Had he devoted more time to surveying the northern end of Lake Victoria and checking his sometimes careless geography, these escapades might have done less damage to his reputation. In fact, the visit made a positive and constructive impression on Buganda. More than the novelty of his white skin and rich presents – including a gold ring and the firearms with which Mutesa killed four cows and a courtier – Speke opened Buganda to western culture, and to Europeans. The moment was right: British interest in Central Africa now embraced not only missionary ventures, the anti-slavery campaign and natural science, but also the exploitation of potential foreign markets, fuelled by the Industrial Revolution.

On 28 July 1862, 65 km (40 miles) east of Mutesa's palace, Speke sighted the Ripon Falls, where the Nile flowed out of Lake Victoria. His claim to have discovered the source of the Nile was still premature, however, unsupported by conclusive evidence, and his statement, 'The Nile is settled', while poetic, was not finally proved until Henry Morton Stanley circumnavigated Lake Victoria in 1875 (see p. 161).

Speke and Grant finally reached Gondokoro in February 1863, long after the planned rendezvous with Petherick. Meanwhile Petherick and his wife had explored

A watercolour of Ripon Falls by Speke, titled 'Na'Mwéri Falls, Uganda' (c. 1862). Speke's claim that Lake Victoria was the source of the Nile was finally proved by H. M. Stanley in 1875.

and traded in the hinterland of the Nile. They returned to Gondokoro five days after Speke's expedition arrived, only to be snubbed by Speke – who later accused Petherick of trafficking in slaves. Speke and Grant were greeted instead by Baker, who went on to discover Lake Albert and would become known as 'Baker of the Nile'.

The hilltop palace of Mukabya Mutesa, Buganda, and one of Mutesa's cows, sketched in watercolour by Speke in 1862.

The Death of Speke

Speke's *Journal of the Discovery of the Source of the Nile* (1863), though fascinating, was flawed by omissions and factual errors. The RGS arranged a debate at Bath between Speke and Burton, in an attempt to settle the controversy over the source of the Nile. Speke detested public speaking and any sort of confrontation. After months of uncongenial literary work and much personal antagonism, he felt depressed and exhausted. He was partly deaf; strain and long periods devoted to writing had affected his still delicate eyesight. On the morning of the debate, 16 September 1864, after some delay, the president of the RGS, Sir Roderick Murchison, announced that Speke had been killed in a shooting accident, near Corsham, the previous day.

Whether Speke committed suicide or shot himself accidentally has always remained a mystery. It seems, however, inconceivable that he meant to kill himself while clambering over a wall in full view of his cousin and his gamekeeper. Besides an extended second edition of *What Led to the Discovery of the Source of the Nile*, Speke had made other exciting plans, including a hunting trip to India and, in 1865, a major expedition to Central Africa financed by the Emperor Napoleon III of France. None of this would indicate the mind-set of a man determined to end his life.

In 1881 Burton finally accepted Speke's discovery, and shortly before he died in 1890 wrote a letter withdrawing every harsh word he had uttered against Speke. A red granite obelisk commemorating Speke was erected in Kensington Gardens in 1866; and on 4 May 1995 a plaque acknowledging Burton and Grant was unveiled at Speke's memorial.

CLARE PETTITT

David Livingstone

AFRICA COAST TO COAST

(1813–1873)

*Africans are not by any means unreasonable.
I think unreasonableness is more a hereditary disease
in Europe than in this land.*

David Livingstone,* African Journal, *1855

It was almost impossible to get hold of tickets to David Livingstone's elaborate funeral at Westminster Abbey on Saturday, 18 April 1874, and Dean Stanley of the Abbey remembered that the event 'called forth a greater amount of popular feeling than any in which I ever took part'. The burial of the 'Weaver Boy who Became a Missionary' was the celebrity event of the year. Pall Mall and Whitehall were lined with grieving men and women of all backgrounds and classes. A children's cut-out scene from 1875 describes him as 'the fearless missionary and explorer, [who] was the first white man to carry the good news of Jesus Christ to vast tracts of darkest Central Africa'. In fact this was only partly true, and Livingstone's fame rested more on his remarkable self-invention than on his missionary success.

Missionary and Explorer

Born in 1813 in a one-room tenement in Shuttle Row at Monteith's cotton mill in Blantyre, near Glasgow, at 10 years old Livingstone was already employed in the mill. The Livingstone family was devoutly religious and highly literate. David argued with his father over his fascination with science and travel books: Neil Livingstone thought such works ungodly. In 1832 both father and son were converted away from the Church of Scotland when they heard the Glasgow Congregationalist Ralph Wardlaw reject the idea that only the predestined elect could hope for redemption, urging instead a liberal theology which allowed the possibility of redemption for all. This would underpin Livingstone's liberal views about Africans later in his life. In 1834 he picked up a pamphlet his father had brought home about medical missionary work in China, and saw a way to reconcile his dream of becoming a doctor with his family's religious beliefs. With characteristic determination, he put himself through medical school at Anderson's College in Glasgow, going back to work at the mill whenever he could to pay for his studies.

He made his first trip to London in August 1838 for an interview with the London Missionary Society (LMS), who accepted him to train to become a medical missionary. In 1840 he met Robert Moffat, a missionary of the LMS on leave in London, who excited him by talk of his mission at Kuruman in northern South Africa. Also in London he heard Thomas Fowell Buxton denouncing the slave trade, and recommending legitimate trade with Africa as a way of ending the cruelty. Livingstone had his hopes set on China as his missionary destination, but the outbreak of the First Opium War in September 1839 prevented this. Instead, he set off, newly ordained and with his brand-new medical diploma in his pocket, for Kuruman on 8 December 1840.

Livingstone did not stay at Kuruman for long. He was disappointed by it and soon took off with another missionary, Rogers Edwards, to visit the Kwena people 400 km (250 miles) to the northeast. In search of a new location for a mission, Livingstone made two more long journeys over the next two years, learning the local language in preparation. Finally, in January 1844 Livingstone and Edwards, together with Mebalwe, an African teacher, established a new mission at Mabotsa; a year later, Livingstone married Moffat's eldest daughter, Mary. However, Livingstone quarrelled with Edwards and founded another mission at Chonuane among the Kwena, whose chief, Sechele, became his pupil and learned to read. The Livingstone family (there were now two children – Robert and Agnes) moved west to Kolobeng, with Sechele, although he soon drifted away from Christianity and back to his African religion.

It was around this time that Livingstone seemed to change his focus from converting the Africans to exploring their beautiful continent. Sending his growing family (they now had a third child, Thomas) back to Kuruman, he set off with a wealthy big-game hunter, William Cotton Oswell, along the Botletle River, which they followed to Lake Ngami (in modern Botswana). The river, which led further north into others, excited in Livingstone the idea of the rivers of Africa forming a vast interlocking communications network. He thought that if he could find a passage by river to the sea,

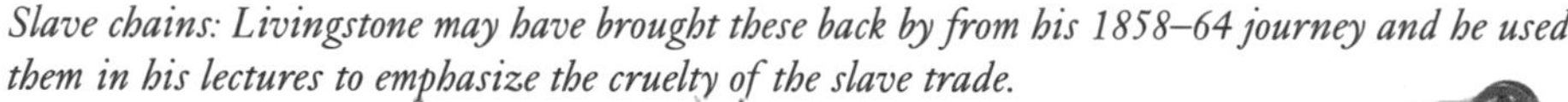

Slave chains: Livingstone may have brought these back by from his 1858–64 journey and he used them in his lectures to emphasize the cruelty of the slave trade.

A touching photographic portrait of David Livingstone and his youngest daughter, Anna Mary, by Thomas Annan. Anna Mary remembered little about her father.

he would discover the key to modernizing this fragmented continent, bringing in legitimate global trade and thus driving out the slavers whom he saw terrorizing the Africans. Returning to Kolobeng, Livingstone promised to wait while Oswell went to procure the boat they needed to explore further. But when Oswell returned with the boat, he found that Livingstone, with characteristic impatience, had already left, now reunited with his family. Oswell managed to catch them up, but two of Livingstone's children were very ill and so they returned to Kolobeng.

In the course of resuming his journey in 1851, Livingstone took a perilous route across a desert which nearly killed his children, but they arrived at the Chobe River. Livingstone and Oswell then met the local chief, Sebituane, before reaching the Zambezi in August 1851. Livingstone rejoiced that he had at last found the great river he needed. Impatient to get on with exploring it, Livingstone first had to accompany his family back to Cape Town; another son, Oswell, was born on the journey. In March 1852, Mary and the children sailed for Britain, where they lived for the next four years in miserable poverty while Livingstone made his epic journey.

Coast to Coast

Livingstone set off northwards and reached Linyanti on the Chobe in May 1853. He was welcomed by Sebituane's son, Sekeletu, but the region was malarial and unsuitable for the mission he wanted to set up, so, with Sekelutu's help, Livingstone set off in November on a prospecting journey up the Zambezi to see if it could form a route

View of the Victoria Falls, Zambezi River, by Thomas Baines (1862). In 1855 Livingstone was the first European to visit the falls, known locally as Mosi-oa-Tunya, 'The Smoke that Thunders'.

west to the sea. Conditions were tough as the rains set in; the party ran out of goods to trade on their way through villages and they abandoned their canoes. When he reached Luanda on the coast of Angola, on 31 May 1854, Livingstone, suffering from malaria, collapsed, but refused to take a ship from there to Britain.

Only by September was he well enough to start back across Africa – the journey back to Linyanti took him nearly a year. In November 1855 Livingstone led another expedition to the Zambezi, this time hoping to find a route eastwards. Very soon, they came to the colossal waterfalls called Mosi-oa-Tunya, 'The Smoke that Thunders', which Livingstone renamed the Victoria Falls, after the British queen. He was excited about the country, feeling he had finally found a suitable place to create his own lasting mission. In December the expedition continued to the Portuguese settlement at Tete (in Mozambique), in the process inadvertently skirting around the cataracts of Quebrabasa, which were to cause Livingstone immense problems later. Livingstone eventually came to the coast at Quelimane, where he started his journey 'home', reaching Southampton on 12 December 1856 to be greeted by Mary.

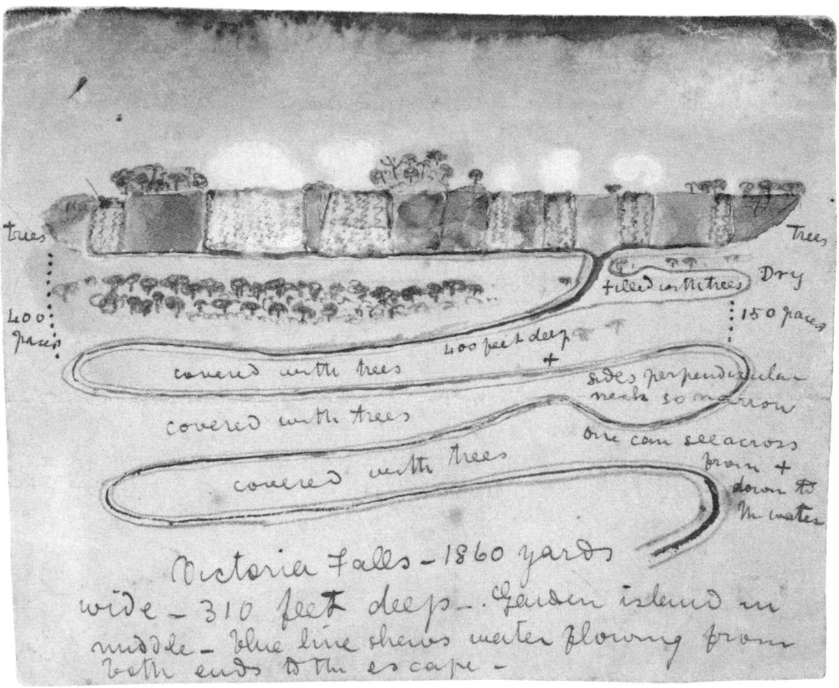

Livingstone's drawing of the Victoria Falls (possibly August 1860). It is typical of his African sketches, which are usually for the purposes of record – he has measured distances in paces and carefully noted the distribution of vegetation in the area and the dimensions of the Falls.

CELEBRITY IN BRITAIN

Livingstone had absolutely no idea how famous he was in Britain until he stepped off the boat. Unbeknownst to him, in 1855, he had been awarded the Royal Geographical Society's annual Founder's Medal. His letters – those that had reached Britain from Africa – had all been published. In lodgings in London Livingstone wrote his book *Missionary Travels and Researches in South Africa* at breakneck speed. It was destined to be one of the biggest bestsellers of the century. He then undertook a schedule of well-attended public lectures and spoke at Cambridge University on 4 December 1857, making an impassioned plea to the young male students in the audience to give themselves to missionary work in Africa. This was to be the speech that launched the ill-starred Universities' Mission to Central Africa (UMCA).

In between being made a Fellow of the Royal Society, receiving honorary degrees, being appointed to a consulate, and having an audience with Queen Victoria, Livingstone was planning a new expedition down the Zambezi river. The LMS had already declined to support his next journey however, sensing, rightly, that Livingstone's real career was now that of explorer rather than missionary. Instead, this time Livingstone was to be sponsored by the British government, which was interested in the potential for trade.

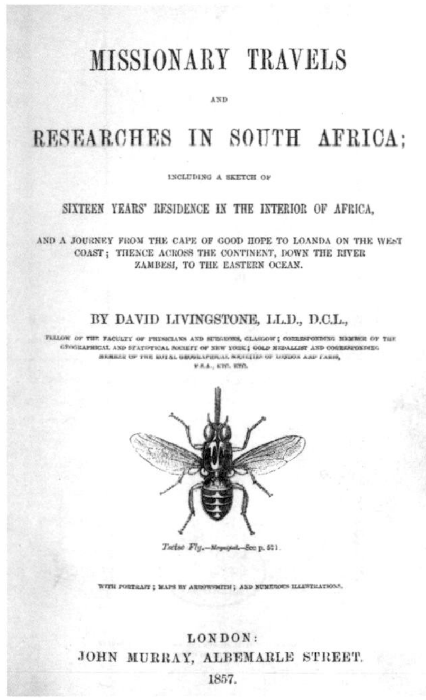

MISSIONARY TRAVELS

AND

RESEARCHES IN SOUTH AFRICA;

INCLUDING A SKETCH OF

SIXTEEN YEARS' RESIDENCE IN THE INTERIOR OF AFRICA,

AND A JOURNEY FROM THE CAPE OF GOOD HOPE TO LOANDA ON THE WEST COAST; THENCE ACROSS THE CONTINENT, DOWN THE RIVER ZAMBESI, TO THE EASTERN OCEAN.

BY DAVID LIVINGSTONE, LL.D., D.C.L.,

FELLOW OF THE FACULTY OF PHYSICIANS AND SURGEONS, GLASGOW; CORRESPONDING MEMBER OF THE GEOGRAPHICAL AND STATISTICAL SOCIETY OF NEW YORK; GOLD MEDALLIST AND CORRESPONDING MEMBER OF THE ROYAL GEOGRAPHICAL SOCIETIES OF LONDON AND PARIS, F.S.A., ETC. ETC.

Tsetse Fly.—Magnified.—See p. 571.

WITH PORTRAIT; MAPS BY ARROWSMITH; AND NUMEROUS ILLUSTRATIONS.

LONDON:
JOHN MURRAY, ALBEMARLE STREET.
1857.

Title-page of Livingstone's Missionary Travels *(1857). The illustration of the 'Tsetse Fly – Magnified' suggests that the book is more 'travels' than 'missionary'.*

THE ZAMBEZI EXPEDITION

The Zambezi expedition left England on 10 March 1858, its members including Livingstone's brother, Charles, and, as expedition artist, Thomas Baines (p. 72). They took with them a steam boat built in sections called the *Ma-Robert*, the African name for Mary Livingstone. Mary herself was also on the expedition, but she was, it turned out, pregnant again, so remained at Cape Town before leaving for Kuruman with her parents. The *Ma-Robert* was not a great success: she needed enormous amounts of fuel to make her steam and the river was so treacherous that she often had to be disassembled and carried. More problems were encountered when they came to the Quebrabasa cataracts, which Livingstone had missed the first time he had travelled

Livingstone's steam-launch the Ma-Robert, *painted by Thomas Baines on 24 May 1858, built for the 1858 expedition to the Zambezi River. She was dubbed 'The Asthmatic' due to the extensive problems she had with her boilers, and had to be replaced in 1861.*

this way. His companion John Kirk realized they were impassable, but Livingstone simply would not accept this.

In any case, Livingstone had settled upon a tributary river to the Zambezi, the Shire, as his new route, believing that his ideal of fertile land for a mission could be realized here. In September 1859 the expedition reached the south end of Lake Nyasa. The British government continued to support the expedition and in 1861 a new boat, the *Pioneer*, was sent to replace the dilapidated *Ma-Robert.* Personal relationships were strained from the first on the Zambezi expedition, however, and Livingstone eventually quarrelled with most of the Europeans who accompanied him.

In February 1861 Livingstone met the UMCA missionaries, who had just arrived from Cape Town, and accompanied them up the Shire River, where they set up a mission at Magomero. Livingstone left to explore Lake Nyasa further. He also now received his new portable steamer, the *Lady Nyassa*, which he had paid for. In March 1862 he learnt of the death of the head of the UMCA mission, Charles Mackenzie, and on 27 April 1862 Mary Livingstone, who had rejoined her husband, also died. Shocked and grieving, Livingstone started a series of frenzied attempts to force his

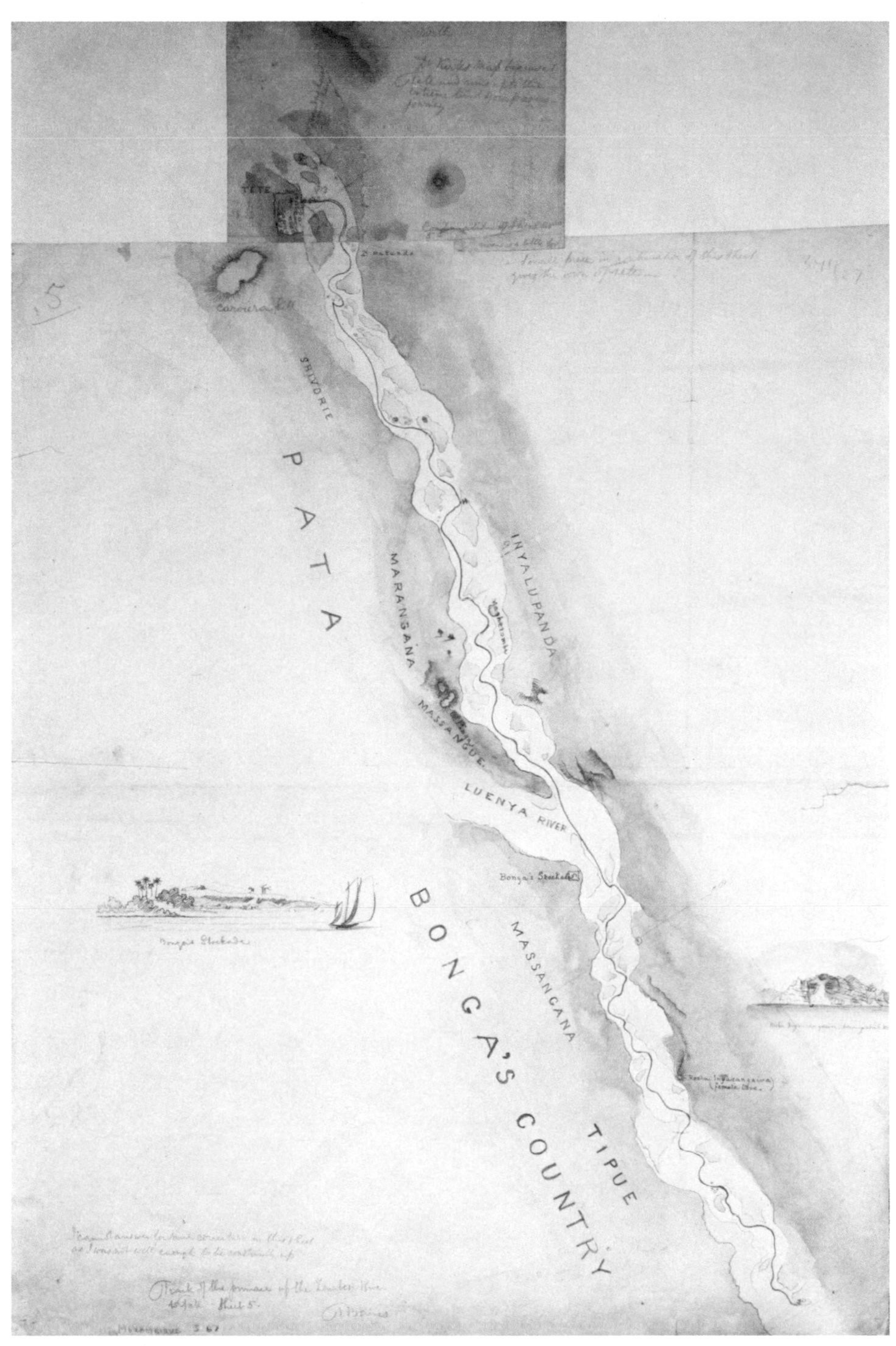

A hand-drawn map by Baines (1859) showing the route Livingstone took down the Zambezi in the Ma-Robert. *Later this same year, Baines was dismissed from the expedition, along with half its European members, after Livingstone argued bitterly with them.*

Photograph taken at Newstead Abbey, the home of the Webbs, in June 1874 during the visit of Livingstone's servants to England after his death. Left to right: Abdullah Susi, Horace Waller, James Chuma, Agnes Livingstone (seated), Mrs Webb, William F. Webb and Tom Livingstone.

boats up the Zambezi and Rovuma rivers. In the end, even he had to give up. In 1863 a drought and slave raids had caused havoc in the Shire Valley, and the river was floating with bloated corpses. Livingstone's expedition suffered from dysentery, and was now recalled by the government. Depressed and angry, Livingstone made his way back to Britain, arriving in London in July 1864.

After the unsuccessful, extremely expensive and lengthy Zambezi expedition (it had lasted over six years rather than the two intended), Livingstone's reputation was at a low ebb. He went with his favourite daughter, Agnes, to stay with his friends the Webbs at Newstead Abbey, where he wrote the *Narrative of an Expedition to the Zambesi and its Tributaries* (1865) in which he tried to excuse himself for the mistakes of the expedition, and to blame others. He was already anxious to get back to Africa, and was now nursing a new ambition: to discover beyond doubt the source of the Nile and so surpass both Burton (p. 80) and Speke (p. 136), who each had theories about it.

The Source of the Nile

This expedition, which set out in 1866, was to include no other Europeans; Livingstone always worked better with Arabs and Africans. He believed Lake Tanganyika might conceal the secret of the source of the Nile, and so he was heading – he thought – towards it, although his measuring apparatus was damaged and inaccurate. One of the servants on the expedition ran away with his medicine chest, and Livingstone – usually tough – was now really ill. Slave raids and violence made progress very slow and difficult. He managed to reach Ujiji, which Burton and Speke had also visited, in March 1869, finding that few of the stores he had ordered had arrived, and toiled on to the Lualaba River, arriving in March 1871. He was so horrified by the massacre of Africans by slave-traders that he spurned the Arab offer of boats to continue and turned back to Ujiji. Here, however, his supplies were so low that he had to live – reluctantly – on Arab help until his famous relief by Henry Morton Stanley (p. 158) in November 1871. Livingstone was no doubt delighted to be greeted with the famous line 'Dr Livingstone, I presume?', and he and Stanley then explored the north end of Lake Tanganyika, failing to find any outlet. Stanley left Livingstone at Tabora on 14 March 1872, later sending him new supplies and porters from the coast.

Livingstone was still feverishly obsessed with the source of the Nile and carried on – weaker and weaker – searching around Lake Bangweulu. He was soon so ill he had to be carried on a litter, and on 30 April 1873 he died at the village of Chitambo. His heart and viscera were buried in an old flour tin under a tree, but his servants decided to embalm his body and return it to the coast and to England. Abdullah Susi, from Shupanga, and James Chuma, a Yao, led the party. It took until February 1874 for them to reach Bagamoyo, where the British consulate arranged for the body to be sent to England. Livingstone was buried in Westminster Abbey in April 1874. Despite his lack of success as a missionary, his questionable judgment on the Zambezi expedition and his failure to find the source of the Nile, Livingstone was mourned and celebrated as a great hero.

David Livingstone did not just explore Africa and then come home again, he lived there and worked alongside Africans. Apart from two trips back to Britain, he spent all his adult life in Africa. His is as much a tale of emigration as of exploration. Much of his writing is from Africa looking at Europe and the 'old civilized countries' as from a distance. This makes Livingstone's style of exploration both unique and complex.

Francis Garnier

AN OBSESSION WITH THE MEKONG

(1839–1873)

Only the construction of a new Empire of the Indies in this ideally located peninsula between India and China can ... guarantee the wealth and grandeur of our [French] nation.

Francis Garnier, 1867

Born in St Etienne and destined for the navy, the young Garnier would be remembered for a nickname – 'Mademoiselle Buonaparte'. It was not a compliment, rather a snub to one whose lofty ambitions were at variance with his diminutive physique. But if what distinguishes the explorer from the traveller is a sense of mission, an obsession even, then Francis Garnier belongs among the giants of geography. Comparisons would often be made with Livingstone (p. 142). In 1871 Garnier and Livingstone were feted jointly by the first International Geographical Congress; in 1873 both men mysteriously disappeared; and in 1874 their tragic deaths were confirmed almost simultaneously. Livingstone was a dedicated missionary, driven by detestation of the slave trade. No less driven, Garnier was a dedicated patriot, obsessed with rescuing the fortunes of France at a time when the benefits of an overseas empire seemed to have eluded her. The acquisition of Indo-China would rectify this. And if anyone inspired the construction of that future 'pearl of empire', it was Garnier.

Like Stanley (p. 158) on the Congo, Garnier pursued his aim by exploring the region's principal river. Wayward, jungle-clad and largely unknown, the Mekong became Garnier's passion. It nearly killed him when for 12 days he lay in a coma, and nearly seduced him when he toyed with 'going native' in lower Laos. Only the satisfaction of mapping each twist of the river over some 2,500 km (1,550 miles) kept him going. 'This constant preoccupation, from which nothing could distract me, amounted to an obsession,' he explains, 'I was mad about the Mekong.'

He was also maddened *by* the Mekong. It was as if the river was bent on disguising its potential, defying France and so frustrating him personally. The idea of a 'Mekong

The Mekong Exploration Commission was overtaken by its second monsoon when entering the Shan states of Myanmar (Burma). With the river in spate, the expedition took to forest trails, themselves flooded by the rains.

Exploration Commission' had been his from the start. In 1859 he had taken part in the French navy's first assault on the Vietnamese coastline. The capture of Saigon, then a small port, provided a bridgehead from where Garnier took it on himself to lobby for the commercial, political and territorial expansion that would make the little colony viable. An 1863 advance through the Mekong delta to Cambodia was a success; its king welcomed French protection. Similar receptions, argued Garnier, could be expected from the states upstream; their produce, both vegetable and mineral, would enrich the colony; and although the course of the river was uncertain, it supposedly traversed Yunnan before plunging into the Asian rainforest and so offered a backdoor waterway into China. Garnier himself would pioneer this future 'highway of commerce'. He needed only the funds and authorization to do so.

Paddle-Boats to Pirogues in Cambodia

Not without official misgivings, the expedition was approved. Aboard two small paddle-driven gunboats the six French officers and 16-man escort cast off from Saigon in June 1866. They chugged up through the delta to Phnom Penh, repaired to the ancient site of Angkor to test their instruments, and then re-embarked just as the monsoon broke. Entering a notorious rainforest at the height of the rains seemed perverse. Leeches were at their liveliest, mosquitoes at their most abundant; dysentery, then malaria, resulted. But Garnier was not to blame. Too junior as a 27-year old lieutenant for command of the expedition, he was officially just surveyor/deputy to *Le Commandant* Doudart de Lagrée. Lagrée, 20 years his senior, knew Cambodia well; and it was he who had concluded that tackling the river in spate was the only way to override its obstacles.

Sure enough, the Mekong soon assumed its true character. Gobs of spume heralded white-water, while the placid surface began to buck and boil. The forest advanced, crowding the banks with tropical foliage. Semi-submerged tree trunks torpedoed the gunboats, whirlpools spun them round, and where rocky islands split the current, such was the force of water that not even boiler-driven paddle wheels could make much headway. Just two days out of Phnom Penh they gave up. Steam-power was no match for the Mekong's rapids.

Instead, the expedition transferred to the long, local pirogues. Normally these were paddled, but against the flood boathooks were plied like punting poles, using such purchase as roots and rocks provided. Known as piking, this painful form of locomotion was how, for the best part of a year, the expedition covered much of the next 1,000 km (620 miles). As a feat of endurance it was exemplary, though less so as one of needless bravado. For as now appeared, the river on whose navigability Garnier had counted was spectacularly unnavigable. No sooner were they past the first rapids than they faced the great Falls of Khon where the Mekong cascades from Laos into Cambodia. Even dolphins had difficulty surmounting this barrier and no boat possibly could. The expedition climbed past on foot and commandeered new pirogues above it. It was 'absolutely insuperable', noted one of the officers; consequently, 'steamers can never ply the Mekong as they do the Amazon, and Saigon can never be united to the western provinces of China by this immense waterway'. The expedition must, as per instructions, be aborted.

Lieutenant Francis Garnier, the inspiration for the Mekong expedition and its eventual leader.

That no such thing happened was entirely due to Garnier. At the rapids he had claimed to have discovered a navigable channel and doubtless would have done the same at the falls. But he never had the opportunity as they coincided with his 12-day coma. Unconscious till they were passed, he neither witnessed their magnitude nor credited the descriptions of his colleagues. On the contrary, his published account implies that the pirogues actually ascended them. Clearly, 'Mademoiselle Buonaparte' was not going to be discouraged by a fluvial anomaly. His strength was returning and with it his resolve. From now on – three months into their odyssey – it was Garnier who began to call the shots.

Through Laos, Burma and China

A case could always be made for pushing on. Lagrée thought it pointless without their letters of authorization from Beijing, which were waiting back in Phnom Penh. Garnier countered this by volunteering to return for them. He did so, tramping an incredible 1,660 km (1,030 miles) in 60 days. Meanwhile, there were tributaries to be explored, gold and silver deposits to be investigated, the potential for plantation crops to be assessed, and political overtures to be made. Better still, retreat was no longer an option; for according to the returned Garnier, Cambodia was in revolt. In effect, China and the Yangtze now represented their only chance of escape.

Vientiane, the once capital of Laos, lay in ruins. They forged on through rapids made more dangerous by the falling river to Luang Prabang. Here at last was something approaching civilization. The king seemed friendly and his womenfolk even more so. They could rest and recuperate while their second monsoon passed. Not so,

In Lower Laos the expedition made a long halt at Bassac (Champassak) and there celebrated the river's annual water festival and fireworks. The spot moved Garnier to plan a local retirement and inspired the expedition's artist, Louis Delaporte, to execute evocative sketches. Redrawn and coloured, they remain the best-known legacy of the expedition.

insisted Garnier. Funds were running low; delay was out of the question. Again they loaded the pirogues and, as they piked round northern Thailand, again the rains overtook them.

Worse followed when the river turned north into Burma's Shan states. Here even Garnier conceded that the rapids were quite impassable. Instead, they hired porters and took to forest trails that were themselves little better than rivers. The Shan chiefs fleeced them – spare trousers were traded for chickens, shirts for cucumbers. Garnier ate alligator eggs ('not entirely disgusting'); the others went hungry. All six officers were now gibbering with malaria, two were incapacitated by infected leech wounds, and Lagrée was barely able to speak. In fact, when, in late 1867, they finally emerged from the forest and reached Kunming, capital of Chinese Yunnan, *Le Commandant* was in terminal decline. He died three months later en route to the Yangtze.

Garnier was absent at the time, making a last abortive bid to relocate the Mekong. On his return he officially assumed the command that he had long since exercised in practice, and on 6 June 1868, two years to the day since they had left Saigon, the expedition surprised the world by presenting itself at the French consulate in the Yangtze port of Hankou.

Death in a Ditch

As news of their reappearance broke, the Royal Geographical Society hailed what was now called the 'Garnier expedition' as 'one of the most remarkable and successful of the century' and awarded him its Patron's Medal in 1870; indeed Garnier himself was 'the century's most gallant and talented explorer'. More medals and plaudits followed. But they came mostly from London. From Paris the response was muted because the expedition's triumphant return coincided with the disastrous 1870–71 Franco-Prussian war.

Garnier joined in the ineffectual defence of the French capital and then sailed back to China in disgust. At a time of national crisis, colonial expansion was out of favour. He wandered up the Yangtze, wrote another book, and was still there when summoned to resume the 'construction' of Indo-China in 1873. Another expedition, this time more warlike, was to sail from Saigon to Hanoi, ostensibly to extricate a French citizen. Garnier interpreted this generously. He seized the Hanoi citadel, hoisted the *Tricolore* and claimed to have 'secured a land of two million souls'. Laos and the Mekong would form its western border, while north Vietnam's Red River offered another 'highway of commerce' to inland China.

This triumph was short-lived. Vietnamese resistance gathered, and on a retaliatory raid across the rice fields Garnier himself was cornered, then slaughtered. He was 34. Embarrassed disavowals of his action followed. They merely delayed the realization of his dreams. In the following decade both Hanoi and the lands along the Mekong were duly coralled into that 'Empire of the Indies' to which his short life had been devoted.

Henry Morton Stanley

IMPERIAL SERVANT

(1841–1904)

He had many faults, some of them even were grave faults,
but they were, I think, chiefly the faults of his qualities,
and without those faults he would not probably have been
possessed of some of the great qualities which made him
so successful in almost everything that he undertook.

Arthur J. Mounteney Jephson, on Stanley

Henry Morton Stanley's rise to fame as an explorer can only be viewed as remarkable. Born out of wedlock in Denbigh, Wales, and christened John Rowlands, he lived in a workhouse between the ages of six and 15. Unable to find a permanent job in Britain, John joined the crew of a ship bound for New Orleans and once there absconded to begin a new life, taking the name Henry Stanley, after a prominent New Orleans cotton broker. After some experimentation he later added Morton. In 1861, while living in Cypress Bend, Arkansas, he joined the Confederate side in the American Civil War. Captured at the battle of Shiloh, he survived a bout of dysentery while confined in the Union prison at Camp Douglas near Chicago. To get out he agreed to enlist with the Blues, and then quickly deserted from a sickbed in Harper's Ferry, Virginia. Following several stints at sea he joined the Federal Navy, and promptly deserted again in February 1865.

With no career in sight, Stanley headed west, and during a stop in St Louis he signed on as a freelance reporter with the *Missouri Democrat*. He met William Harlow Cook, another aspiring reporter, and the two decided to seek their fortunes by crossing Asia from west to east. In New York they convinced Louis Noe, Stanley's partner in deserting the navy, to come along, and in July 1866 the trio departed for Smyrna (Izmir), Turkey, arriving at the end of August. However, they had not travelled far before being imprisoned by a group of robbers. Set free through the intervention of the local governor and thankful to be alive, they abandoned the Asia adventure.

After a brief visit to relatives in Wales, Stanley again crossed the Atlantic and was soon back with the *Missouri Democrat*, which sent him to cover government attempts to end hostilities with the Native American tribes of the west. Stanley then decided to try his luck in New York, and, by a stroke of good fortune, he managed to get an inter-

A studio photograph of Stanley with his gun-bearer, Selim, and personal servant, Kalulu, taken in Zanzibar in 1872, after his Livingstone expedition.

view with James Gordon Bennett, Jr, owner and editor of the New York *Herald.* A brief conversation led to Stanley being told he could cover a British invasion of Abyssinia. He would, however, have to absorb the costs, with compensation being paid depending on the acceptability of the stories. They proved more than that. Indeed, he scooped the other reporters when his dramatic accounts reached readers first. Other assignments for the *Herald* followed. Then, on 28 October 1869, a meeting with Bennett took place in Paris, at which Stanley said he was told to 'Find Livingstone'. First, though, he would have to write an array of dispatches along a route from Egypt to India, and it was not until 12 October 1870 that Stanley left Bombay for Zanzibar.

From Reporter to Explorer

An array of problems delayed the departure from Zanzibar for Bagamoyo on the mainland, and Stanley finally began his march inland on 22 March 1871. He had no

A watercolour by Catherine Frances Frere of some of the Zanzibar and other Africans of Stanley's party, sketched at the Government House, Cape Town, 1877.

intention of doing any exploration – his only goal was to find Livingstone as quickly as possible and tell the world about it. Yet it was a difficult journey and Stanley did stumble across the previously uncharted Lake Gombo on the way to the Arab trade centre of Tabora. And after the improbable meeting with Livingstone at Ujiji in November, the two sailed to the northern shore of Lake Tanganyika and ended the debate about its being part of the White Nile watershed by showing that the Rusizi River flowed into, rather than out of, the lake.

On his return to Bagamoyo, and having sent supplies to enable Livingstone to continue his search for the source of the Nile, Stanley boarded ship for England, expecting accolades for finding and rescuing the good doctor. Instead, he encountered a hostile establishment headed by the Royal Geographical Society that attacked him for not being a true explorer and for having fabricated letters from Livingstone. Stanley's American connection, newspaper style of writing and occasional impolitic statements added to the invective aimed at him. By the end of the year, though, he had prevailed and his book, *How I Found Livingstone*, became an instant bestseller.

Still a reporter at heart, Stanley returned to Africa in late 1873 to cover the British campaign against the Asante in the Gold Coast. At its completion, with yet more stirring stories added to his credits, he set off for England and on the way heard of Livingstone's death. It is clear that the doctor had touched him deeply and, indeed, triggered a change in Stanley's priorities. He would now finish the Nile quest and in the process open up Africa to commerce, Christianity and civilization. This led to the formation of the combined Anglo-American Expedition, sponsored by the *Daily Telegraph* and *Herald*, with its epic 999-day crossing of Central Africa in 1874–77. In terms of exploration, Stanley became the first European – perhaps the first person – to circumnavigate Lake Victoria and thus validate John Hanning Speke's contention that it was the source of the White Nile. Afterwards, by connecting the Lualaba River to the Congo River, he solved another long-enduring geographical puzzle and added many new place names to the map of Africa.

Stanley's exploits caught the attention of King Leopold II of Belgium, who was interested in building up an empire in Africa, and during two stints between 1879 and 1884 he set up and connected stations along the Congo River for a so-called International African Association. It was, in fact, bogus, as Stanley suspected, but he believed Leopold to be a philanthropist and thus went ahead with the task, earning the name

A collection of Stanley's personal items: his hand-made cap, pith helmet and mended boots, a pygmy arrow broken in half and a section of the tree under which he first met David Livingstone at Ujiji.

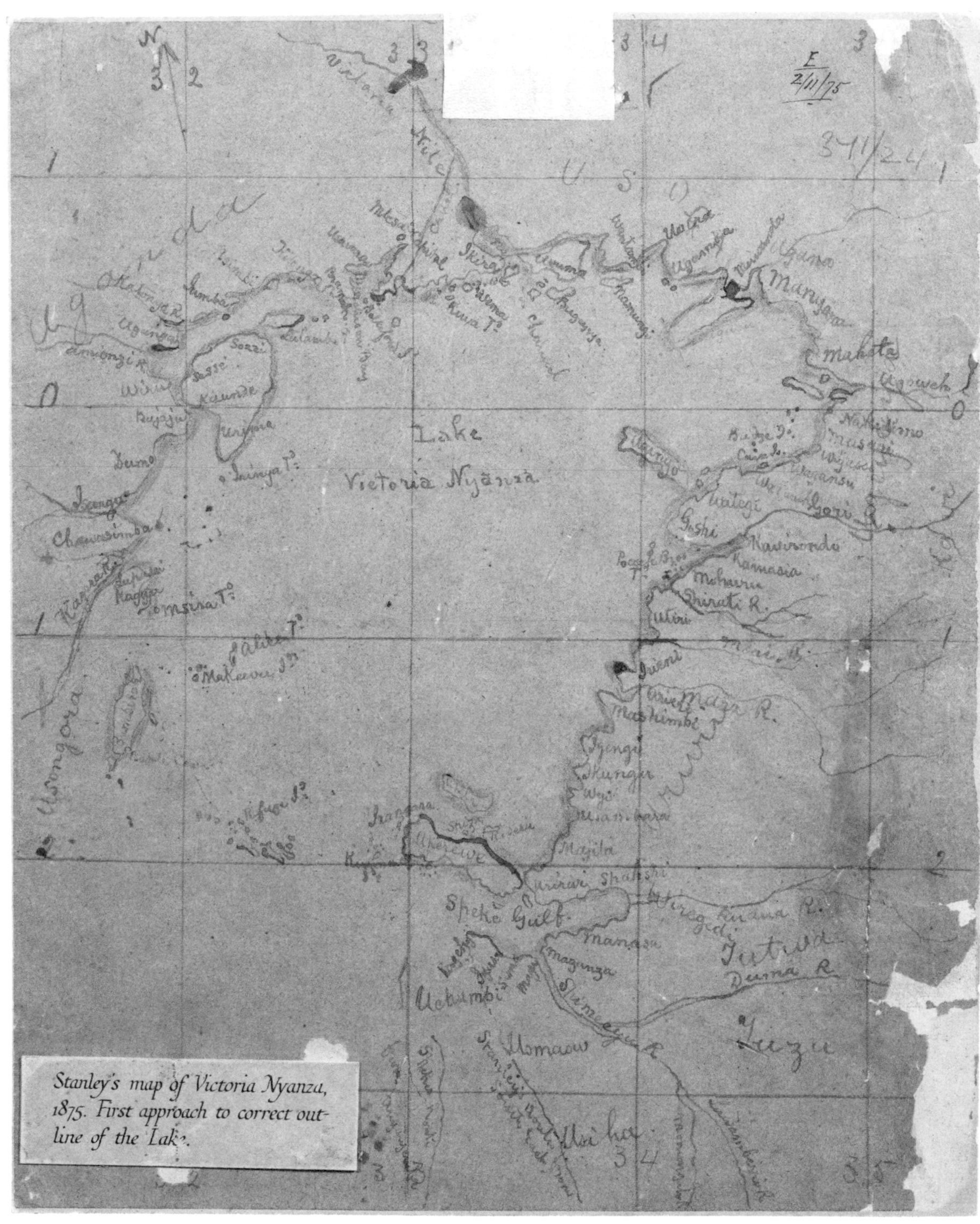

Stanley's map of Victoria Nyanza, 1875. First approach to correct outline of the Lake.

After Stanley had found Livingstone at Ujiji, the pair spent four months together and sailed Lake Tanganyika, ascertaining that the Rusizi River flowed into not out of the lake and that therefore it could not be the source of the Nile.

Bula Matari, or 'breaker of rocks', for his hard-driving style. Little time existed for exploration, but Stanley did venture along the Fimi River and plotted Lake Leopold II, now Mai Ndombe.

Stanley's last African adventure was as leader of an 1887–89 expedition to rescue Emin Pasha (Eduard Schnitzer), thought to be trapped in Sudan, desperately holding out against the forces of the Mahdi which had earlier taken the life of General Gordon at Khartoum. In this Stanley succeeded. On the way in he became the first European to describe the Ituri forest and the lands west of Lake Albert. During the return, he is credited with putting Mount Ruwenzori on the map, and thereby locating the fabled Mountains of the Moon; he also added the Semliki River and Lake Edward.

An Ambiguous Reputation

In terms of bringing to light formerly unknown lands and peoples and filling in 'blank spaces' on European maps, Henry Morton Stanley stands tall among explorers of

Stanley's hand-drawn sketch map of Lake Victoria after his circumnavigation in 1875, which proved it to be one body of water and confirmed Speke's claim that it was the long sought-after source of the Nile; this is the first time that the lake had been mapped at all accurately.

Africa, and, indeed, the world. However, there have been reservations about him and his methods. He has often been accused of having lied repeatedly, and it's clear he did fabricate much about his early life, though exaggerations in an attempt to regale readers with adventure stories are perhaps forgivable. More serious, and with greater substance, is the allegation of brutality towards the men on his expeditions. Stanley was prone to outbursts of temper and on many occasions he ordered whippings, a common practice by caravan leaders at the time to enforce discipline. And, in a few instances, he oversaw executions for acts deemed treasonable to the expedition. To an ever-increasing extent, Stanley acted the role of general.

This leads to the oft-made charge that Stanley commanded large, well-equipped armies that ran roughshod over anyone in their way. However, on the Livingstone expedition his small caravan fought no battles on the journey in or out; similarly, no violence was used creating the stations along the Congo River. Stanley had only a small armed force at his disposal, and, anyway, he knew violence would work against the creation of conditions necessary for the establishment of the free trade that was his primary objective. In 1874–77 and 1887–89, Stanley did command what amounted to armies, at least to begin with, and two episodes during the former expedition have continued to haunt his image.

The first involved the Wanyaturu or Warimi of central Tanzania. Seeing the expedition as potentially hostile – a reasonable speculation given previous experiences with strangers – they launched two attacks. After successfully repulsing them, Stanley ordered his men to engage in a scorched-earth tactic that produced in his words 'a now silent and blackened valley'. The second was an act of retribution against the inhabitants of Bumbire Island in Lake Victoria. Stanley and a small party had been detained there after visiting King Mutesa of Buganda. In fear for their lives, they escaped. Later, on the way back to Buganda and enhanced by a large contingent of soldiers, Stanley orchestrated an attack from the water that overwhelmed the island's defenders. While it is true that he said no to a landing, thus avoiding a likely massacre, the whole episode could have been avoided by simply sailing past Bumbire, as the inhabitants now lacked the capacity to threaten his party.

In addition, Stanley recorded 32 battles while going down the Lualaba and Congo rivers. By this time, though, his force had been considerably reduced and there is no evidence that he started any of them. As Stanley noted, it was a case of fight back or die. Stanley's journeys through the Ituri during the Emin Pasha Expedition involved numerous small-scale conflicts that resulted in deaths and sometimes the disappearance of whole villages. The search for food under near starvation conditions

Stanley, with his wife Dorothy, at the window of the special Pullman Car provided for his 1891 lecture tour of the United States. After all his expeditions and travels Stanley settled in England, becoming a member of Parliament.

occasionally led members of the expedition to initiate hostilities. One such resulted in a massacre, but produced very little to eat. Stanley wasn't there at the time and only learnt about the incident later. Sometimes forgotten are battles with the Wasukuma as the expedition marched with Emin towards the coast. They raged for several days until a Maxim gun did its job. The men then burnt all the villages in the vicinity; Stanley and the other Europeans became known as *wazungu wakali*, 'vicious whites'.

One thing Stanley should not be indicted for is the horror that became the Congo Free State. While he created the infrastructure around which Leopold built his fiefdom, what ultimately happened was not his doing, and, indeed, Stanley often warned the king that violence would be counter-productive to the kinds of developments designed to profit Belgians and Congolese alike. Later, it must be admitted, he had to bury his head in the sand to ignore the king's involvement in what was taking place.

Today, as during his lifetime, the name Henry Morton Stanley evokes contrasting responses. Some still see it as belonging to a heroic explorer who exhibited great courage in the face of dangers that should have cost him his life on many occasions. Others view it attached to a man representing the worst of the 19th-century European penetration of Africa. One hundred years from now it is likely to do the same.

POLAR ICE

The Arctic, the edges of its ice and its rich marine life, were well known for centuries. The Inuit and other indigenous peoples who have lived for millennia at the very northern extremities of human survival, had learnt its ways and how to hunt and fish its waters. The Vikings knew it well, too, and sailed vast distances around it in search of new lands. In the middle of the 18th century a theory was propounded that there was open sea in the centre of the Arctic Circle and, if reached, a direct route to the Pacific would be discovered. Two Royal Navy ships, led by Captain Constantine Phipps, were sent in 1773 to survey the possibilities and although they reached only 80° 48', their discoveries helped subsequent travellers.

The North Pole remained elusive for well over 100 years. Most effort went into the search for the fabled Northwest Passage. Among the numerous expeditions, notably tragic was John Franklin's attempt in 1845 with two large steamers and 129 men, which famously disappeared. Meanwhile, some progress towards the Pole was being made. The Magnetic Pole, then over land near the Boothia Peninsula, was located by James Ross in 1831; and in 1875–76 George Nares commanded the last naval expedition into the Arctic with two ships, reaching 82° 29'.

It was not until the late 19th century that the great age of polar exploration began. Two Norwegians led the way. Fridtjof Nansen, building on the growing awareness of powerful currents that circled the pole, set out in his specially designed ship, the *Fram*, in an attempt to drift there. When that didn't work, he and one companion left the ship and tried to sledge to the Pole, only to fail again after getting to 86° 13' and, astonishingly, managing to walk back all the way to land. Nansen's protégé, Roald Amundsen, was to become the first to bring a vessel through the Northwest Passage, in 1906, before turning his attention to the North Pole, but since that was claimed by Frederick S. Cook and then Robert Peary, at the last minute he decided to head south instead.

The British Antarctic Expedition, 1910–13: as much as striving to be first to reach the South Pole, this also had a scientific purpose. In this photograph by Herbert Ponting, members are working a 'pram' through the ice in an attempt to reach the Emperor Penguin colony.

Members of Nansen's polar expedition: Sigurd Scott Hansen, Fridtjof Nansen and Otto Sverdrup taking a rest on the Fram*'s afterdeck, while attempting to drift with the ice to the North Pole.*

The desolate Arctic and Antarctic wastes were seen as the ultimate physical challenges for mankind in the mastery of the planet. Instead of being motivated by greed for conquest or the subjugation of nations, the later polar explorers battled only with the elements. And, both in the north and in the south, they had a single specific location as their target: the Pole. National pride was central to the race that now developed. The Americans were determined to succeed in the north, while the British were pre-eminent in the south. Ernest Shackleton and Robert Falcon Scott are the best-known names from this era and they strove mightily to reach the South Pole. Edward Wilson travelled with them both, eventually dying on the return with Scott, after their party had been defeated by Amundsen. Wilson deserves his place among the greats because, as well as being the bravest of the brave, he was a scientist, doctor, naturalist and artist. One of the geological specimens he kept to the last in the tent where he died proved that the Antarctic continent had once been warm.

Wally Herbert, who lived and travelled 50 years after the days of these legends, proved to be arguably the greatest of all polar explorers. After criss-crossing Antarctica as a surveyor, he turned his attention to the north and pulled off the longest and most significant trans-polar expedition of all time. Unintentionally, and unaware of doing so at the time, he and his team probably also became the first people to reach overland the exact location of the North Pole, Robert Peary's achievement in 1908 being now seriously questioned.

Fridtjof Nansen

ARCTIC EXPLORER AND DIPLOMAT

(1861–1930)

Maybe they have heard it is a glorious enterprise; but why? To what end?... But their eyes are riveted upon the ship, and perhaps there dawns before their minds a momentary vision of a new and inconceivable world, with aspirations after a something of which they know naught.

Fridtjof Nansen, **Farthest North,** *1898*

In all the annals of exploration, the name of Dr Fridtjof Nansen holds a singular distinction; unlike those who traded everything – their fortunes, their scruples and quite often their sanity – for the laurels of polar heroism, Nansen retained all three. His stature as a man of culture and the arts, a humanitarian and a citizen of the world, might indeed have completely superseded his Arctic accomplishments, had these not been so extraordinary.

How did a man, the son of a well-to-do lawyer who might have enjoyed a life of quiet comfort, come to find his calling in the vast emptiness of the Arctic? Born in 1861 in Store Frøen, Nansen excelled in science and drawing, studying both at the University of Oslo and eventually majoring in zoology. Early in his career, he spent four months on a Norwegian sealer sailing the eastern coast of Greenland; it was with this voyage that his passion for the far north began. He was then appointed curator of the Bergen Museum, where he worked for the next six years, also becoming an expert Nordic skier. It was there that he conceived his plan to make an unprecedented crossing of the interior of Greenland on skis. In the summer of 1888, along with five handpicked men, among them Otto Sverdrup, Nansen embarked on a 41-day journey across gaping crevasses and daunting mountains, reaching an elevation of 2,745 m (9,000 ft). After a difficult descent, the team arrived at last at Ameralik Fjord in October, returning to Norway to universal acclaim.

The march across the inland ice – a photograph taken during the expedition to Greenland in the period July 1888 to May 1889.

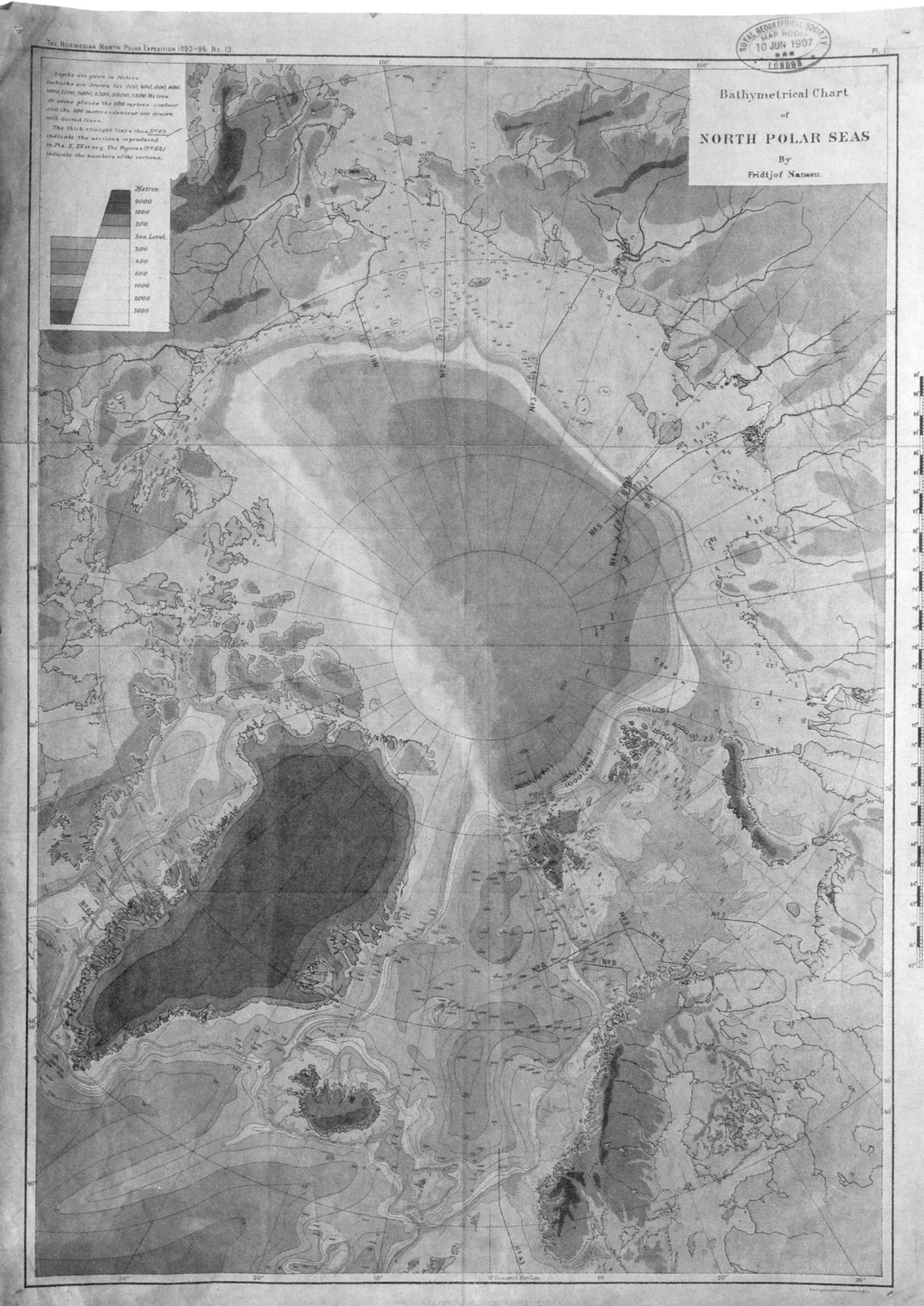

Royal Geographical Society Map Room 10 JUN 1907 London
Arctic Gen. 2

Drifting to the Pole

Fresh from this triumph, Nansen readily obtained the backing he needed for his next, still more ambitious undertaking. Knowing that the polar icecap was itself in constant motion, he set out to commission a ship that was specifically intended to be caught in, and survive, the icepack. By moving *with*, rather than *through* the ice, he hoped to reach the Pole itself. Designed by the leading naval architect Colin Archer to meet Nansen's specifications, this ship was the *Fram* ('Forward'); with her heavy oak planking and extensive interior bracing, she would be the strongest wooden vessel ever built.

Many were openly critical of Nansen's plan. Among the most vociferous was the American explorer Adolphus W. Greely, who declared it to be hazardous to the point of recklessness, but that – in any case – he believed the region contained a large land-mass hundreds of miles in diameter; moreover the idea of an indestructible ship was nonsense. In this opinion he was joined by such luminaries as explorer and botanist Sir Joseph Hooker, Admiral Sir George H. Richards and Sir Allen Young. Nansen had his revenge by quoting their criticisms in his book describing his voyage.

OPPOSITE *A bathymetrical chart recording the depth of the North Polar Seas drawn by Nansen, from his North Polar Expedition, 1893–96.* BELOW *The* Fram *caught in the ice: Nansen's idea was to allow his ship to be trapped and then carried to the Pole by drifting with the currents.*

The *Fram* sailed from Vardø, a small town in the far northeast of Norway, on 24 June 1893. Nansen found the ship handled the ice admirably, twisting and turning 'like a ball on a platter' and finding channels where no other ship could. They passed south of Novaya Zemlya and traversed the Kara Sea; on 22 September, they entered the polar ice in the Nordenskjøld Sea. Just as planned, the drift was carrying them to the north and west, but it reversed itself two days later, then resumed, then shifted again. Far from moving in a continuous northwesterly rotation, the polar ice twisted its way through conflicting influences of ocean currents, winds and the earth's rotation. Thus, while the overall drift did – excruciatingly slowly – carry their vessel in the right direction, they could not reach the Pole.

Nansen then made a bold decision: together with Hjalmar Johansen, he would make an overland dash, leaving the rest of his crew to await release or rescue, though neither was likely for at least a year. The decision was made in November of 1894, and they spent the winter preparing. Nansen re-read the published accounts of the ill-fated Franklin expedition of 1845, all 129 members of which had perished in the Arctic. From the view of hard experience, he admired these men anew; despite their technical limitations, they were men of 'grit' and courage. After all, he wrote, 'it was not their fault to have been born in a country where the use of snowshoes is unknown'.

The Attempt Overland and Return

Nansen and Johansen finally departed the *Fram* on 14 March, 1895; with them they took three sledges, two bamboo-framed kayaks, and 28 dogs. Nansen had calculated that, with enough food for the dogs for 30 days, they could get on for another 50 by gradually killing the dogs and feeding them to the survivors; with 80 days, they could surely 'arrive somewhere'. They sledged northwards through a maze of pressure-ridges, frustrated by the southward drift of the ice, which undid much of their progress. Finally, on 8 April, convinced that to go further would make return impossible, Nansen called a halt. They stood at 86° 14', further north than any human beings had ever stood – and yet it did not seem a moment of victory.

The return trip was longer, and more trying, than either man could have possibly imagined. It would be more than 70 weeks, including a winter spent on an unknown island surviving on walrus blubber and polar bear meat, before they made it back. They had allowed their watches to run down and so could not calculate their longitude. It was not until a chance encounter with the British Jackson-Harmsworth expedition, sent to survey Franz Josef Land, far to the east of their goal of Svalbard, that they realized where they were. Hitching a ride on Jackson's ship, they returned to

Nansen using his special apparatus for measuring deep-water temperatures on the North Pole expedition. The original caption for this photograph was 'Deep Water Temperature. "Up with the Thermometer!" July 12, 1894'.

their starting point at Vardø on 13 August 1896, scarcely a week before the *Fram* itself – left in the capable hands of Sverdrup – arrived at Skjervøy, all hands safe and sound.

In his subsequent diplomatic career, Nansen served as the first ambassador in London of an independent Norway (1905–08), while also undertaking several important oceanographic expeditions. After the First World War, he became deeply involved in the League of Nations. As High Commissioner for Refugees in 1921 he created the 'Nansen Passport' for stateless persons, which was eventually recognized by 52 countries. In 1922, he was awarded the Nobel Peace Prize. Nansen died on 13 May 1930, at his home Polhøgda ('The Polar Height') in Lysaker, Norway.

Edward Wilson

SCIENTIST, DOCTOR, NATURALIST, ARTIST

(1872–1912)

Words must always fail me when I talk of Bill Wilson.
I believe he really is the finest character I ever met.

Robert Falcon Scott, Journals, 22 October 1911

In the early 20th century Antarctica was the last unexplored continent and Edward Wilson was in the vanguard of its exploration. A naturalist, artist and doctor he was the only officer to go with Scott on both his Antarctic expeditions. Wilson took part in many of the early voyages, discovering the horrors of sledge-hauling at sub-zero temperatures. With Scott and Shackleton, he achieved 'Furthest South' in December 1902, and his fascination with Emperor Penguins resulted in an extraordinary sortie, the first ever in the Antarctic midwinter, to obtain specimens of their eggs. In 1912 he reached the South Pole with Scott and three companions. All five British explorers died on the ill-fated return.

Wilson was born in Cheltenham to a family of 'doers': a great-grandfather made a fortune in railways and land; his mother was artistic and also an author; and an uncle, Major General Sir Charles Wilson, commanded the attempt to rescue Gordon of Khartoum. But as a young man Wilson did not plan for business, the army or exploration. He studied medicine at Cambridge and St George's Hospital, London. A serious respiratory illness, diagnosed as tuberculosis, made his preferred career as a surgeon inadvisable and the offer of the post of doctor, zoologist and artist on the *Discovery* expedition led by Scott, venturing to explore and scientifically record the mysteries of Antarctica, was tailor-made for him. Scott wrote later that Wilson's appointment was one of the things he had the greatest cause to be thankful for.

DISCOVERY, 1901–04

The *Discovery* expedition opened up the Antarctic interior and made real scientific, geographical and topological discoveries. Wilson, a famously hard worker, painted and drew, pursued his medical and zoological studies, contributed to work on the ship,

Title-page of The South Polar Times, *volume 1, April 1902, edited by Shackleton with artwork by Wilson. All the crew could contribute to the journals, copies of which were produced, after the expedition, at seven guineas each, to help the expedition funds.*

"DISCOVERY"

THE

SOUTH POLAR TIMES.

APRIL · 1902

Discovery *in winter quarters, McMurdo Sound, in an undated watercolour by Wilson. Wilson made many paintings on this expedition, striving to capture the fiery orange/lemon sky, the pale blue light and the colours of the ice.*

collected meteorological records and took part in expeditions. In addition, his capacity for conciliation contributed greatly to the harmony of the expedition. Exploration can reveal discordant egos. Wilson was deeply religious; he wanted to serve his fellow-man. He was a facilitator and never aspired to leadership.

In art, Wilson followed John Ruskin's precepts of factual representation, which he thought more important than interpretative work. On *Discovery* he made over two hundred paintings and meticulous, accurate drawings of the Ross Barrier, the landscapes of Victoria Land, and the birds and animals of Antarctica. He was the last major expedition artist: technical developments in the field of photography were soon to make cameras practical as a way of recording the stillness and the beauty of the unknown continent.

The Ross Barrier is an ice shelf the size of France, hinged on to the landmass. Its nature was unknown when *Discovery* reached Antarctica and Scott's Southern Journey of 1902 provided the first evidence to support this conclusion. Scott unexpectedly chose Wilson as his companion for this attempt to reach furthest south; clearly, he felt at ease with this clever, supportive man. Wilson wanted a third member and Ernest

Shackleton his friend, later famous in Antarctic history in his own right, was chosen. Their start was delayed because of an outbreak of scurvy (vitamin C deficiency) in other members of the ship's company. This delay made the South Pole an impossible goal although the three still hoped to make significant inroads into the interior.

The Southern Journey started with support teams and 19 dogs which pulled so well that Scott sent the support teams back earlier than planned, leaving the trio, their dogs and sledges to continue over the Barrier. But after their hopeful start, progress soon degenerated into mindless endurance, as they slogged over the flat, white landscape. The three relayed for 29 days, covering 3 miles for every mile advanced southwards. When land eventually appeared in the southwest they decided to steer towards it. Wilson was relieved, thinking anything more promising than a tedious plod to make a southern record. They eventually achieved 82°12', where they had to turn back because of dwindling food supplies. They could not get on to the land from the Barrier because of a huge chasm that separated the two. Wilson noted tide cracks, thus suggesting that the Barrier was in fact, a floating ice-shelf. They had not achieved as much as they had hoped, but they had a significant 'Furthest South' and recorded the vast mountains of Victoria Land to the west of the Barrier.

Wilson made several more expeditions before *Discovery* returned to New Zealand in 1904. The finding of Emperor Penguin eggs confirmed that, despite the freezing temperatures, gloom and howling winds, Emperors bred in Antarctica. Wilson needed specimens of newly laid eggs for his research, and his failure in this respect is thought to be a reason for his returning later to Antarctica. Notwithstanding, his achievements were significant. He had explored furthest south, recorded the wildlife of Antarctica, made suggestions about the true nature of the Ross Barrier and produced the first observations of the mountains in the interior of Victoria Land.

Shortly before leaving on *Discovery*, Wilson had married the love of his life, Oriana Souper. She was waiting for him in New Zealand, 'as beautiful as ever', and the couple had a delayed honeymoon there, a land they immediately loved and hoped to return to.

Emperor Penguin eggs painted by Wilson. The life cycle of these birds became Wilson's overriding scientific interest on the Discovery *expedition.*

Wilson working up a sketch on the Terra Nova *expedition. The photograph is by Herbert Ponting, the camera artist on the expedition, who created many beautiful images of Antarctica.*

Wilson was first and foremost a scientist and his work on his return to England was entirely suited to his habits of patient, careful observation. In 1905 he was appointed Field Officer to the Grouse Commission, set up to find the cause of a disease decimating red grouse on the moors of northern England and Scotland (the sport was hugely important to the Scottish economy). Characteristically hard working, Wilson haunted the moors by day and night, closely observing the birds. He confirmed the cause, a threadworm, and suggested measures to minimize infestations. In 1907, he received an unexpected offer from the exuberant Shackleton to return to Antarctica as his Second-in-Command. Wilson refused: it was not in his nature to abandon unfinished work. His authoritative Grouse Report finally appeared in 1911; Wilson never saw it published.

TERRA NOVA, 1910–13

Wilson sailed again for Antarctica in 1910 on Scott's *Terra Nova* expedition as Chief of Scientific Staff, a busy and onerous post. He had little time for painting, but took part in two important missions, one purely scientific – a sortie in the Antarctic midwinter to obtain specimens of Emperor Penguin embryos – the second, the assault on the Pole itself.

Having unexpectedly discovered on the previous expedition that Emperors bred in the Antarctic midwinter, three men – Wilson, 'Birdie' Bowers and Apsley Cherry-

Garrard – now struggled against appalling odds to reach their breeding colony. The five-week expedition proved worse than even Wilson could have imagined. The men pulled in darkness over a snow surface that resembled sand, and always in bitter cold – the temperature was well below freezing and was once recorded at –59°C (–75°F). Wilson wanted newly laid eggs to investigate theories that birds were descended from dinosaurs and that early embryos showed evidence of this evolution. He finally obtained three eggs only. A blizzard trapped the trio in the hut that they had built above the penguin colony, whirling away their canvas roof and their tent. For two days they lay entombed in snow, without food or drink, but singing hymns. Their recovery of the tent and return to base was miraculous. Scott wrote lyrically that the effort was heroic: a tale for his generation. The exploration has been criticized – the connection between birds and dinosaurs was not made and it was only months before the assault on the Pole. But Wilson would have defended himself stoutly. This was a scientific expedition that could potentially result in great achievements and he showed great determination to push through with it.

The British now knew they were in a race for the Pole with a Norwegian team led by Roald Amundsen (p. 181). They started their own attempt in November 1911, later

Wilson, Bowers and Cherry-Garrard after their return from the winter journey to Cape Crozier in 1911. They were frostbitten and exhausted.

Sketch of the pyramidal tent. Only one man could stand comfortably and they shared a sleeping bag.

than the Norwegians because of the ponies. Scott followed Shackleton's route of 1908. He kept to his own publicized plans of sending small groups back in sequence from the 16-man party. Wilson wrote regularly to Oriana, telling her how he hoped to be chosen for the Pole attempt. The British thought that they had beaten the Norwegians, assuming that they too would be following Shackleton's route, so the appearance in the distance of a speck that materialized into a black flag, on 16 January 1912, was the cruel end of their hopes and dreams. The Norwegians had in fact beaten them by a month.

The return was doomed. Dogged by malnutrition, low body temperatures, fluid loss, and wasting of body fat and muscle, they marched north. The final unhappy outcome was sealed by exceptionally low Barrier temperatures in the early months of 1912. The first man to die, Chief Petty Officer Evans, suffered from all the above, possibly complicated by a bacterial infection from a cut in his hand, sustained while working on the sledges. 'Titus' Oates died next. His final words, that he was going out and might be some time, resonate still. Wilson, Scott and 'Birdie' Bowers, died slowly together in their tent, 18 km (11 miles) from the next food cairn.

On 12 November 1912, in the Antarctic spring, the explorers' bodies were discovered, together with their graphic records of the struggle to the Pole and of the doomed attempted return. Wilson's letters were calm and hopeful. They must have been of some comfort to Oriana who, cruelly, first heard the news shouted out by newspaper hawkers. Wilson looked forward to the next life. 'Don't be unhappy – all is for the best. We are playing a good part in a great scheme arranged by God himself and all is well.' At first the country was stunned by the tragedy, but as details of the explorers' heroism were blazoned around the world, pride and inspiration at the men's achievements partially replaced grief. The flames of the Heroic Age of Antarctic Exploration had been fanned.

RUSSELL POTTER

Roald Amundsen

A BURNING AMBITION TO REACH THE POLES

(1872–1928)

Strangely enough the thing in Sir John Franklin's narrative that appealed to me the most strongly was the sufferings that he and his men endured. A strange ambition burned within me to endure those same sufferings. Perhaps the idealism of youth, which often takes a turn towards martyrdom, found its crusade in me in the form of Arctic exploration.

Roald Amundsen, **The North West Passage,** *1908*

In the history of those who have explored both the Arctic and Antarctic, the accomplishments of Roald Amundsen stand unequalled. The first to traverse the fabled Northwest Passage by ship, the first to reach the South Pole, and quite probably the first to set eyes – albeit from the air – on the North Pole as well, Amundsen lived to fulfil the dreams of the men whose narratives he so admired, completing the circle with a mysterious disappearance amid the ice that set the seal of tragedy upon his great accomplishments. And yet, during his lifetime, he was rarely accorded the accolades given other polar heroes: the British snubbed him (at the Royal Geographical Society, news of his attainment of the South Pole was greeted with three cheers – for his dogs); the Americans resented him; and although his laurels were welcomed in Norway, he never enjoyed the sort of adulation accorded Nansen (p. 169). Part of the reason may have been that, in personal terms, he was a somewhat cold and isolated man, whose strength of character was edged by a pride intolerant of even the slightest hint of disloyalty. He also admired and embraced the methods of the Inuit, an approach that greatly aided his efforts even as it seemed an affront to British explorers of a generation that took a dim view of native culture and regarded men rather than dogs as the ideal motive force.

Roald Engelbregt Gravning Amundsen was born on 16 July 1872 in Borge, Østold, in what was then a Norway under Swedish rule. His father was a shipbuilder and so he might have seemed born into an ideal trade for an explorer; his mother, however, recognizing his intellectual gifts, wanted him to become a doctor. He promised to follow her wishes, while at the same time making surreptitious preparations for what he felt was his true career. Her death when he was 21 enabled him to leave

Amundsen on skis during the Belgian Antarctic Expedition of 1897–99. When the expedition became trapped in the ice, Amundsen helped ensure their survival by hunting for fresh meat.

university and embark upon his dreams; four years later, in 1897, he volunteered for the Belgian Antarctic Expedition, where he served alongside the American doctor Frederick A. Cook. When their ship, the *Belgica,* became trapped in the ice, they became the first explorers to overwinter in the Antarctic. This unplanned sojourn was turned to advantage by Amundsen, who embarked on a series of forays, studying the sea ice, designing and constructing tents, and hunting seal and penguin. He introduced his shipmates to Norwegian-style long skis and snowshoes, which they found superior to the Canadian models. Amundsen was also of vital assistance to Cook in maintaining a steady supply of fresh meat, which he insisted they eat, a policy that almost certainly preserved the lives of the crew.

The Northwest Passage

His appetite for polar adventure thoroughly whetted, Amundsen set about planning his own expedition, seeking to fulfil his boyhood dream of traversing the Northwest Passage. Yet despite the romantic associations of this goal, Amundsen was anxious to maintain a solid scientific justification for his undertaking, and emphasized that magnetic observations, particularly determining the location of the North Magnetic Pole, were the paramount goal of the expedition. He secured the blessing of leading experts in terrestrial magnetism, and – more importantly – that of Nansen, whose stature as Norway's leading polar explorer was already secured. As with most such undertakings, money proved the most difficult ingredient. Having obtained a well-built fishing trawler, the *Gjøa*, in Trömso, Amundsen was forced to go into debt to cover the costs of re-outfitting her and laying in supplies. He assembled a crew of just six men beside himself, with provisions for five years, as he anticipated wintering over for two or three seasons, and set sail under cover of darkness on 16 June 1903 – just ahead of the debt collectors who had threatened to seize the ship the next morning.

In many ways, although inspired by British Royal Navy expeditions in search of the Passage, especially that of Sir John Franklin, Amundsen's plan was their complete opposite. The British sent large ships in pairs in case one were lost; Amundsen had only one tiny vessel, with a crew a fraction of the size of Franklin's. Naval crews relied entirely upon ship-board stores, while Amundsen planned on hunting and as much fresh meat as possible. The final and most dramatic contrast was in their respective attitudes towards the Inuit. Though they accepted their help when in dire need, British explorers conceived of the 'Esquimaux' as primitives from whom little could be learnt. Amundsen, though he too believed that European civilization was superior in most respects, knew that the Inuit's thousands of years of collective experience was invaluable for anyone hoping to live and travel efficiently in the polar regions.

Amundsen's progress through Lancaster Sound followed Franklin's route closely, including a visit to the graves of some of Franklin's crew at Beechey Island. Following the path determined by his magnetic instruments, he proceeded from there southwest through Peel Sound. Then, in a departure from Franklin's presumed route, Amundsen steered to the east, rather than the west, of King William Island. This led him through increasingly shallow waters; near Matty Island, the *Gjøa* ran aground, and Amundsen was forced to jettison 25 cases of dog pemmican. The experience provided clear evidence that Franklin's ships, which rode far deeper in the water than Amundsen's tiny vessel, could never have managed this route.

As they steered cautiously along the southeastern coast of King William Island, Lieutenant Hansen, who was in the crow's nest, called out that he had spotted 'the finest little harbour in the world'. Amundsen dubbed it Gjøahavn (Gjoa Haven), and for the following two winters it would be their base of operations. Since the current position of the magnetic pole was within 145 km (90 miles), Amundsen considered it ideal for magnetic observations. It was not until well into the autumn that they had their first encounter with local Inuit. Food was exchanged and later caribou-skin clothing; Amundsen, as well as his men, had a full head-to-toe outfit and he quickly realized that it was far superior to European dress in warmth, comfort and durability. Nevertheless, he frequently spoke of them as a 'Stone Age' people, and took measures to prevent his men from having personal liaisons with their wives, lest the invisible but vital line between his civilized view of the world and their primitive one be crossed.

Two winters at their snug little harbour on King William Island proved ample for the observations Amundsen had planned, and, despite his efforts to distance his expedition from the Inuit, it was with a certain feeling of sadness that he and his men finally bade farewell to the place. Amundsen completed the rest of the Passage without encountering any extraordinary difficulties, a fact which he attributed to good planning, although to the English, who had struggled after the goal for centuries, it seemed almost unfair. The only complication came at the end when, on his arrival at Fort Yukon, Amundsen discovered that there was no telegraph with which he could

Two Gjoa Haven Inuit, Praederik and his wife Draga, in their igloo. From a photograph taken during Amundsen's Northwest Passage Expedition, 1903.

announce his triumph to the world. He was forced to sledge south some 320 km (200 miles) to Eagle City. Unfortunately for him, one of the operators copied the wire to a newspaper reporter, and his hopes to sell exclusive rights to his story were dashed. Nevertheless, the coverage he received cemented his claim to fame; the Royal Geographical Society awarded him its Patron's Medal in 1907, and the Norwegian *Storting* voted 40,000 Kroner to defray his expenses.

The Race South

Never one to rest long on his laurels, Amundsen quickly set about plans for an expedition to the North Pole, using his new-found fame to get things moving quickly. In a deeply touching gesture of support, Nansen offered him the use of the *Fram*, and the same suppliers who had previously threatened to impound the *Gjøa* were eager to have their names attached to this mission. Yet as both Cook and then Robert Peary laid claim to the North Pole, Amundsen suddenly changed his plans, waiting until the *Fram* was underway to inform his crew that the South Pole, rather than the North, would be their goal. He took the time to send a telegram to Captain Scott, who had already set out on his own, well-publicized expedition with the same aim, but otherwise let no one, not even his backers, know of his plans.

Amundsen's men showing off their improvised homemade 'patent goggles' in the dining area of Framheim, their base camp in Antarctica.

Amundsen and his crew, equipped with a portable shelter and 97 well-chosen dogs, arrived at the Bay of Whales on 2 January 1911, where he established a camp he named Framheim. He began at once laying in depots for his polar trek, chafing at the long, slow arrival of Antarctic spring. He launched his first attempt prematurely on 8 September, but was forced to retreat in the face of temperatures as low as –58°C (–73°F), in which two dogs froze to death and his men suffered severe frostbite. A second effort was begun on 19 October, reaching the Queen Maud range on 11 November. After a difficult ascent of the Axel Heiberg glacier, they made camp and set about butchering two dozen of their dogs, using the meat to feed the remaining 18.

A Norwegian flag taken by Amundsen on his expedition to the South Pole, as seen flying above the tent at the Pole in the photograph opposite.

They pressed south across hazardous crevasses, enduring days of poor visibility in which Amundsen was forced to navigate by dead reckoning. Happily, a burst of sunlight on 8 December enabled observations, which showed them to have reached 88°16'. Less than a week later, on 14 December 1911, they reached the Pole itself. Amundsen spent three days there, establishing a camp he dubbed Polheim and making extensive observations to confirm the location of the Pole. On their return trip they travelled mostly by night, moving more quickly with lightened loads, and reached Framheim on 25 January. Although he had reached the Pole first, Amundsen was shocked when he heard of Scott's death, remarking that he 'would gladly forgo any honour or any amount of money if thereby I could have saved Captain Scott from his terrible death'. Still, many in Britain felt that Amundsen had not quite played fairly, having started in secret under false pretences, and relied on dogs rather than men for motive power.

Flight over the North Pole

Amundsen took little time to savour his triumph, embarking upon a modified version of his earlier North Pole plans, using the ship *Maud* to attempt a Northeast Passage. Despite careful planning, his hopes of getting the *Maud* ensconced in the polar pack ice met with failure, and he returned to Norway, turning his attention instead to polar aviation. The idea of reaching the Pole by air was not a new one, but technical difficulties had doomed earlier efforts. S. A. Andrée's famous attempt by balloon in 1897 had ended in his death, and Walter Wellman's endeavours using a dirigible in 1907 and 1909 had been costly failures. No stranger to air travel – he had obtained his pilot's licence in 1912, the first in Norway – Amundsen hoped to launch an expedition using planes equipped with ski-runners.

His first attempts ended abruptly when the plane's undercarriage collapsed on landing. Further attempts were hampered by lack of money, until Amundsen discovered an able friend in the industrialist Lincoln Ellsworth. Ellsworth provided funds for the acquisition of two specially modified Dornier Wal seaplanes, and Amundsen recruited skilled pilots; he and Ellsworth would serve as navigators. The planes left Spitsbergen on 21 May 1925 and enjoyed a smooth flight as far as 88° north, a polar aviation record, by which point they had exhausted half their fuel. A landing attempt proved disastrous, when one of the planes was damaged beyond repair. Amundsen oversaw repairs on the remaining plane, which took several weeks; by the time they managed to take off and return to Spitsbergen, they found that they had long been given up for dead.

Much as had Sir John Ross before him, Amundsen found that a surprising return from a supposed grave was an enormous source of fame. Convinced that the fuel limitations and fragility of fixed-wing craft were the problem, Amundsen revived the idea of a voyage by airship. He sought the assistance of Colonel Umberto Nobile, who had designed long-range airships for the Italian air force. On the condition that he himself serve as pilot and that five Italian crewmembers be included, Nobile agreed. Frustratingly, just before Amundsen's airship the *Norge* set out in May 1926, the American pilot Richard Byrd embarked on his own flight to the Pole. Byrd's flight, which began at Spitsbergen and lasted only 16 hours, is now widely doubted to have

The successful explorers at the South Pole, 14 December 1911. Amundsen himself is on the left. The photograph was taken by Olav Bjaaland and this is a reproduction of the only known contemporary print of this image to have been made from the original camera negative.

A crowd of people cheer Amundsen's expedition as it takes off from Spitsbergen on board the airship, the Norge, *in May 1926 for a flight over the North Pole. Despite an earlier claim by Richard Byrd, Amundsen is now considered to be the first person to have achieved this.*

reached the Pole, but at the time his claim was given considerable credence. The *Norge* departed two days after Byrd's flight, and enjoyed a remarkably smooth and uneventful flight to the Pole, arriving at 9.55 a.m. on 11 May. The ship continued across the polar icecap, and despite some concerns with ice formation on its outer envelope, managed a safe landing at Teller, Alaska, on 14 May after a flight of just over 70 hours. It was the culmination of Amundsen's career, but his triumph was marred by Nobile's insistence that the credit belonged to him, and to Italy.

Putting aside his understandably bitter feelings, Amundsen acted quickly when he heard that Nobile's airship *Italia* had crashed during a second North Pole voyage two years later. He secured a plane and pilot from the French government and took off on 18 June 1928 despite poor visibility. His plane is presumed to have crashed somewhere north of Bear Island in the Barents Sea, but searches have so far failed to find it.

Wally Herbert

THE LAST GREAT ARCTIC EXPEDITION

(1934–2007)

A pioneer has an unspoken responsibility to bring back something of value from one's travels – a map, a unique discovery, or specialist knowledge that contribute to mankind's understanding of our planet – but therein lies a dilemma: if one finds paradise, should one reveal its secrets to one's fellow man? It is not an easy choice; when one discovers a place of beauty, one becomes responsible, in many ways, for its future.

Wally Herbert,* The Polar World, *2007

Three things are expected – or at least hoped for – from a polar explorer. The first is the tenacity and presence of mind necessary to the task of exploration itself; the second is the ability to write a narrative that gives drama and form to an expedition account; the third is a visual sensibility, the knack for picturing – in sketches, photographs or paintings – the strange world encountered. Not everyone excels in more than one of these areas; Wally Herbert stands almost alone as a master in all three. The leader of what is widely regarded as the last great Arctic expedition, and perhaps – given that man would set foot on the moon only a few months later – the last great journey on earth, Herbert devoted his later career to research, writings and paintings, leaving a lasting legacy unlike any other polar figure of his day.

Self-portrait by Wally Herbert, executed with pencil and scalpel. Through his images he captured the spirit of the polar world.

Herbert, famously, credited his initial interest in the poles to a newspaper which, quite literally, fell on his head from an overhead compartment on a bus. It contained a notice asking for volunteers for the Falkland Islands Dependency Survey (FIDS; later the British Antarctic Survey). The year was 1954, and FIDS was a fertile training ground for polar explorers. It was there that Herbert learned the delicate art of dog-driving, a skill essential to long-distance crossings over ice and snow, and there that he began – when other work was not pressing – to employ his tiny art kit, which consisted of a paintbox and three brushes.

One endeavour that brought art and science together for Herbert was the making of relief maps. In the early days, these were prepared using a sheet of artist's foil which had been thinly coated with ink. Then, patiently and with infinite care, a surgeon's scalpel was used slowly to scrape away the paint in such a way as to highlight the topography. As part of the team which prepared the very first accurate maps of the Queen Maud Range, Herbert perfected his skills as surveyor and mapmaker; in later years, he adapted these same methods for portraiture, making use no doubt of these many hours spent carefully rendering shadow and light.

Herbert's time in Antarctica was a rich and rewarding apprenticeship – but for what? As he lamented at the time, little remained to be explored in Antarctica, where no journey was without at least some precedent – but what of the north? His skills in sledge-travel could be readily applied there, and he might benefit from the use of Inuit dogs and local expertise. And, though it was similarly a frozen world, the Arctic had at its heart not a landmass, but rather a vast, slowly whirling mass of ice, whose vicissitudes were only partly understood.

Herbert's 'field sketch' relief map of the Queen Maud Range, Antarctica; he helped to produce the first accurate maps for huge areas of this largely unexplored land.

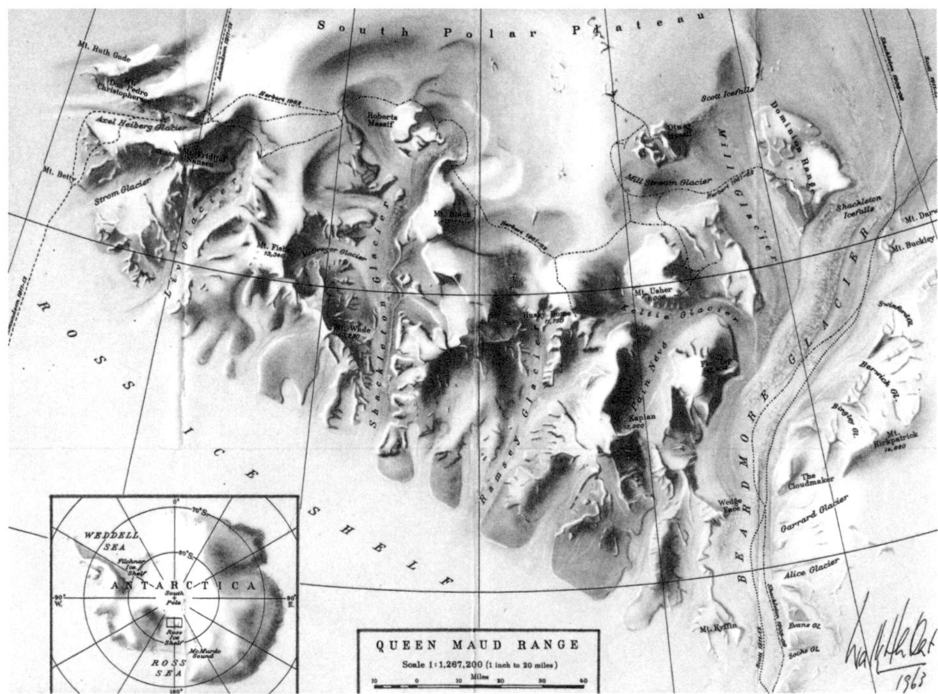

Landing on Svalbard 1969: *this painting by Herbert depicts the final landfall of the British Trans-Arctic Expedition as they completed their historic crossing of the North Polar icecap by its longest axis.*

Crossing the Polar Icecap

At the time, Herbert firmly believed that one of his heroes, Robert Peary, had already reached the North Pole, but the polar icecap had never been crossed on foot by its longest axis. Such a crossing would require starting earlier than usual in the season, as soon as the February sun could spare a scant two hours of daylight. After that would come a long trek through dangerously mushy summer ice, with the goal of first reaching the so-called 'Pole of Inaccessibility', that part of the sea ice furthest from any land. Next would come a fixed winter camp, borrowing Nansen's idea of harnessing the slow drift of the polar icecap to move slowly eastwards. Characteristically, Herbert downplayed the Pole itself as an attainment: 'We shall go to the pole, I hope, but this will be incidental'.

With him Herbert took three trusted men, each chosen carefully for his background and personal qualities. Foremost among them was polar glaciologist Dr Roy 'Fritz' Koerner, with whom Herbert had worked at Hope Bay in Antarctica. The team

A photograph of the winter camp taken during the British Trans-Arctic Expedition, around January 1969. At this time the expedition was behind schedule, but they later made such good progress that they reached the end of the journey on the exact day that Herbert had planned.

also included Antarctic geophysicist Allan Gill, as well as Ken Hedges, an army doctor. They departed from Point Barrow on 21 February 1968, but their initial progress through the constantly moving ice was slower than planned. Herbert was obliged to extend their travel further into the summer months, when conditions would be at their worst. After crossing 80° of latitude, they encountered a long series of leads in the ice which forced them off track by more than 128 km (80 miles). After finally reaching their summer camp on 4 July 1968, they found themselves at an auspicious point for taking advantage of the ice-drift. Indeed, over the summer they were carried along at a rate of 2.4 nautical miles a day – a better speed than they had managed throughout their last two weeks of ice-travel.

Yet a still greater challenge awaited them the following season, when, four days out of camp, Gill stumbled in a slush-hole and injured his back. The exact nature and severity of the injury were difficult to determine; in a series of tense radio exchanges with the expedition's committee at the Royal Geographical Society, Herbert argued as best he could that it would be better to have Gill recuperate than to try a risky rescue operation. He was overruled, and Weldy Phipps, a veteran Canadian bush pilot, made a rescue flight from Cornwallis Island, only to be turned back due to ridged ice that made landing impossible. Although this meant a premature winter camp, Gill made a full recovery, and once again it seemed that fate had weighed in on Herbert's side.

The end of the winter found them significantly behind schedule; in order to make up for lost time, Herbert planned a series of forced marches that began in complete polar darkness. By early April they were nearing the North Pole, though the constant drift of the ice necessitated maddening detours; as Herbert later recalled, finding the Pole was 'rather like stepping on the shadow of a bird hovering overhead'. Nevertheless they did reach it, on 6 April 1969 – 60 years to the day after Peary's claimed attainment. The remainder of their journey was covered in record speed, such that they arrived at Tavleøya Island in Svalbard on the very day – 29 May – that Herbert had estimated in his plan five years earlier.

Later Life

Accolades for Herbert's achievement poured in from around the world; British Prime Minister Harold Wilson hailed it as 'a feat of endurance and courage which ranks with any in polar history'. Although overshadowed in the press by the first manned moon landing soon after, it remains an unparalleled journey, one never attempted since. Herbert then planned a circumnavigation of Greenland, which though unsuccessful brought him closer to the culture and peoples of West Greenland.

As fate would have it, Herbert's attainment of the Pole, which he himself downplayed, took on new significance in the light of questions about Peary's 1909 claim. Approached by the National Geographic Society, and with unprecedented access to Peary's personal diaries, after much soul-searching Herbert agreed to examine the evidence. It was only gradually, and to his own lasting disappointment, that he found compelling evidence that Peary had not reached the Pole in 1909, and – perhaps worse – that he'd known it. Herbert's account was published as *The Noose of Laurels* (1989), and while it has not completely quieted the controversy, it effectively diminished support for Peary's claim. In his later years, Herbert finally returned to his brushes and paintbox, producing a significant body of art representing his life and career as an explorer; his final book, *The Polar World*, was published after his death in 2007.

DESERTS

Deserts have always drawn explorers. The challenge of surviving in the extremes of heat and dryness can be as seductive as overcoming the trials of cold and ice. Heinrich Barth stands out above the others. His companions kept dying on him, but he was invincible. Carrying just a compass, watch and two pistols, speaking fluently the language of each region he passed through and taking copious notes, he was a model explorer. A true scholar, he revealed the truth about the fabled city of Timbuktu and published a massive book of his travels, which still remains an authoritative work on the Sahara and its peoples 150 years later.

In Australia, the existence of rivers tantalized explorers with the possibility of a body of water and fertile land in the interior, but most simply petered out in endless sandy wastes, which many died trying to cross. Charles Sturt searched in vain for an inland sea on three epic expeditions. Although he never found it – how could he? it did not exist – he did unlock many of the secrets of Australia's heartland and its network of rivers.

The Arabian deserts attracted eccentrics, and none perhaps were more odd than Major Miss Gertrude Bell, whose ironic legacy today is that she virtually single-handedly brought about the modern state of Iraq. As much a political animal as an explorer, she travelled courageously to Hail, where she was the first to record details of a harem from the inside. Harry St John Philby claimed to have made the first 'true' crossing of the Empty Quarter and he, too became expert on Arabia, travelling huge distances by camel. He fell out with the British government and

Gertrude Bell on horseback at Kubbet Duris funerary monument, Lebanon, during her first trip to the desert in 1900. Bell's subsequent travels in the Middle East were to make her a legendary figure in the exploration and politics of the region.

Ralph Bagnold and his party of eight camped by their Model A Fords at the foot of a crescent dune in southern Egypt in 1932. On this expedition they travelled over 8,000 km (5,000 miles) across country where no vehicle had been before. Although much of it was 'bad going', they had no serious breakdowns.

ended his life in relative disgrace (although this was nothing in comparison with the ignominy of his son, the traitor spy Kim).

Ralph Bagnold virtually invented modern desert travel. The Sahara is far and away the largest desert on earth and Bagnold began to explore it in 1926, taking Model T and Model A Fords to places no one had considered attempting to reach by vehicle before. He was also a fine scientist and he made many discoveries about how dunes work, as well as locating archaeological sites. Later, in the Second World War, he was to create the Long Range Desert Group.

Wilfred Thesiger loved deserts and travelled across many in Africa and Asia. Once, when he briefly joined an expedition of mine in the Borneo rainforest, we asked him what he thought of it. He replied that he 'preferred an environment where water was more appreciated'. He is best known for his book *Arabian Sands*, which captured the spirit of the Empty Quarter in a way no one has done before or since.

Heinrich Barth

CROSSING THE SAHARA

(1821–1865)

In matters of science and humanity all nations ought to be united by one common interest, each contributing its share in proportion to its own peculiar disposition and calling.

Heinrich Barth, **Travels and Discoveries,** *1857–58*

Of all the many desert explorers of the 19th century who made their names in the burning sands, the German Heinrich Barth was surely one of the greatest, remarkable as much for what he was not as what he was. Today it has become fashionable to decry much of the British-led exploration of the world as imperialist in ambition, whatever its more noble motivations. Not the least of these was an attempt to suppress the slave trade, so much of which passed through the swathes of Sahara where Barth won lasting fame in the annals of African exploration.

Unlike some of his perhaps more dashing contemporaries in the field, Barth was a highly accomplished scholar and linguist; his anthropological research is rightly regarded to this day as a definitive survey of the African lands, peoples and languages he encountered. His crowning work, the *Travels and Discoveries in North and Central Africa: being a Journal of an Expedition undertaken under the Auspices of H. B. M.'s Government, in the Years 1849–1855*, reveals the inner workings of an intensely humane figure, ahead of his time in the respect shown to the Africans among whom he travelled, the numerous friendships he made among them and his fascination with their history, cultures and languages. It ran into five volumes and 3,500 pages and remains an essential reference point. Little wonder that his prodigious achievements are commemorated to this day in the institute in Cologne named after him, which 'is dedicated to the spirit of Heinrich Barth who laid the foundations of interdisciplinary research in Africa with his travels and publications'.

Barth was born in Hamburg in 1821 and read Classics at Berlin University, where he studied under such intellectual luminaries as the geographer-scientist Alexander von Humboldt (p. 232), the magisterial 'scientific' historian Leopold von Ranke,

Frontispiece from an account of the progress of the Central African Expedition published in 1854, with a map of the routes taken, portraits of the four expedition members and vignettes of scenes through which they passed; Barth is bottom left.

Map of part of
AFRICA
showing the
PROGRESS OF THE EXPEDITION
under
Messrs. Richardson, Barth, Overweg & Vogel
in the years 1850..1855.
From Official & private sources compiled by
Augustus Petermann, F.R.G.S.
Geographical Miles.
MEDITERRANEAN SEA
Gulf of Sidra
TRIPOLI
BARCA
SAHARA
FEZZAN
COUNTRY OF THE TIBBUS
GREAT DESERT
AIR OR ASBEN
SUDAN
BORNU
Lake Tsad
BAGIRMI
ADAMAUA
BENIN
GULF OF GUINEA
ROUTES.
Richardson, Barth, Overweg & Vogel 1850..55
Hornemann, 1798.
Ritchie and Lyon, 1818. 1820.
Oudney Denham & Clapperton, 1822. 1825.
Clapperton and Lander, 1825 & 1826
Lander, 1830 (The same journey was repeated by Allen and Oldfield in 1833.)
Dickson 1851.
Native Routes.
JAMES RICHARDSON
ADOLF OVERWEG
HEINRICH BARTH
EDUARD VOGEL

Friedrich von Schelling the philosopher and the philologist Jakob Grimm. Such figures and others provided the young Barth with the intellectual strength he later used so profitably in the field. He became fluent in French, Spanish, Italian and English, languages to which he later added Arabic in preparation for his great African journeys, which would take him through Islamic lands. He graduated in 1844, at the zenith of European exploration of Africa, led in large part by the British at a time when the venerable Royal Geographical Society conducted its own research and sent expeditions to every corner of the globe. Among these British travellers of the 1820s were Dr Walter Oudney and Lt Hugh Clapperton, veterans of a successful expedition that charted the shores of Lake Chad, explored the (Libyan) oasis of Ghat and brought back a wealth of political, commercial and ethnographical information. Willingly or not, Africa was opening up to the outside world.

Portrait of A'bbega and Dyrregu, former slaves liberated by Overweg and brought to Europe by Barth.

First Foray into Africa

Barth wasted little time joining the quest. After studying Arabic in London, he embarked on his first African journey in 1845, heading east from the Moroccan port of Tangier, across Barbary and the Libyan jewel of Cyrenaica, to Egypt, where he was set upon and wounded by robbers, the very stuff of 19th-century travel adventures. He ascended the Nile as far south as Wadi Halfa before crossing the Sinai desert into Palestine, travelling onwards and extensively through Palestine, Syria, Turkey and Greece, returning at last to Berlin in 1847 with a significant journey under his belt. Two years later, he published a record of the expedition, the rather modestly titled *Wanderings Round the Mediterranean.* With this impressive debut he had won his spurs and was now ready for something altogether more serious.

Of the British band of African explorers, one man in particular was to play a defining role in Barth's subsequent career. James Richardson, a passionate, headstrong and irascible campaigner against the slave trade, had already led a pioneering North African expedition which resulted in his spirited account *Travels in the Great Desert of Sahara in the Years of 1845 and 1846.* Disgruntled by the premature termination of his first mission, in 1849 Richardson was commissioned by Lord Palmerston to make a 'more extensive expedition through the Northern Parts of Africa to the Great

Desert of Sahara and further south if possible to Lake Chad, in order that a more intimate knowledge may thus be obtained of the state of those Countries ... and also with a view to substitute legitimate Commerce for the Traffic in Slaves in the Interior of Africa, by encouraging an exchange of the Productions of those Countries for the Production of Europe'. In short, it was to establish 'regular and secure' communications between the Mediterranean and Niger – an ambition virtually impossible to achieve without the use of aircraft.

The Central African Expedition

Diplomatic manoeuvrings in London, spearheaded by the Prussian ambassador and wholeheartedly supported by Alexander von Humboldt, resulted in the appointment of Barth and his Prussian colleague the astronomer Dr Adolf Overweg to Richardson's second mission. This was the mammoth Central African Expedition of 1850–55, which would result in Barth's celebrated discoveries. As the expedition's official papers put it: 'Mr Richardson will be accompanied by two Prussian Gentlemen, Dr Barth, a distinguished African Traveller and a member of the University of Berlin, and Dr Overweg, a Geologist and a member of the Geographical Society of Berlin. These Gentlemen have been selected by the Prussian Government to accompany Mr Richardson; but they are equally with Mr Richardson travelling on the Service and under the Protection of the British Government.'

The grandly titled expedition moved south from Tripoli in early 1850. Problems beset the explorers from the start, with health a constant concern. The party passed through the Garian Hills and traversed the featureless wasteland of the Hamada al Hamra (Red Plain) before reaching the historic oasis of Murzuk, a long-established centre of the Saharan slave trade, and continuing south to the remote settlement of Ghat, today close to the border between Libya and Algeria

After travelling onwards through the Aïr Mountains to Agades, the party divided into two groups after disagreements, brought on in part by Richardson's unpredictable and autocratic style of leadership; tact was never his strong suit. After the split, Barth pressed on to Kano, while Richardson headed east before succumbing to fever and exhaustion on 4 March 1851 in Ungurutuwa, six days' march from Kukawa, west of Lake Chad. 'My way of looking at things was not quite the same as that of my late companion, and we had therefore often had little differences', wrote Barth diplomatically as he gazed at the impatient Englishman's grave beneath a fig tree, 'but I esteemed him highly for the deep sympathy which he felt for the sufferings of the native African, and deeply lamented his death'. Barth now assumed command of the expedition. Together with Overweg, he surveyed land to the north, west and south of Lake Chad. Eighteen months after Richardson's untimely death, Overweg too passed away near Lake Chad. Had it not been for the courage and vision Barth showed after two of his most important colleagues had died, the expedition would have been an expensive failure, both in lives lost and money spent. As it was, like all the best explorers, Barth pressed on undaunted.

In addition to the Saharan journeys, impressive enough by themselves, Barth surveyed the country around Lake Chad and Bagirmi and Timbuktu to the west, south as far as Cameroon. Adept at languages and fascinated by the local histories and vocabularies he was compiling, he made prolonged journeys among the ancient sultanates of Bornu, Kano, Sokoto, Gando, Nupe and Timbuktu.

To reach the fabled city of Timbuktu itself he assumed the guise of a travelling Muslim by the name of Abd el Kerim ('Servant of the Merciful'). 'By this means', he wrote, 'I won the esteem of the natives, who took such a lively interest in my well-

Barth's arrival at Timbuktu, in September 1853: his careful, sensitive and scholarly conduct during his stay in this legendary city ensured his survival, unlike some earlier travellers, and also revealed the full range of skills that made him the complete explorer. This plate, drawn by J. M. Bernatz from a sketch by Barth , appeared in volume 4 of Travels and Discoveries *(1857–58).*

being that, even when I was extremely ill, they used to say, "Abd el Kerim shall not die.'" His sensational arrival in Timbuktu in 1853 was worth the ruse. It led to his confirmation of earlier reports by the French explorer René Caillié. He was also able to show that the upper Benue empties into the River Niger and the Shari empties into Lake Chad. Among his many achievements was the first survey of the middle section of the Niger, one of the great puzzles of African exploration. Generous-spirited, endlessly curious and humane, Barth struck up good relations with a number of African leaders and scholars; in Timbuktu his friendship with Ahmed al Bakkay al Kunti, a renowned spiritual leader, almost certainly saved his life.

Barth also formed a strong bond with his beasts of burden. Unlike a good number of his peers, he refrained from making the usual vituperative denunciations of the camel, one of nature's most vilified creatures. His appreciation of this much maligned animal still brings cheer to anyone who has made long journeys with camels.

> *I am rather afraid that Europeans often make camels stupid by their own foolish treatment of them, whereas I was wont to treat this noble animal, which had carried myself or the heaviest of my things all the way from Tripoli, as a sensible companion, giving it in the beginning the peel of the oranges I was eating, of which it was particularly fond, or a few of my dates (for which it did not fail to turn round its beautiful neck) ... Its fidelity will ever remain in my memory as one of the pleasantest recollections of my journey.*

When Barth finally returned to England in 1855, after another traverse of the Sahara, he had been out of contact for so long that the British government assumed he was either dead or missing. In fact, he had been immersed in his studies.

Achievements and Acclaim

While the physical aspect of this single expedition was astonishing – he notched up a breathtaking 16,000 km (10,000 miles) of overland travel – it was the intellectual results that laid the foundations of his greatness as an explorer. Barth was nothing if not methodical in his studies, exhibiting a mental stamina that matched his physical bravery during the arduous treks across inhospitable terrain.

Although *Travels and Discoveries in North and Central Africa* may not have been everybody's cup of tea – much of the reading public considered it fearfully dull on publication in 1857–58, and with the diminished attention spans of today it is a stretching read – it is a masterpiece of historical, geographical, topographical, anthropological, commercial and philological research, enlivened considerably by magnificent, highly evocative plates. On many levels Barth returned with more complete

Interior of a Musgu dwelling, south of Lake Chad in present-day Nigeria. During his travels Barth witnessed a Bornu raid on Musgu – a brutal example of the Trans-Saharan slave trade in action.

information on the Sahara and Sudan than previously known to Europeans. His penetrating research into the history of the places and peoples he visited included the discovery of the *Tarikh as Sudan* ('History of Sudan') and a history of the kingdom of Bornu. In the Lake Chad area alone he was able to compile 40 distinct vocabularies of African languages. The Royal Geographical Society, quick to appreciate the value of his five-year expedition, awarded him its Victoria Medal; the British government made him a Companion of the Order of the Bath.

After a journey to Asia Minor in 1858, the 1860s saw Barth hard at work on his collection of Central African vocabularies. In 1863 he was made a professor of geography at Berlin University and president of the Berlin Geographical Society, an inspired choice. He died in 1865, aged just 44.

His work stands as a monument to the possibilities of open-hearted exploration. As he wrote in the preface to his magnum opus:

> *If ... I have succeeded in placing before the eyes of the public a new and animated picture, and connected those apparently savage and degraded tribes more intimately with the history of races placed on a higher level of civilization, I shall be amply recompensed for the toils and dangers I have gone through.*

He succeeded admirably.

A sketch showing a rock art panel of engravings and petroglyphs (in the background) amid the sandstone cliffs at Wadi Telsaghe (Telizzharen), Libya, 1850. Barth was fascinated by these 'admirably executed' drawings and sculptures.

A herd of elephants near Lake Chad, 1851. Barth's surveys around Lake Chad produced much useful knowledge, and a map of Central Africa sent back during his expedition was described as 'the most comprehensive and complete … of any single African traveller'.

Charles Sturt

QUEST FOR AN INLAND SEA

(1795–1869)

I would rather that my bones had been left to bleach in that desert than have yielded an inch of ground I had gained at so much expense and trouble.

Charles Sturt,* Narrative of an Expedition into Central Australia, *1849

Over three decades, Charles Sturt's respectable life as a government administrator was both enlivened and threatened by his obsession with finding an inland sea in Australia's interior. His three expeditions were epic affairs, with heat, thirst and exhaustion bringing either death to his men or the agonies of endurance. But his achievements, including his journey down the great waterway of the Murray, were clouded in his mind by his inability to find the sea of his dreams.

Sturt was born in India in 1795, the eldest son of a judge. He was educated in England and gained a commission as an ensign in the 39th Regiment. As a captain he embarked with a detachment in charge of convicts on board a ship bound for New South Wales, arriving in May 1827. In Australia he was made military secretary to the governor, Sir Ralph Darling, and soon sought permission to lead an expedition into the centre. Sturt had become entranced by the mysteries of Australia's geography and the great unknown of the interior and wanted the honour of solving them. In 1818 John Oxley had charted a series of inland rivers in New South Wales, but had been bogged down in marshlands. The idea remained that an inland sea lay beyond the horizon.

SEARED BY DROUGHT

Sturt received approval to trace the course of the Macquarie River and left Sydney on 10 November 1828. He had selected an experienced explorer, Hamilton Hume, as his deputy, and a party of three soldiers and eight convicts. In December they started beside the headwaters of the Macquarie, through country seared by drought and heat, and established the northern limits of the vast Macquarie marshes that had thwarted Oxley. Rather than attempting to penetrate the sea of reed beds and waterways, they turned west and came to the Bogan River, following a course that was little more than a series of water-holes. On 2 February 1829, to their amazement, they came upon a 'noble river' flowing southwest. Sturt named it the Darling River. They rushed eagerly

The sandy wastes and far horizons, the heat and oppression of loneliness of the Australian inland are depicted in this watercolour by S. T. Gill, based on a sketch by Sturt for the frontispiece engraving accompanying his account of his last journey, Narrative of an Expedition into Central Australia, *published in London in 1849.*

down to the water to quench their thirst, but found it to be salty and undrinkable. They followed the Darling downstream for seven days, at which point Sturt and Hume agreed that the appalling heat, the swarms of flies and lack of good water made it too difficult to continue. Returning to their base at Mount Harris, they then went west to trace the Castlereagh River north until it, too, joined the Macquarie River. To complete the picture they returned down the eastern side of the Macquarie marshes.

Sturt had sketched the main outlines of the northern New South Wales river system and had discovered the previously unknown Darling River, but had not found any good country. Most vexingly, he had not reached an inland sea; he was convinced, however, that the secret would be unlocked by following the course of the Darling. The Governor was looking for more productive land and decided that Sturt should investigate the more southerly, but still inland-flowing, Lachlan-Murrumbidgee River system. Sturt was instructed that he should proceed to the more southerly reaches of the Darling only if the Murrumbidgee proved impassable.

A New Quest

On 3 November 1829 Sturt and his party set out and reached the limits of settlement, near today's Gundagai, before heading off into unknown country. They came to the Murrumbidgee amid scenery which Sturt described as 'wild, romantic and beautiful'; the river here was 25 m (82 ft) wide and fast flowing. This time Sturt had brought a collapsible 8-m (26-ft) whaleboat, but decided not to risk it in the wild waters and they slogged along the bank with their bullock drays. Finally, on 6 January 1830, Sturt committed the whaleboat to the reed-infested waters of the Murrumbidgee and chose seven men to accompany him on 'the desperate adventure'. The whaleboat eventually cleared the reed beds and was thrust along by the fast-flowing current, through over-arching trees which occasionally reached down to head height.

On 14 February they were astonished to be carried with great force into what Sturt called a 'broad and noble river'. He named it the Murray, after the Secretary of State for the Colonies, Sir George Murray. The party floated on in comfort down this 'high road', disturbed only by an assembly of armed and painted Aborigines on the

Sturt came across and sketched this camp established by a group of itinerant Aboriginals of Central Australia while on his second expedition. His sketch was rendered into watercolour by S. T. Gill. The Sturt expeditions had many such encounters.

Depot Glen: a wash drawing by Charles Sturt of the place on the Darling River where he and his party were marooned while on his final expedition in 1844. With access to the only permanent water in a parched country, they lived for six months in an underground bunker.

bank. The men loaded their guns and prepared for trouble, but an Aboriginal whom Sturt had befriended upstream emerged from the bush and persuaded the tribal leader to let the boat pass. Soon after that they came to a junction with a river flowing in from the north and Sturt rightly concluded that it was the Darling.

The glide downstream through open country was made increasingly uncomfortable by a lack of fresh food and their inability to stomach any more of the river fish known as Murray cod. Eventually the river petered out in a large and shallow lake, named Alexandrina for the princess, the future Queen Victoria. Having trudged over sandhills to the southern ocean, they realized with disappointment that the channel to the river was too shallow for shipping. They now faced the awful prospect of a haul upstream of 1,500 km (900 miles) against a steady current, with only a little flour and salt meat per day, though the killing of some swans brought a welcome change of diet. Rowing in shifts from dawn to dusk, it took 32 days to get back to the Murrumbidgee, which had a faster current that was almost impossible to row against.

Sturt wrote of his men: 'Their arms appeared to be nerveless; their faces became haggard, their persons emaciated, their spirits wholly sunk.' Arriving back at their starting point he sent his two strongest men to the nearest station, some 120 km (75 miles) away. On 18 April, when the last ounce of flour had been served out, the pair stumbled back with supplies enough to revive them for the last journey to safety.

A Last Chance

His hope of finding an inland sea diminished, but not extinguished, Sturt's life settled to a generally disappointing round of officialdom, punctuated by illness that sent him back to England and temporarily blinded him. His restoration to health was completed by marriage to Charlotte Greene in 1834, and the couple returned to Australia.

In 1843 Sturt, by now reduced to the lowly position of registrar-general in South Australia, decided that his last chance for personal recovery lay in making a claim on the British Colonial Office for special consideration. He still believed in the inland sea and prepared a plan for exploring and surveying the entire unknown interior of the continent. The plan was reduced to a proposal to penetrate the centre of the continent and attempt to establish the existence of a mountain range, but it gave Sturt his chance for glory and vindication.

On 10 August 1844 Sturt left Adelaide with 15 men, 6 drays, a boat and 200 sheep. They followed the Murray-Darling route north and found permanent water at Depot Glen – the only water in a drought-parched country. However, they were trapped by the weather and lived there for six months in an underground bunker, 'locked up … as effectually as if we had wintered at the Pole'. The heat and a diet of mutton and damper (bread) brought great suffering and cases of scurvy. All were severely affected and the second-in-command, James Poole, died. Finally, they were saved by heavy rain; they then moved northwest and built a structure which they called Fort Grey. From here Sturt made a last dash 800 km (500 miles) inland to seek for his longed-for sea. Instead, he was stopped by wave after wave of sand dunes, and then the immense rocky plain, now known as Sturt's Stony Desert. Back at the Murray River he next wanted to make a last trip inland with John McDouall Stuart (who was later to traverse the continent) but was over-ruled. The party started for Adelaide, with Sturt stricken with an attack of scurvy on the way, and arrived there on 19 January 1846.

There was honour and satisfaction in Sturt's later life. Back in England he was made Colonial Secretary, completed a published account of the last expedition and received the Founder's Medal from the Royal Geographical Society in London. On retirement he lived at Cheltenham, England, although he applied unsuccessfully for the governorship of both Victoria and Queensland. In 1869, at the instigation of friends, he sought a knighthood but died before the formalities were completed. Queen Victoria permitted his widow to use the title Lady Sturt.

The Murray River, which he saw as useless for shipping, did become the great inland waterway of Australia, carrying passengers and vast cargoes during the 70 years or so of the riverboat era.

Gertrude Bell

POETRY AND POLITICS IN THE MIDDLE EAST

(1868–1926)

Some power in her linked the love of the East with a practical aim that became a dominating purpose ... that she endured drudgery, was never dismayed by continual disappointment and never allowed her idealism to turn to bitterness, shows a strength of character rare indeed among those of the English for whom the East has become a passion.

The Times, *13 July 1926*

Step into the Royal Geographical Society's Ondaatje Theatre, probably the finest auditorium and one of the most daunting speaking venues in London, and the names of the great explorers of the past arrayed around the walls convey a humbling thrill and sense of magic: Burton, Franklin, Scott, Shackleton, Speke, Stanley. Few women are commemorated here, however, for exploration in this heroic age was, with few exceptions, a man's world. Yet one name in particular breaks that mould: Gertrude Bell, Arabist, explorer, mountaineer, archaeologist, writer, poet, intelligence expert and, as if this was not enough to occupy a life tragically cut short at 57, co-founder of the modern state of Iraq.

A photograph of Bell and Fattuh standing in front of a tent at camp, Deghile, Turkey, June 1906, towards the end of a punishing journey that started in Aleppo and ended in the Turkish city of Konya, via the course of the Tigris in Iraq.

Bell, born to an immensely wealthy and well-connected English industrialist's family in 1868, made a habit of amassing a prodigious collection of firsts. She was the first woman to achieve a First in Modern History at Oxford; the first woman to be awarded a prize by the Royal Geographical Society; the first woman officer in British military intelligence; and she made an important first ascent in the Alps. With this sort of CV, hard-won in a largely male world, her subsequent

The great rock-cut tombs at Petra (including the Palace Tomb and Corinthian Tomb), with Bell's camp in the foreground. Fearless and hardy as a traveller and explorer, Bell was also an accomplished and indefatigable archaeologist.

dedicated opposition to the Suffragettes and the extension of the vote to women comes as something of a surprise.

Like many British Arabists and desert explorers, Bell succumbed early to the pull of the East. At 32 she made her debut in the desert, a camel trek across Syria. Of the Orient she wrote: 'I find it catching at my heart again as nothing else can, or ever will, I believe, thing or person'. Love was not entirely elusive, but those she loved either died before she was able to marry them, were married themselves, or both.

She therefore joined that fascinatingly troubled band of British desert explorers – together with her contemporary T. E. Lawrence and successor Wilfred Thesiger (p. 225) – whose professional successes in the sands were never matched by personal happiness. This exacted a heavy price. Professionally triumphant, Bell remained personally unfulfilled throughout her life. She dabbled in the emotional world with a couple of doomed, unconsummated love affairs, but the sexual companionship of a soul-mate eluded her.

'There is poetry and beauty in solitude', a friend once told her. There was, there often is, but Bell didn't always want it. In fact, she craved a husband and children and admitted to her inner circle that she was merely 'carrying on an existence'. But what an existence! This virtually indomitable woman was sustained by stupendous personal reserves of energy and willpower. She possessed an ability to inspire and make friends around the world, coupled with a fierce intellect and felicitous talent for Eastern languages. 'Say, is it not rather refreshing to the spirit to lie in a hammock strung between the plane trees of a Persian garden and read the poems of Hafiz', she wrote in one of the more than 1,600 wonderful letters to her friends and family. Within two years of learning Persian she was translating its greatest writer. Her rendering of Hafiz's poetry into English is widely regarded as the finest and to many she was the leading Orientalist of her day. No less an authority on Persian literature than Edward Browne pronounced her work 'probably the finest and most truly poetical renderings of any Persian poet ever produced in the English language'.

To Hail

Bell's landmark Arabian journey of 1913–14 saw her strike out alone from Damascus to the stronghold of Hail in the Nafud Desert of what is today Saudi Arabia. She had already made numerous intrepid voyages, but this was a formidable expedition, undertaken in part to escape the turmoil of her relationship with the married army officer Charles Doughty-Wylie, later recipient of a posthumous Victoria Cross for gallantry at Gallipoli in 1915.

Louis Mallet, the British ambassador in Constantinople and a friend of 20 years standing, maintained the classic Foreign Office attitude to a traveller setting out for remote parts: he disclaimed all responsibility. Undaunted and armed with a three-inch theodolite, Bell pursued her dangerous journey, having signed documents eschewing protection from either the Ottoman or British authorities. Before setting out on the expedition, she had taken lessons in surveying techniques and map projections from the Royal Geographical Society.

While travelling south, she confided her thoughts in a letter to another well-placed friend, Valentine Ignatius Chirol, who was the former Foreign Editor of *The Times*.

> *I have known loneliness in solitude now, for the first time, and in the long days of camel riding and the long evenings of winter camping, my thoughts have gone wandering far from the camp fire into places which I wish were not so full of acute sensation. Sometimes I have gone to bed with a heart so heavy that I thought I could not*

carry it through the next day. Then comes the dawn, soft and beneficent, stealing over the wide plain and down the long slopes of the little hollows, and in the end it steals into my dark heart also ... that's the best I can make of it, taught at least some wisdom by solitude, taught submission and how to bear pain without crying out.

In December 1913 she was in volcanic country between Jebel Druse and Wadi Sirhan, discovering a Roman fort, then stopping at Qasr al Azaq to copy an inscription of Diocletian, the 3rd-century Roman emperor. Her eventual arrival in Hail, having negotiated the tortuous sand dunes of the Nafud Desert, coincided with the height of the noble Rashid family's internecine war. She was placed under what amounted to house arrest. A combination of judicious behaviour and inimitable grandeur prevented anything untoward happening to her. No European had set eyes on Hail since 1893, and only one woman – Lady Anne Blunt – had been there before.

Bell returned to Britain with copious information on the tribes between the Hijaz railway on the western flank and the Sirhan and Nafud to the east, as well as acute insights into relations between the Rashids and Sauds, rivals for power in the Arabian peninsula. Together with the mapping and surveying of the terrain she had conducted, this was intelligence of the greatest value for London, which was also seeking information on routes for the advance of the British Army into Palestine. The RGS recognized her extraordinary achievement by awarding her its Founder's Medal.

Bell's caravan of men and camels at the city walls of Hail, Saudi Arabia, March 1914. Of her many journeys in the Middle East, the expedition to this fabled city was by far her most perilous and successful, requiring all her talents as surveyor, explorer, intelligence expert and diplomat.

ABOVE *Townspeople in the streets of Hail, in a photograph by Bell.* BELOW *Turkiyyeh – a Circassian woman sent to Muhammad al Rashid as a gift. Bell met her in Hail and recorded: 'She is worth her weight in gold, as I have come to know. She is a chatterbox of the first order and I passed an exceedingly amusing hour in her company.'*

MIDDLE EASTERN POLITICS

From 1915 Bell was the interpreter of all reports from Central Arabia. Two years later, by now with a wealth of Middle Eastern experience under her belt, she was appointed Oriental Secretary to the colonial administrator Sir Percy Cox and settled in Baghdad. 'We shall, I trust, make it a centre for Arab civilization and prosperity', she wrote to her father as British troops entered the city with General Maude in March 1917.

Bell threw herself into Middle Eastern politics with gusto. Her wide-ranging intellect, linguistic talent and unconquerable will, together with an anachronistic fearlessness amid hair-raising adventures in a foreign world even more male then her own, were credentials unmatched by her contemporaries. There are times when Bell makes Lawrence of Arabia look like a dilettante.

Ibn Saud's visit to Basrah, 1916 (left to right: Abdul Aziz Ibn Saud, Sir Percy Cox and Gertrude Bell). Bell was a brilliant, if unconventional, civil servant.

Hardly surprisingly, she was not popular with all her colleagues. Her behaviour while working for Sir Arnold Wilson, Civil Commissioner for Iraq, writing letters undermining the official British position to all and sundry, would have seen her sacked by any boss today. Sir Mark Sykes, one half of the Anglo-French team which in 1916 drew the infamous Sykes-Picot line carving up the region between the two colonial powers, described her uncharitably in a letter to his wife: 'Confound the silly chattering windbag of conceited, gushing, flat-chested, man-woman, globe-trotting, rump-wagging, blethering ass!' She did not suffer fools.

The end of the First World War presaged the remaking of the defunct Ottoman empire into something a little neater and more orderly. At least that was the idea. And so came the state-making which so thrilled Bell, the delineation of Iraq's borders – encompassing Kurds and Sunni and Shia Arabs – which remains so problematic to this day. Then there was the equally gratifying procession of ambitious sheikhs sweeping through her office and home. 'They are the people I love,' she wrote, 'I know every tribal chief of any importance throughout the whole length and breadth of Iraq.'

She did, but with Iraq created and King Faisal installed on the throne, Bell had practically outlived her usefulness to His Majesty's Government by the mid-1920s. She felt the diminution in her status keenly, and there was no family of her own to fall back on. For a while, the National Museum which she founded and her position as Iraq's Director of Antiquities – another first – sustained her. But it was not enough. Her heart rebelled against the solitude, no longer so poetic. An overdose of sleeping pills on the night of 11/12 July 1926 ended it. She was buried in the British Anglican Cemetery in Baghdad.

In 1980, as the Royal Geographical Society celebrated its 150th anniversary, there were plans to honour Gertrude Bell in one of a commemorative set of postage stamps featuring great British explorers. One can only imagine her reaction if she had learnt of the Foreign Office's response: it vetoed the proposal for fear of offending Saddam Hussein.

JOHN URE

Harry St John Philby

A PASSION FOR ARABIA

(1885–1960)

I didn't hear what you said, but I entirely disagree with you.

Philby, quoting his own perversity, in Arabian Days, *1948*

From the moment of his birth in Ceylon in 1885 until his death in Lebanon in 1960, Harry St John Philby was an Englishman who was more at home abroad than in his own country, and more committed to foreign causes than to those of his compatriots. His father was a coffee planter and an unsatisfactory husband, who left his wife to bring up their children in England without him. But Philby was clever enough to win a scholarship to Westminster School and an exhibition to Trinity College, Cambridge, where – after taking a First in Modern Languages – he went on to study oriental languages and passed into the Indian Civil Service. However, from an early stage in his career he was found to lack the commitment and team-spirit required in conventional public service. He was seconded to the Mesopotamian expeditionary force, and later arranged to have himself seconded again – this time to head a mission to Ibn Saud, the ruler of Nejd in central Arabia. By now Philby was a fluent Arabic speaker and had already developed that enthusiasm for desert travel that was to form the keystone of his reputation as an explorer.

Crossing Arabia

In 1917, Philby persuaded Ibn Saud to provide him with an escort to accompany him across Arabia to the port of Jiddah on the Red Sea. In completing this journey (which did not involve the Empty Quarter of Arabia) he achieved a memorable crossing of Arabia from coast to coast, and his feat was widely acclaimed. In Jiddah he met Sharif Husain, the leader of the Arab revolt against the Turks in the First World War and the associate of Lawrence of Arabia. After the war, Philby was again seconded – this time to Baghdad to work in the administration of the newly formed state of Iraq (where Gertrude Bell (p. 209) was his field controller); but once more disagreements on policy and clashes of personality forced him to move on, first to Transjordan and then out of public service altogether.

He now settled in Jiddah and set up a trading company while acting as an adviser to Ibn Saud. But increasingly his attention was focused on what he most enjoyed and

Philby, with entourage, Jiddah, 1917–18. Having travelled by camel from the Persian Gulf to Riyadh, Philby arranged for an escort to accompany him from there to Jiddah, thus completing a crossing of Arabia from coast to coast.

did best – exploring the deserts of Arabia. For the next several decades he concentrated on making a series of remarkable journeys, culminating in his crossing of the Empty Quarter in 1932. Philby was to claim that this crossing – from north to south – was the first 'true' crossing of the Empty Quarter, although Bertram Thomas had crossed it two years earlier by a slightly shorter and arguably less arduous route from south to north. Philby's route took him from Hufhuf through Naifa, and then west for over 1,930 km (1,200 miles) across entirely barren and unexplored desert, eventually arriving at Mecca. The distance between wells could be as much as 644 km (400 miles), and water had to be poured into the camels through their nostrils as there was

A photograph of Jiddah taken by Philby around 1917. Philby first visited the city in 1917/18 as part of the British mission to Ibn Saud. Later, in 1926, he settled there and ran a trading company, though his real passion was the exploration of Arabia.

nowhere for them to drink, and even they were becoming dehydrated. His escort came near to mutiny, but he pressed on – subsequently emphasizing all these difficulties – determined to prove to the world that his achievement was superior to that of Thomas.

Philby had certain advantages over Thomas. While the latter had been accompanied by Rashid tribesmen, who were excellent guides but who had long-standing enmities with some of the Bedouin tribes they encountered en route, Philby went with the eventual blessing of the king of Saudi Arabia (his patron Ibn Saud) and so enjoyed a measure of protection not granted to Thomas. Philby also had by then acquired one further great advantage in dealing with the king, and indeed with the entire Arab world: he had converted from Christianity to Islam. There is little reason to think that matters of faith had much to do with Philby's conversion, which appears to have been motivated by considerations of personal advantage. He even accepted a second wife – 45 years his junior and by whom he had two sons – as a present from the king. Just as he abandoned his faith, so he also abandoned considerations of British national interest by helping to negotiate an oil agreement between the Saudis and an American oil company in 1933 – a considerable set-back to British interests in the region.

Although Bertram Thomas had already crossed the Empty Quarter of Arabia, Philby claimed his was the first 'true' crossing, from north to south and following a difficult route with only very infrequent wells. This photograph by Philby shows the expedition riding along the dune range of Bani Zainan before setting off across the waterless desert.

Recognition and Alienation

Unsatisfactory as Philby had shown himself to be as a public servant or a colleague, he nonetheless was proving to be an explorer of great merit. Travelling by camel across the Arabian deserts, he was assiduous in taking notes of everything of interest: geographical place names, geological features, archaeological inscriptions, temperatures, altitudes, astronomical observations, compass readings, distances – nothing escaped his meticulous attention or comprehensive recording. He wrote numerous articles and several books publishing the results of his researches.

As a consequence of all this industry, Philby received recognition from all the principal institutions concerned with such matters: the Royal Geographical Society awarded him their Founder's Medal and the Royal Asiatic Society awarded him their Richard Burton memorial medal; the British Museum and the Royal Botanic Gardens, Kew, as well as many foreign academic bodies also honoured him with awards or prizes.

None of this spared him from falling seriously out of favour with the British government at the time of the Second World War. He had long been known as an avowed pacifist who had stood as an anti-war candidate in a British by-election in 1939, but during the war from the sanctuary of Saudi Arabia he became ever more strident in his denunciations of British policy, and when he was rash enough to visit India he was arrested and sent back to imprisonment in England under wartime regulations. After the war he returned to his former life in Arabia, but the new king there was irked by Philby's criticisms of his regime and he had to go into exile in the Lebanon. It was there that he died in 1960, while staying with his son Kim Philby, who was shortly to be revealed and denounced as a Soviet double-agent who had worked for the Russians while employed by MI6 in Britain. What had been disaffection and awkwardness in the father had turned into treason and treachery in the son.

Philby had some claim to the inscription on his gravestone that he was 'the greatest of Arabian explorers', though Bertram Thomas and Wilfred Thesiger (p. 225) might well have disputed this. Certainly as an explorer he had the distinction of immersing himself more deeply in the language, lore and customs of Arabia than possibly any Englishman has done before or since. His contribution to exploration will be remembered with admiration by many, but with affection by few.

Philby taking a bath at Naifa well, Rub' Al Khali – the Empty Quarter – 1932, with Zaid the cook helping and the dinner tray used as a bath.

Ralph Bagnold

FORD CARS OVER THE DUNES

(1896–1990)

Travels among the ruins of desert kingdoms and the crocks and querns of prehistoric tribes; beyond them among creeping dunes, petrified forests and sand seas, beyond the last bone of man or mouse.

R. A. Bagnold, **Libyan Sands**, *1935*

The Eastern Sahara, or Libyan Desert, is the size of India. It is the largest expanse of severe aridity on earth. The central figure in its exploration was Ralph Bagnold, a man who was small and wiry, shy by nature, discerning and sociable with his friends, extremely practical around the house and in creating scientific instruments, and a keen climber and snooker player.

In 1915, during the First World War, Bagnold joined the Royal Engineers and was sent to France. After the war he studied engineering at Cambridge before returning to the army in 1921. In 1926 he was posted to Egypt and it was during his leaves, and building upon the experience that Dr John Ball and others had gained in using Model T Fords for desert exploration during the war, that he developed his passion for desert exploration by motor car.

The Expeditions

In the winter of 1873–74, Gerhard Rohlfs had led a German expedition that attempted to cross the Great Sand Sea, as the Eastern Saharan dunes are known, from Dakhla to Kufra. However, no expedition capable of making precise observations had penetrated this area of enormous dunes since then. The general view was that this terrain was just too difficult for motor vehicles. Bagnold was keen to test this supposition. In November 1929, together with five colleagues, he motored southwestwards from Cairo into dune country before turning southeastwards to Ain Dalla and thence back to Cairo. Ain Dalla was a crucial location for those intending to voyage into the dunes, for it was a source of water. They took three vehicles and their Ford touring car's performance was so remarkable that by the end of the journey Bagnold was

Bagnold's Camp 9 of 1929 in the Great Sand Sea, with typical car tracks over a 46-m (150-ft) high whaleback dune.

confident of getting across any dune country. The car also had a low petrol consumption, could carry a reasonable payload and gave promise of a self-contained range of action of 1,900 km (1,180 miles). This was the way forward. The 1929 journey proved that the Great Sand Sea could be penetrated by a simple, two-wheel drive car.

The experience had been so instructive that in October and November 1930 Bagnold decided to attempt a more ambitious journey. This expedition left Cairo on 13 October and made for Ain Dalla again. From there in four-and-a-half days they travelled nearly 600 km (370 miles) over the dunes of the Sand Sea. Bagnold plainly became smitten by them:

> *We travelled in an unstable world of bare curving sand high above the rock. Strangest of all was the unnatural regularity of the dunes. They are identical in character and details of form, maintain their geometrical straightness throughout their great length, and are parallel to one another to within 2 deg[rees]. We felt always in the presence of vast purposeful organisms, slowly creeping southwards through the ages, engulfing all that might have been in their way.*

One of the Fords, with a stripped down body and fitted with containers for carrying fuel and water.

The second part of the journey involved travelling down to Uweinat, where water was available, and then across to Selima and Wadi Halfa before taking the Darb Al Arba'in road to Kharga, Asyut and Cairo. In 34 days they travelled almost 5,000 km (3,100 miles). The day's run, even in the most difficult dune country, never fell below around 100 km (62 miles).

The fact that such distances could be achieved safely and quickly can be put down to four devices that enabled the cars to penetrate the deepest recesses of the desert: sand tracks for extricating bogged down vehicles; sun compasses for navigating in featureless desert; condensers to reduce water loss from boiling radiators; and broader tyres. After the introduction of the Model A Ford in 1927, they used so-called 'air wheels' which were 23 cm (9 in) wide and were excellent in soft going – the original Model T had tyres that were under 8 cm (3 in) wide. In addition, the cars had to be adapted so that weight was minimized and the risk of damage to stores due to vibration and bumping was reduced. Special box bodies were constructed. Everything had to fit tightly and yet be easily off-loaded. They found that the best unit of packing was the 8-gallon wooden petrol case, holding two 4-gallon tins. As far as possible all stores, whether food, spare parts, tools or petrol, were packed in these cases, which were a convenient size and weight.

Giant sand ripples at the foot of the Gilf Kebir in southwest Egypt, 1929–30. It was not until 1938 that Bagnold succeeded in finding a way to drive up to the top of this plateau.

In 1931 Bagnold returned to England after serving in India, and with Bill Shaw hatched the idea of going on an enormous journey to the northwest of Sudan and the unexplored frontier regions bordering the French province of Chad. It was decided to go as a party of eight in four Model A Fords. The first objective of this 1932 expedition was to reach Uweinat, the meeting point of the Egyptian and Libyan frontiers. Uweinat was to be the base where large stores of petrol and food could be dumped for a 1,900-km (1,180-mile) journey westwards into the Sarra triangle (a tongue of then Sudanese territory which juts towards the Tibesti Mountains and was ceded to Italy in 1934) and for a slightly longer journey southwards to the Sudanese settlement of El Fasher, and then back to Cairo via Wadi Halfa. While at Uweinat the party scaled the summit and explored the volcanic craters between Uweinat and the Gilf Kebir.

All in all this was a lengthy, cheap and successful trip. As Bagnold was to relate:

> *The whole journey totalled over 6,000 miles, including the two runs from Kissu to Selima and back. Of this distance more than 5,000 miles was over country with no existing tracks. Much of it was very bad going for cars, being covered either with large stones and boulders, or, in the south, with hidden water runnels of hard mud. Apart from the cracking of one of the main engine-supporting brackets, which occurred within sight of the Tibesti Mountains and which was partly responsible for our decision not to go farther west, no serious fault occurred to any of the four cars, which at times were twisted and bumped about unmercifully.*

It was entirely appropriate that in 1935, the Royal Geographical Society, which had supported the 1929, 1930 and 1932 expeditions, awarded Bagnold its Founder's Medal for all he had accomplished to date.

Explorer as Scientist

Thereafter Bagnold served in the Far East, but was taken ill with 'tropical sprue' (a digestive complaint) and was discharged from the army. However, he now embarked on a career in scientific investigation at Imperial College, London, with the aim of understanding sand movement and dune development, conducting the first experiments with a wind tunnel. In 1938 he decided that he needed to validate the work he had been doing on sand movement in his wind tunnel against real world conditions and returned to the desert accompanied by archaeologists and surveyors. The journey took them to Uweinat, the Gilf Kebir and the Selima Sand Sea.

Most of the time Bagnold's fieldwork involved waiting for a sand storm to occur so that he could witness and measure sand grains in action, but he also wanted to do 'a bit of long-needed exploration'. His objective was to drive on to the top of the Gilf Kebir. Its cliffs had deterred this ambition in the past, but Bagnold and his colleague, Ron Peel, managed to find a way up. This sandstone plateau, only discovered in 1926 – even though it is the size of Switzerland – became the subject of detailed scientific scrutiny.

When the Second World War started Bagnold returned to the army and used his unique experience to establish the Long Range Desert Group, to commit 'piracy on the high desert' and to harry the Axis forces in North Africa. Bagnold may have been the greatest of the explorers of the Libyan Desert, but there were other formidable contemporaries, including the surveyors John Ball and Patrick Clayton, and, above all, the subject of *The English Patient*, Count László Almásy, an Austro-Hungarian.

One feature of the Bagnold expeditions is that besides exploring new regions and developing new techniques for desert travel he also had time for science. Some expeditions can be self-indulgent stunts in which alpha males display their virility. Not so with Bagnold. His team made remarkable discoveries that included the profusion of archaeological sites in the desert and evidence of profound changes in past climatic conditions. Bagnold wrote his classic book on dunes in 1941 and it is still much cited today. Remarkably for a soldier and explorer he was made a Fellow of the Royal Society.

Bagnold using his equipment to measure the movement of sand in a storm near the Gilf Kebir in 1938.

ALEXANDER MAITLAND

Wilfred Thesiger

SPIRIT OF THE EMPTY QUARTER

(1910–2003)

Journeying at walking pace under conditions of some hardship, I was perhaps the last explorer in the tradition of the past.

Wilfred Thesiger, **The Life of My Choice,** *1987*

Wilfred Patrick Thesiger was born on 3 June 1910 in Addis Ababa, where his father was Minister in charge of the British Legation. He lived there until he was nearly nine. Thesiger always insisted that his childhood in Abyssinia (as he often referred to modern Ethiopia) profoundly influenced the whole of his life and instilled in him a longing for 'colour and savagery'. In 1919 the family returned to England, where Thesiger's father died of a heart attack the following year. Thesiger was educated at a preparatory school in Sussex, followed by Eton and Magdalen College, Oxford; he boxed for the university and graduated in 1933 with a degree in modern history.

Journeys in Ethiopia, Sudan and the Sahara

In 1930, while he was still at university, Thesiger attended the coronation of the emperor Haile Selassie in Addis Ababa. There he met Robert Cheesman, a British officer who had travelled in Arabia, who encouraged him to explore the Awash River and discover where it ended. Thesiger accomplished this successfully in 1933–34, aged 23. Because of his youth and inexperience, coupled with the risk of being murdered by hostile tribesmen, Thesiger regarded this journey through the territory of the Danakil (or Afar) people as the most dangerous he ever undertook; he also became the first European to traverse the forbidden Sultanate of Aussa.

In northern Darfur, where Thesiger served in the Sudan Political Service from 1935 to 1937, he learnt to ride camels and to treat his followers as companions rather than servants. Until 1940 he was accompanied everywhere by Idris Daud, a teenage Zaghawa and reprieved murderer, the first of many tribal youths who shared Thesiger's semi-nomadic lifestyle. Camel journeys to Jabal Maidob and Anka wells in Sudan, and to Bir Natrun in Libya, gave Thesiger his first experiences of the true desert. To prove himself he once rode 185 km (115 miles) in 24 hours. His beautiful

Thesiger's party on his second crossing of the Empty Quarter, January 1948. In this vast sand desert, the dunes in a chain known as Uruq al Shaiba reach heights of over 215 m (700 ft).

Bisharin camel, Faraj Allah, had 'charming manners' and let him 'do anything with it'. Such a claim was typical of Thesiger, who asserted that his family's achievements were unrivalled, his upbringing incomparably happy and his schools the finest in England.

Thesiger's 3,330-km (2,000-mile) journey in 1938 from Sudan across the Sahara to Tibesti, a range of extinct volcanoes, involved no danger or hardship comparable to the Danakil country, or his later crossings of the Empty Quarter, but was arduous, and more demanding than journeys in Syria and Morocco in 1936 and 1937. It tested Thesiger's endurance, though without seriously risking his life. No European had approached Tibesti from the east; nor had any English traveller been there before him. 'It is not easy', Thesiger commented, 'to be the first Englishman nowadays.'

Arabia and the Empty Quarter

In 1945 Thesiger joined the Middle East Anti-Locust Unit searching for locust outbreak centres in southern Arabia. This led to his greatest journeys: two epic crossings of the Empty Quarter 'the most important experience of [my] life'. On these journeys Thesiger was accompanied by Bin Kabina and Bin Ghabaisha of the Rashid, who became his inseparable companions during his five years in Arabia. A self-confessed romantic, Thesiger travelled in the overland tradition of the past. Unlike St John Philby (p. 215), who would listen to the test-match scores on a radio, Thesiger during his journeys never wanted any contact with the outside world.

Thesiger's first crossing of the Empty Quarter, in 1946–47, began and ended at Salala, a township on the coast of Dhaufar. Travelling north to Dhafara and Liwa, his party and their exhausted camels climbed the Uruq al Shaiba, a chain of dunes more than 215 m (700 ft) high. For a fortnight they struggled on between brackish wells, forced to endure agonizing thirst, hunger verging on starvation, numbing fatigue, biting cold nights and scorching sun by day. Thesiger was the first European to reach the Liwa oasis, the first to have visited the fabled quicksands of Umm al Samim. He wrote: 'To others my journey would have little importance ... It was a personal experience, and the reward had been a drink of clean, tasteless water. I was content with that.'

With six companions, including Bin Kabina and Bin Ghabaisha, Thesiger crossed the Empty Quarter a second time, from January to March 1948. Together these crossings explored vast areas of the desert untravelled by Thesiger's only predecessors, Bertram Thomas and Harry St John Philby in 1931 and 1932. At Sulyail, Thesiger was imprisoned briefly by order of Ibn Saud, but was released thanks to Philby's personal intervention. Enraged by his infidel presence, fanatical tribes had vowed to kill him. Thesiger's party might still have perished had they not found drinkable water at Umm al Adwa, near the Jabrin oasis, originally located and mapped by St John Philby and Robert Cheesman. In 1949–50 Thesiger travelled in the interior of Oman, journeys which involved considerable danger from tribes loyal to the Imam, but relatively little hardship.

Thesiger wearing a headcloth, long Arab shirt and silver-hilted Omani dagger, and holding a camel stick; the Empty Quarter, March 1948.

Attempting to explain his motive for making such dangerous journeys, and the satisfaction they gave him, Thesiger confessed he was thrilled by the lure of the unknown and the challenge to resolution and endurance. 'Yet those travels in the Empty Quarter', he wrote, 'would have been for me a meaningless penance but for the comradeship of my Bedu companions.'

Photography and Writing

Thesiger's exceptional gifts as a photographer and writer brought him increasing fame. Until his first book, *Arabian Sands*, was published in 1959, however, his achievements were known mainly to diplomatic circles, or geographical societies. As an explorer, traveller, writer and photographer, Thesiger inspired (and still continues to inspire) adventurous men and women who journey not only in Africa and the Middle East, but also in other parts of the world not linked directly with him.

Thesiger used photographs to document his journeys. In Ethiopia he photographed the Danakil; in Sudan in 1935–40 he photographed Darfur's Muslim tribes, pagan Nuer on the Upper Nile and Nuba wrestlers in Kordofan, as well as the big game he had shot. He used a box camera, then a Leica, one of four he owned in succession. Thesiger viewed his books and photographs as by-products of his travels and until the Second World War, photography had remained a pastime. Photographs Thesiger took in Arabia after the war showed a marked improvement, both artistically and technically. This may have resulted from studying Freya Stark's photographs in *Seen in the Hadramaut* in 1938 and realizing the possibilities of close-up portraiture, light and shadow. Thesiger liked Freya, and admired her, but said that, for him, reading some of her books was like 'eating a dinner composed of nothing but trifle'.

As a boy of 12 Thesiger had begun to keep diaries, and it was a habit he continued throughout his life. Diaries, and letters to his mother and brothers, were a literary equivalent of the photographs he used to record his journeys. Together they gave him the details he needed to write his articles, lectures and books. Fond as he was of company, Thesiger was a private individual and, when writing *Arabian Sands*, to begin with found great difficulty in conveying not only physical experience, but the innermost thoughts and feelings 'shut up in himself with stern determination for half an active lifetime'. *The Marsh Arabs*, published in 1964, described Thesiger's seven years during the 1950s in the photogenic, reclusive world of the Ma'dan in southern Iraq. His canoemen, Amara, Hasan and Sabaiti, played roles similar to that of Idris Daud in the Sudan, and by Thesiger's Bedouin companions in Arabia.

ASIA AND AFRICA

Young Bakhtiari tribesmen, Iran, 1964. That year Thesiger joined the Bakhtiari nomads on their annual migration through the Zagros Mountains.

During the 1950s Thesiger travelled at intervals among the mountains of Pakistan, Afghanistan, Nuristan and Morocco. He returned to Ethiopia in 1959–60, undertaking long journeys on foot with mules across the south, then the north. Soon after, he made the first of many camel safaris to Lake Rudolf (now Lake Turkana) in the Eastern Rift Valley Province of Kenya and he continued to travel extensively in northern Kenya during the next 15 years.

In 1977 he ventured further, joining Gavin Young on a voyage round the islands of Indonesia – the setting for Joseph Conrad's Eastern novels. In 1983 he rode with ponies and yaks for six weeks across Ladakh. After this journey Thesiger lived an increasingly sedentary life at Maralal in Kenya with his Samburu and Turkana 'families', sharing one or other of the houses he had built for Lawi Leboyare, Laputa Lekakwar and 'Kibiriti', his adoptive 'sons'.

By 1992 Thesiger's sight had failed so much that he gave up photography and could no longer write unaided. When first Laputa, then Lawi died in 1994 and 1995, instead of ending his days at Maralal as he had intended, Thesiger returned permanently to England. He died in Surrey aged 93, after a short illness, on 24 August 2003. The journeys Thesiger made on foot with baggage animals and local tribesmen spanned 50 years, and included many remote areas of Africa, Arabia, the Middle East and western Asia. When he was 89 he had paid a final visit to the United Arab Emirates. By then he had long been acclaimed the 20th century's greatest traveller and one of its most celebrated explorers.

LIFE ON EARTH

The most important purpose of exploration must be scientific research. Baron Alexander von Humboldt showed the way to study everything, at a time when that was still possible. His output was phenomenal as, with his long-suffering companion Aimé Bonpland, he spent five years travelling throughout much of Central and South America, collecting and analysing everything they saw. Humboldt was also an indomitable climber and for a long time it was thought that he had almost surmounted the highest peak in the world, until it was proved that some of the Himalayas were higher than Chimborazo.

Botanical painting was a way for women to explore in times when such things were not done by ladies. Marianne North started late, at over 40, but she made up for it by becoming one of the most resolute and perspicacious of all flower painters. In the course of her extensive and often arduous travels, she painted throughout the tropics and we are fortunate that her fine collection is preserved at Kew.

Alfred Wallace was another of the giants of scientific travel. He spent four years collecting in the Amazon before moving to the Far East, where he spent eight years and did some of his finest work. While lying in his hammock suffering the pains of malaria, the idea of the survival of the fittest came to him. He immediately wrote to his friend and mentor, Charles Darwin, who had been sitting on the theory for some 20 years. Generously, Darwin shared the glory with Wallace, whose paper was presented to the Linnaean Society in 1858. Nothing in the field of evolution – or science – would ever be the same again.

Botanical studies inspired another great explorer, Frank Kingdon-Ward, who spent nearly 50 years on 25 expeditions to Tibet and the eastern Himalayas. He discovered and brought back to Britain many beautiful plants now familiar in our gardens, though the conditions he travelled in and the close encounters with danger he faced were far removed from safe horticultural surroundings.

In the Americas Humboldt and Bonpland collected over 60,000 specimens, a great many of them previously unknown, and described and illustrated them in their extensive publications.

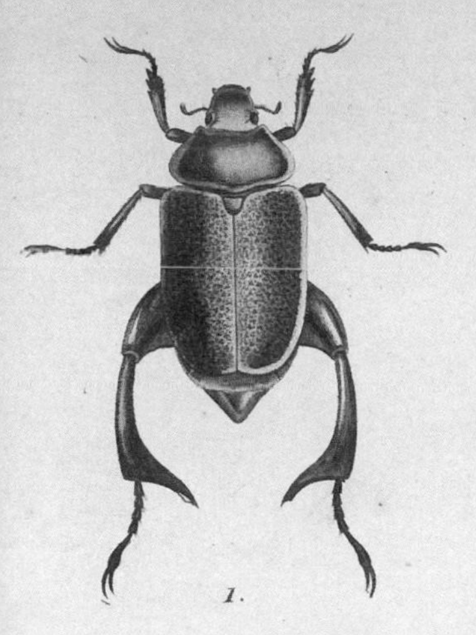

1.

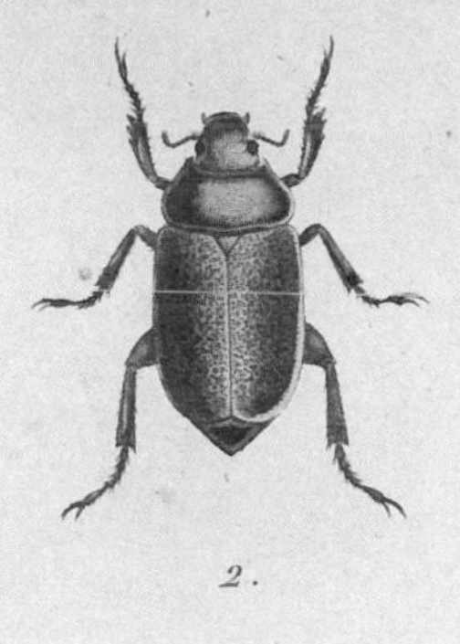

2.

3.

4.

5.

6.

7.

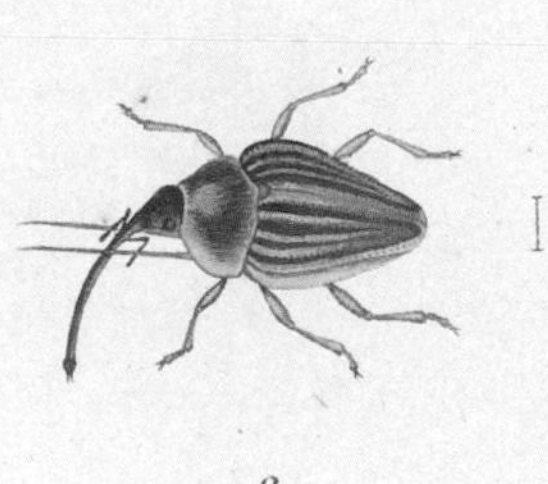

8.

10.

11.

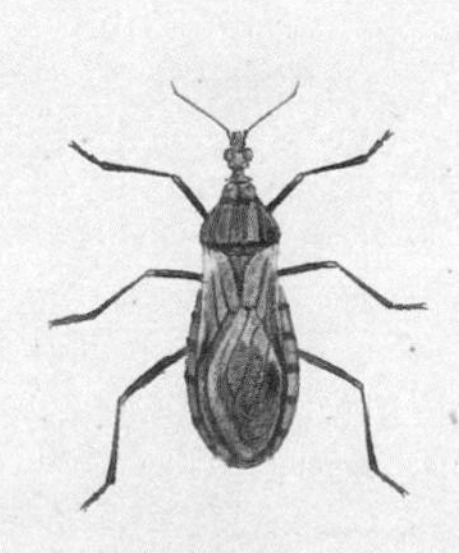

12.

9.

Alexander von Humboldt

THE GREATEST SCIENTIFIC TRAVELLER

(1769–1859)

I believe that you are fully right in calling Humboldt the greatest scientific traveller who ever lived.

Charles Darwin, letter to J. D. Hooker, 6 August 1881

Alexander von Humboldt was not only a heroic traveller and pioneering scientist, he also merits the title of being the last great universal man and can be viewed as the founder of the modern science of ecology. Humboldt was born in Berlin in the age of enlightenment on 14 September 1769; Napoleon, Wellington, Chateaubriand and Cuvier were born the same year. As a young university graduate he travelled to England with his great friend Georg Forster, who had sailed with James Cook (p. 46) as a scientific illustrator, and together they visited Sir Joseph Banks to see his brilliant herbarium and botanical library.

A Phenomenal Work Rate

Humboldt then enrolled into the Freiberg School of Mines in 1791. He threw himself into the intensive studies, but devoted any precious spare time to his own natural history investigations. He wrote of these student days: 'I have never been so busy in my life. My health has suffered as a consequence, though I am on the whole very happy', ending with the statement 'I am in a profession that must be followed passionately to be enjoyed' – which sums up his approach throughout his life. His first job was as an inspector of mines; in this he travelled extensively and managed to turn abandoned mines into profitable works and open a training school. Humboldt's study of gases in the shafts resulted in his invention of miners' breathing apparatus and four types of safety lamp.

Humboldt was a talented artist: this is a self-portrait of 1814.

He was 26, well educated, well connected and had boundless energy. He put his creativity to use in some extraordinary self-experimentation. In order to understand what he called 'animal electricity' Humboldt had experimented on frogs, and plants. But to prove the point he applied the electrodes to himself.

> *I raised two blisters on my back, each the size of a crown-piece.... When the blisters were cut and contact was made with the zinc and silver electrodes, I experienced a sharp pain, which was so severe that the trapezius muscle swelled considerably, and the quivering was communicated upwards to the base of the skull and the spinous processes of the vertebra.... Frogs placed upon my back were observed to hop.... The phenomenon was so extraordinary that I repeated it.*

Humboldt's work rate was phenomenal. His 4,000 experiments included applying electrodes to the cavity left by one of his pulled teeth, which almost led him to inventing the first electric battery. He noted at the time: 'How can you stop a man wanting to find things out and understand the world around him? In any case, a wide variety of knowledge is vital to a traveller.'

Independence and Preparations

Humboldt's mother died in 1796 leaving him a fortune; this allowed him to resign from the mining industry and begin to make plans for his scientific travels. He was so keen to set out on his explorations that in April 1798 he agreed to join the 'half mad, half genius' Lord Bristol on his expedition to the Nile. While Humboldt was in Paris to collect scientific instruments, however, Napoleon invaded Egypt and Lord Bristol was arrested in Milan – and that ended that scheme. He then met one of his boyhood heroes, Louis-Antoine de Bougainville (p. 40), who asked Humboldt to join his new five-year French government scientific expedition that would travel around the world. Humboldt wasted no time. In two weeks he was ready and received orders to embark on board the ship. But at the last minute the expedition was cancelled when the government realized that they could not afford it.

'A man can't just sit down and cry, he's got to do something', he declared, and decided to organize his own expedition to North Africa with the botanist Aimé Bonpland. This partnership was to become one of the most significant in the history of exploration. But they faced yet more difficulties. Humboldt's idea was that they should sail to Algiers, overwinter in the Atlas Mountains and then meet up with a pilgrim caravan crossing the desert between Tripoli and Cairo. They were making arrangements for a ship when they learnt that all passengers arriving at Algiers from France were being thrown into a dungeon immediately on arrival. Still anxious to travel, in December 1798 they decided to walk to Spain. This time they did actually leave, and spent the six-week journey to Madrid making scientific observations, proving, among many other things, that the interior of Spain was a high plateau and that maps of the area were out by miles.

A plate illustrating Rhexia speciosa *in botanical detail. Humboldt considered that what he called plant geography was one of his greatest contributions to science.*

An Epic Expedition

Humboldt's reputation and contacts may make it appear simple, but it is remarkable that after a very short time in Madrid he was able to meet the king of Spain and petition him for support for an expedition to South America. The king granted the pair official permits and made arrangements for them to board the *Pizarro*, with all the equipment that Humboldt had by now acquired, and they set sail from La Coruña in May.

The passage to South America was fairly typical of its time. The *Pizarro* was overcrowded and there was a typhoid outbreak, but Humboldt was impervious to disease, sea sickness and any amount of discomfort. Nothing could distract him from his science and he spent the time onboard making astronomical, oceanographic and meteorological observations.

On arrival at Cumaná, in Venezuela, Humboldt and Bonpland were made welcome by the governor and provided with a house and staff. Humboldt later reflected: 'This was the first spot we set foot on in a land I had been dreaming about since I was a boy. In my mind's eye it is not to all the wonders of the Cordilleras that I return most often, but to Cumaná and its dusty soil.' His notes at this time show him to be almost bursting with new experiences: 'Naked Indians, electric eels, parrots, monkeys, armadillos, crocodiles, amazing plants, reading my sextant at night by the light of Venus'. But his joy was balanced by his disgust at the slave trade: his house was near the town square where slaves shipped in from Africa were sold. For the rest of his life Humboldt openly criticized the slave trade.

After seven weeks, Humboldt and Bonpland set off on a two-month field trip into the highlands, where Humboldt recorded new species of birds and insects, explored a cave system as far as his local guides would dare take him, recorded local language and culture, experienced his first earthquake and a fabulous meteor shower, and survived an attack by a 'crazed half-breed'. In November 1799 they sailed to Caracas.

Their large house in the city came complete with staff and instant acceptance into the best of local society. Astronomical observations were impossible because of the weather, so Humboldt instead made the first recorded ascent of the Silla of Caracas, which at 2,424 m (8,000 ft) is the highest peak in the area. Humboldt's loathing for the trade did not prevent him using 18 slaves to carry his bags for the climb.

In February 1800 they left Caracas to travel inland and it wasn't long before Humboldt had a chance to pursue his interest in animal electricity. He had already tried to get the coastal Indians to capture an electric eel for him, but they were terrified of them. Inland, he found that the people in the Calabozo area fished for them by using horses as bait, by rounding up as many horses and mules as possible and driving them into pools where they were attacked relentlessly by the eels. Some of the horses collapsed and died, while others that tried to escape were driven back into the water and would either drown or survive because the eels had discharged their limited supply of 650 volts. Surrounded by dead and barely alive horses, the Indians could then safely collect the temporarily discharged eels. Humboldt and Bonpland spent a lively four hours receiving shocks while experimenting on and dissecting the eels, which left them both with 'a weakness in the muscles, a pain in the joints and a general malaise until the following day'.

'Animal electricity' had long fascinated Humboldt and on his journey through South America he was keen to study in detail electric eels, or gymnoti as they were called locally. He received a 'dreadful shock' when he accidentally stood on one lying on the ground.

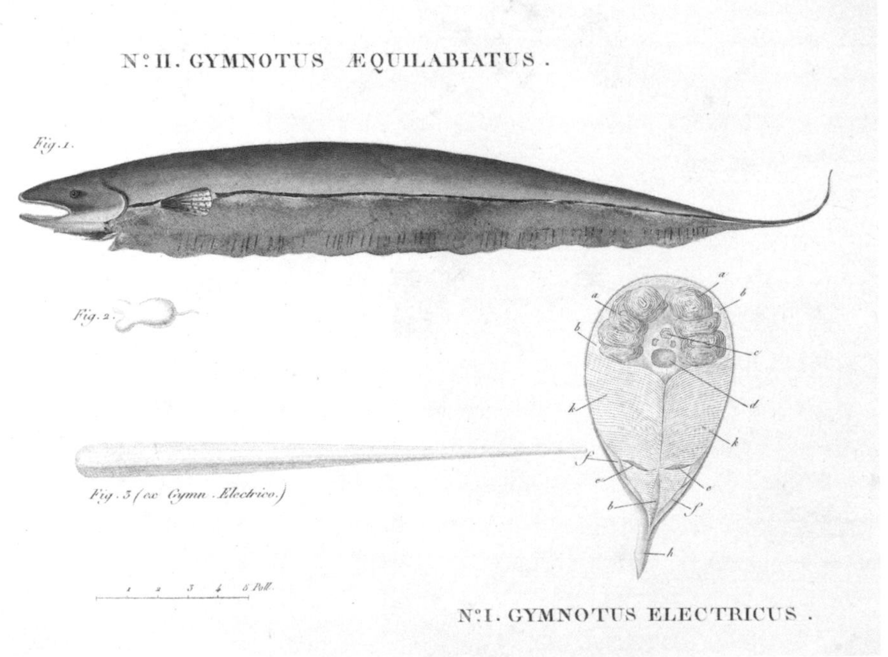

Chimborazo, an inactive volcano in Ecuador, was thought to be the highest mountain in the world when Humboldt and Bonpland climbed it. Although they failed to reach the summit they did achieve a world altitude record. This aquatint is after a sketch by Humboldt.

After this crossing of the *llanos*, or highland plains, they embarked on an ambitious 2,400-km (1,500-mile) river trip to map the course of the Orinoco River. By the time they returned to Angostura they had not only visited the Casiquiare Canal, which forms the connection between the two huge river systems, the Orinoco and the Amazon, via the Rio Negro, but had also accurately mapped these rivers, made extensive magnetic readings and collected 12,000 specimens, including species of plants new to science and some human skeletons. The pair had been through many incredible experiences – they had paddled and portaged the boats through some of the most inhospitable and remote areas on earth, had almost starved to death and been reduced to eating ants, they were bitten to near madness by insects and had lived with mud-eating, drug-taking tribes. Even so, in his enthusiasm, Humboldt could not stop himself exaggerating the journey by reporting excitedly that he had travelled over 9,600 km (6,000 miles) and had hardly ever entered a hut without encountering the horrible remains of repasts on human flesh.

From Angostura they returned to Cumaná by August 1800, sick from fever and with over a third of their priceless specimens ruined by the extreme humidity. With the success of the Venezuela river systems exploration behind him, Humboldt did not rest, and he and Bonpland sailed to Cuba in November 1800; in March 1801 they were back in Cartagena to travel on to Lima for a two-year expedition in the Andes.

The journey inland turned into another epic river adventure – 805 km (500 miles) through dense forest with the Rio Magdalena in full spate. Once more they were plagued by insect bites and eight of their 20 Indians were sent back suffering from tropical ulcers and exhaustion. Humboldt and Bonpland stayed healthy, however, and arrived in the river port of Honda ready for the high plateau journey to Bogota (Colombia). In September 1801 they left for Quito. The customary manner for mining officials to travel difficult parts of the track was to be carried by *cargueros*, Indian bearers: the locals would be saddled up with a chair-type contraption and the officials were thus transported. Humboldt and Bonpland refused this option and walked.

Having arrived in Quito (Ecuador) in January 1802, they spent the next six months studying the region's volcanoes. At that time there was no understanding of the effects of altitude and Humboldt had to abandon his first climb on Pichincha because he felt unwell and passed out. Nothing daunted, he made a second attempt and, after some falls through crevasse bridges, reached the summit. Humboldt was extremely fit and climbed Pichincha again the next day to make more observations. He and Bonpland followed this with an attempt on Chimborazo, but were unable to get beyond a steeper section overlaid by soft snow and stopped at 5,878 m (19,286 ft). For the following 30 years Humboldt held the record as the man who had climbed higher than anyone else. In his old age, when the surveys of the Himalayas showed that Chimborazo was not in fact the highest peak in the world, Humboldt was understandably disappointed and wrote 'All my life I have imagined that of all mortals I was the one who had risen highest in the world – I mean on the slopes of Chimborazo!'.

Wherever he travelled, Humboldt was always a meticulous observer of everything he encountered. The magnetic measurements he took on his way to Trujillo on the Pacific coast were used as a reference for all geomagnetic studies for the following 50 years. He also learnt from local farmers about the rich fertilizing properties of guano, and it was Humboldt who brought this discovery back to Europe.

After spending some time in Lima, in December 1802 he and Bonpland sailed for Mexico via Guayaquil. Humboldt of course pursued his never-ending studies: his measurements of sea temperature off the coast of Peru revealed the current that was named after him (now also known as the Peru Current). They reached Acapulco in

Mexico in March 1803 and spent a year travelling to volcanoes, studying Aztec culture and visiting mines. In March 1804 they sailed to Havana and then on to Philadelphia, where Humboldt made a visit to the US President, Thomas Jefferson. Humboldt had been inspired by Jefferson and felt it was essential to meet him. The two men spent about a week together, discussing among other things the Lewis and Clark expedition (p. 64), marking the finale to Humboldt's greatest expedition. In June 1804 Humboldt and Bonpland sailed for Bordeaux.

Paris and the 'Improbable Years'

The epic five-year expedition had cost Humboldt a third of all of his money. He now had over 60,000 specimens and a vast amount of zoological, geophysical, astronomical, geological, oceanographic and cultural data. Humboldt always said that his aim was 'to collect ideas rather than objects', and it took him 30 years and multiple volumes to distil and publish the results of his South American journey, later translated from French into English as *Personal Narrative of Travels to the Equinoctial Regions ... during the Years 1799–1804.* Since it was funded mostly at his own expense it not surprisingly also caused him financial problems.

After his return from South America Humboldt had settled in Paris, and with the help of a pension approved by Napoleon, he lived there for the next 24 years. As ever, he moved in the finest scientific, social and political circles and thrived in the city. But his love of Paris was not as great as his restless love for travelling and discovery, and in 1805 he undertook a six-week journey across the Alps with the French scientist Gay-Lussac to make magnetic and atmospheric observations. He also had plans for what he called 'the second great task of my life' – a scientific expedition to northern Asia. In 1811 he hoped to leave for Siberia, Kashgar and Tibet, but Napoleon's invasion of Russia put an end to his plans. He returned to Berlin in 1827, his drive to explore undiminished. To gain support for his Russian expedition he made trips to London and on one of these he spent an hour under the Thames with Isambard Kingdom Brunel in a diving bell; after the ascent to the surface he suffered burst blood vessels in his chest and coughed up blood and had a nose bleed until the next day.

In April 1829, at the age of 60, Humboldt left for St Petersburg and in just under six months he arrived back in Berlin having travelled 18,500 km (11,500 miles). Once more he made extensive astronomical, geological and geographical observations and proved that diamonds could be found in Russia. He also organized a network of magnetic and meteorological stations across Russia, work which convinced Europe, Britain and America to do the same, creating a worldwide network.

On his return from South America, Humboldt spent the next 30 years writing and publishing the results of all his investigations and observations. He described this small New World monkey or tamarin and named it Simia leonina, *though it is not certain exactly which species it represents.*

Humboldt now revived one of his earlier ideas and began writing the hugely ambitious *Kosmos*, a massive work in which he sought to bring together and record everything known about science and nature and the connections between different branches – 'a physical description of the universe' no less, in which he would demonstrate the unity of nature. It took him 25 years, with the first volume published when he was 76 and the third when he was 81 (a period he called 'my improbable years'); the fifth and final volume was half complete when Humboldt died just before his 90th birthday.

Humboldt's contributions across all the scientific disciplines were truly pioneering, and numerous plant and animal species, geographical features, places and universities are named after him.

Of himself, Humboldt said:

> *There are only three important and most characteristic achievements I have contributed. The geography of plants and the natural painting of the tropical world connected with it. The theory of isothermal lines. The observations concerning geomagnetism, which have resulted, at my suggestion, in the establishment of magnetic stations throughout the whole planet.*

Humboldt certainly earned all the accolades and acclaim he received and his influence on many branches of science is still felt today.

Marianne North

INTREPID NATURALIST AND BOTANICAL ARTIST

(1830–1890)

I got very chilled one day when trying to paint, so went for a walk up and down the edges of the cliffs for four miles and back. It was very beautiful … here were many berries, but no flowers; and I felt the happier for it, as the scenery itself was enough to study at once. The wind was bitter, and the waves beat on the shore like the real sea.… I sat and wondered if I should ever get home to England and see my gallery finished.

Marianne North, describing in her diary an island in Lake Wakatipu, New Zealand, 1881

Marianne North did not begin the activity for which she is famous until she was over 40 years old. It was the death of her father, to whom she was devoted, that launched her solo quest to document the rare flora of the remote regions of world. During her two remaining decades she amassed a large collection of specimens for the Royal Botanic Gardens at Kew and painted almost 1,000 canvases, which are now displayed in a pavilion she built at Kew and at the British Museum. Few women ventured as far from home as did North. Consumed by her self-imposed task to collect and paint rare and exotic plants she slogged through jungles, hiked mountains, trudged along mud-choked tracks, rafted rivers and endured bugs, snakes and heat. It is fitting that five of her discoveries are named for her.

A CHARMED EARLY LIFE

North was born in Hastings, southern England, into a family of wealth and culture. Her mother had inherited a considerable fortune and her father, Frederick North, was a Liberal Member of Parliament who moved in the political and intellectual circles of the day and belonged to the clubs that were probing new scientific fields. North received little formal education, but family friends included artists and scientists. One, a well-known botanist and Director of the Royal Botanic Gardens at Kew, Sir William Hooker, presented young Marianne with exotic plants to encourage her pursuit of botanical painting. She shared her botanical passion with her father and sister, and during their prolonged rambles around Europe, North studied drawing and painting with a series of artists. Oil painting was her preferred medium: 'I have

Doctor humming birds visiting Leonotis nepetaefolia *in Jamaica. North's pairing was prescient: the iridescent long-tailed doctor bird, a favourite subject of local folklore, became the national bird of Jamaica, and the leonotis is now celebrated for its healing qualities.*

never done anything else since, oil-painting being a vice like dram-drinking, almost impossible to leave off once it gets possession of one'.

After her mother's death in 1855, North looked after her father as she had promised to do. Not marrying, she retained control of her fortune, and was thus able to fund her later exploration. For the next 14 years Marianne and her father travelled relentlessly throughout Europe and the Holy Land, diaries and sketchbooks in hand. During a hiking trip in 1869 Frederick North fell ill and she brought him home to Hastings to die. She was devastated at his loss. Painting and travelling the world in search of rare and exotic plants became her solace.

ON THE ROAD

Her longing for distant travel had begun long before, with William Hooker's gifts of tropical flowers, and so now, aged 41, she began a series of protracted journeys that would last the rest of her life. Encouraged to venture further afield by the explorer Lucie Duff Gordon, whom she had met in Luxor, Egypt, Marianne decided to break the bonds of Europe and realize 'the dream of going to some tropical country to paint its peculiar vegetation on the spot in natural abundant luxuriance'.

Harvesting sugar-cane in Brazil: as amazed as North was by the rich variety of natural life she encountered in Brazil, she was not oblivious to the iniquities of slavery in the fields and mines.

In 1871 she accepted an invitation to visit America, a journey that would set a pattern. Thanks to Sir Joseph Hooker, Sir William's son, as well as Charles Darwin and other friends, she had introductions to the most influential people wherever she went. They in turn facilitated her sojourns in the wild. She travelled alone and her first solo journey began in Boston. Importantly for Marianne she met Mrs Elizabeth Agassiz, who had just returned from a long trip to Brazil with her polymath husband, Louis. Their collection of plants whetted North's appetite to visit the tropics.

With winter coming on she gladly embarked for Jamaica. North suffered in cold weather, enduring what she called her 'old pain' (rheumatism), and she was always happiest in hot climates. Outside Kingston she found a ramshackle house covered in vegetation where she spent a happy solitary month painting. Next was Brazil, where she stayed in a hut in Minas Gerais for a 'blissful' eight months. No matter the discomfort of the travel – how rough, how long – her focus remained on the plants, and these never disappointed her: 'I had delightful rambles and always found new wonders on every expedition'. In fact she much preferred plants to people.

North's painting of landscape, vegetation and people in South Africa. She marvelled at the 'perfectly new world of vegetation in Kafirland', with occasional clearings with beehive-shaped huts whose inhabitants were 'the grandest figures in red drapery and feathers'.

Portrait of Marianne North in Ceylon by Julia Margaret Cameron. North was fascinated by Cameron, whose 'oddities were most refreshing'.

It was not for nothing that her memoirs were called *Recollections of a Happy Life.* Her years of travel were a litany of descriptions of her many adventures scaling cliffs, crossing swamps and rafting rivers to reach the plants she wanted, with little regard for danger. She saw and experienced the world through a veil of vegetation which enthralled her no matter what the circumstance. While painting a coco de mer tree in the Seychelles she had to perch precariously on boulders to get a better view, recording that she 'rested my painting board on one of the great fan leaves, and drew the whole mass of fruit and buds in perfect security, though the slightest slip or cramp would have put an end to both the sketch and to me'. Another time, after a long hard journey through the mountains she wrote she would stick 'to my rule of not going willingly where I could not see my feet'. In Kalutara, Ceylon (Sri Lanka), in 1876, she was returning to her easel set under a tree and saw something green on her chair, waving in the wind. She did not have her glasses on and thought someone had left her a specimen, but as she reached her hand out towards it a poisonous snake took off. 'Since that day', she reflected, 'I have always worn spectacles'. Also while in Kalutara, North met and became friends with the photographer Julia Margaret Cameron.

North's good humour must have been infectious, as she was well received wherever she went. Many came to her aid, including a governor who sent carriages to take her over rough and dangerous roads, a police driver who made her tea beside the 'Black River, where the water was worthy of its name' and a soldier who used 'his fine long sword to decapitate the leeches which stuck to me'. In Borneo she had an introduction to the White Rajah of Sarawak, and became a good friend and travelling companion of the Rani, Margaret Brooke. The rajah arranged her month-long stay in a hut near a swamp, where her cook worked his way through a chicken coop. She wrote that she spent a 'delicious' time painting and only reluctantly returned when she ran out of chickens and her 'bread turned blue'. While in Sarawak North discovered the largest-known carnivorous pitcher plant, *Nepenthes northiana.* It became the first of five plants (the others are *Northea seychellana,* a tree in the Seychelles; *Crinum northianum,* an amaryllis; *Areca northiana,* a feather palm; and *Kniphofia northiana,* an African torch lily or red hot poker), named in her honour.

In 1878–79 she spent a year and a half roaming throughout India, searching for plants that were associated with Indian literature. She painted more than 200 canvases of plants and sites, including frangipani planted near graves so that their flowers covered the dead, mango wood which Hindus used to burn the dead, and night jasmine that was planted around temples for its sweet scent. In the course of her remarkable travels she also visited Japan, Java, the East Indies, Africa, Australia, New Zealand, Chile and the Seychelles.

Her sister Catherine, who published her memoirs, remarked:

> *She seemed to bear a charmed life. She could apparently sit all day painting in a mangrove swamp, and not catch fever. She could live without food, without sleep, and still come home after a year or two, a little thinner, with a more careworn look in the tired eyes, but ready to enjoy to the full the flattering reception which London is always ready to give to any one who has earned its respect by being interesting in any way.*

The largest-known pitcher plant, Nepenthes northiana, *from Borneo, named after North.*

After a few years she decided to exhibit her paintings. The popularity of her show at London's South Kensington Museum gave her the idea of building a gallery to display her paintings permanently. In 1879 she contacted Sir Joseph Hooker to offer not only her collection but also the funds to build a special building to house them. When he accepted she commissioned another friend, the well-known architect James Fergusson, to design the building, which would include rooms for a gardener. She collected 246 different specimens of wood from all her travels to panel the rooms and painted the friezes around the doors. Today Kew displays some 832 paintings depicting 727 genera and nearly 1,000 species. A further several hundred of her paintings of India can be found at the British Museum.

North returned from her last trip to Chile, in 1884–85, now worn out and plagued with illnesses she had picked up from years of hard travel. She died at Alderley in Gloucestershire in 1890 at the age of 59.

Legacy

North was an early conservationist, clearly aware that the images she was capturing were fleeting. Seeing the swathe cut by lumberjacks through a stand of magnificent California redwoods she wrote: 'It broke one's heart to think of man, the civilizer, wasting treasures in a few years to which savages and animals had done no harm for centuries.' In the preface to the official guide to the North Gallery in 1892, Joseph Hooker, Director of Kew Gardens, said of the subjects of her paintings: 'these species ... are already disappearing or are doomed shortly to disappear before the axe and the forest fires, the plough and the flock, of the ever-advancing settler or colonist. Such scenes can never be renewed by nature.'

North's work is an important element in the botanical record in part because she recorded the plants in situ, often in conjunction with birds, insects and sometimes people. She was one of the truly fortunate people who discover what they love to do, have the means and the courage to follow their passion, and the gift to share their discoveries. She also linked her work to one of the outstanding botanical centres in the world, thus ensuring her legacy for all time.

Hedychium gardnerianum, *a ginger lily, and a sunbird, India. One of North's goals in India was to paint plants associated with Indian religion. Flowers of the ginger lily, native to the Himalayan foothills, were made into garlands to adorn a young girl believed to be the incarnation of the goddess Kumari, during the eight-day festival of Indrajatra honouring Indra, the Hindu god of rain.*

Alfred Russel Wallace

THE SURVIVAL OF THE FITTEST

(1823–1913)

... should civilized man ever reach these distant lands, and bring moral, intellectual, and physical light into these virgin forests, we may be sure that he will so disturb the nicely balanced relations of organic and inorganic nature as to cause the disappearance, and finally the extinction, of these very beings whose wonderful structure and beauty he alone is fitted to appreciate and enjoy.

A. R. Wallace, **The Malay Archipelago,** *1869*

Alfred Russel Wallace was born in Monmouthshire on 8 January 1823. The family moved to Hertford in 1826, where Alfred attended the grammar school until he was 14. After a brief spell living with one brother, John, in London, he began his apprenticeship as a surveyor to another, William, in 1837. He spent nearly seven years with him, latterly in Wales, carrying out survey contracts. The open-air life suited him, and he became interested in geology and natural history, embarking on a regular programme of self-education, as well as benefiting from the Mechanics' Institutes. For just over a year he was a schoolmaster in Leicester, where he met Henry Walter Bates, who introduced him to the delights of beetle-hunting. After moving back to Wales, Wallace for a time threw himself into a flurry of survey work – railway contracts were temporarily lucrative.

But his intellectual curiosity was beginning to dominate. Books of travels absorbed him, notably Alexander von Humboldt's *Personal Narrative of Travels in South America* (p. 232) and Charles Darwin's *Journal* from his voyage on the *Beagle.* Then in 1845 he read *Vestiges of the Natural History of Creation* (by Robert Chambers) and found that the central message, the transmutation of species, chimed with his own thinking. He and Bates exchanged monthly lists of 'captures', and when Bates came to stay in Wales they hatched a scheme for a joint expedition. 'I should like to take some one family to study thoroughly, principally with a view to the theory of the origin of species', Wallace wrote to Bates. They decided to head for the Amazon, paying their expenses by selling specimens through a London natural history agent, Samuel Stevens.

To the Amazon

After spending a week practising shooting and skinning birds, Wallace and Bates left Liverpool in April 1848. Arriving in Pará (modern Belém, Brazil) they rented a house just outside the city, and soon settled into a relentless routine – collecting early in the morning, skinning, preserving and pinning the specimens during the heat of the day, then writing up their notes in the evenings. Butterflies, other insects and birds formed the bulk of their collections. They were working, commercial naturalists, desperate to establish their credentials and to set up a system that would fund their more ambitious travel plans. An expedition up the Tocantins River proved a useful learning experience. Wallace had the usual run of accidents of the naive explorer: a fierce attack by wasps; a rash grapple with an alligator he had assumed dead; a nasty hand wound when his gun discharged after jamming in the boards of the canoe. He also decided that he and Bates would separate and cover different areas, having persuaded his own younger brother to join him. Herbert travelled to Pará with the botanist Richard Spruce, and in August 1849, the brothers made the 645-km (400-mile) voyage up the Amazon to Santarém. Wallace was exulting in the exercise, the pure air and the good, simple living. He pursued butterflies – describing *Callithea sapphira* as 'the most beautiful thing I have ever taken' – and puzzled about the distribution of species: after collecting on both sides of the river, he realized that it might act as a boundary for some species.

Growing in confidence, Wallace now wanted to explore less-developed territory. By the end of 1849, he had reached the junction of the Amazon with the Rio Negro and based himself at Barra (modern Manaus). Herbert had decided that collecting was not his metier, so Alfred set off with a local trader, heading for the Falls of São Gabriel and beyond, where the Rio Negro interlocked with the Orinoco river system. Wallace began to collect and draw the fishes systematically. After arriving at Guía, he

Photograph of Wallace with his friend Frederick Geach, dated 1862 and taken in Singapore just before Wallace's return to Britain.

Pencil sketch of Ancistrus gibbiceps, *a fish from the Rio Negro, from one of Wallace's notebooks. The notebook with the fish sketches was one of the few records that Wallace managed to save from the disastrous fire on the* Helen.

diverted to the Serra de Cobati in search of the 'gallo de serra', the colourful cock of the rock bird. This hunting trip was especially illuminating – instead of directing the Indians to catch specimens for him, Wallace followed in their footsteps, and realized, as his gun caught on overhanging branches and his shirt-sleeves snagged in the hooked spines of climbing plants, that they looked on him 'as a good illustration of the uselessness and bad consequences of wearing clothes upon a forest journey'. He spent some months in Javíta, which he found a kind of Utopia, apart from the sandflies, and then canoed up the Vaupés, where he was delighted to find himself 'in the presence of the true denizens of the forest'. Wallace recorded the customs, dances and language of these forest people, and longed to pay an extended visit; besides, he had counted 30 species of orchid in an hour's ramble and realized that he could buy live specimens of monkeys and parrots for a few cheap goods. There was also a rumour of a white umbrella bird – any rare bird was a powerful lure for him. Returning to Barra to send off a batch of specimens and buy more supplies, he learnt that his brother was dangerously ill with yellow fever at Pará. Persuading himself that he was too far away to help, he retraced his route as far as São Joaquim, only to succumb to a violent and recurring fever; he thought himself 'almost at the point of death'.

Wallace never lacked resilience, or determination, but his illness and anxiety about his brother did affect him. Once he had recovered, he retraced his route further up the Vaupés, through or around some 50 falls, until he reached Mucura, where, he felt satisfied, no European traveller had been before him. He mapped the area as well as he could, though his boiling-point thermometers, for altitude, were lost or broken, and he only had a pocket surveying sextant. He blamed the delay caused by his illness for the dearth of animals. The fruit season was past, the fish were less numerous and the white umbrella chatterer seemed not to exist. But he acquired as many live animals as he could and set off. At Pará he learnt about his brother's death and visited his grave.

In July 1852 Wallace sailed for England. Three weeks out, the ship caught fire and everyone had to take to the lifeboats. Wallace grabbed a random selection of belongings, including his drawings of fish and palms, and watched while the ship burned, along with three years of journals, a large portfolio of drawings, and his collection of monkeys and birds. After bobbing about near Bermuda, the survivors were rescued by a ship which eventually limped into Deal; here the beef-steak and damson tart was a pleasant change from the biscuits and water diet of the previous few days.

Wallace reckoned he had lost £500 worth of specimens; even worse, his own private collection, which he had kept with him the whole four years, was gone. Fortunately, his agent Stevens had insured the collections for £200, so Wallace was not destitute. He was 29, and an incurable optimist. He was soon doing the rounds of the learned societies, attending meetings, and giving papers and presentations, including one to the Royal Geographical Society. He scoured his memory, made the best of his decimated written records and put together *A Narrative of Travels on the Amazon and Rio Negro*. His success as a collector, and his thinking about plant and animal distribution in connection with the evolution of species, gave him the confidence to consider an even more ambitious journey. Back to the Amazon, and the Peru he had never reached? Australia? He lobbied Sir Roderick Murchison and the Royal Geographical Society and secured a free passage east. In April 1854 he arrived in Singapore, with a young assistant, Charles Allen, and began his eight years of wandering in the Malay Archipelago, the 'central and controlling incident' in his life.

Borneo and the Orang-Utans

Singapore formed an excellent base, largely because of its key position on the shipping route to Europe. As in Brazil, Wallace began by exploiting the resources close to hand and then experimented with short side trips, spending two months in Malacca and climbing Mount Ophir. But Borneo beckoned, offering comparatively untouched collecting grounds, and an invaluable contact in Rajah Brooke, the ruler of Sarawak. Wallace arrived in November 1854. He sat out the rainy season in a small house at the foot of Santubong mountain and fired off a key paper, 'On the Law which has Regulated the Introduction of New species', which included the challenging statement that 'Every species has come into existence coincident both in time and space with a pre-existing closely allied species'. This was a theory he had discussed with Bates and Spruce, though the vital component – the 'how' – was missing.

While this missive slowly made its way to London, Wallace moved his operational base to the Simunjon River, where a coal works was opening up the virgin forest. He had a small, two-roomed house built, and settled down to serious collecting for nine months in the best location he ever found. In a single day he captured 76 different species of insects and beetles, of which 34 were new to him. Other delights included the magnificent bird-winged butterfly, which he named *Ornithoptera Brookeana* after the Rajah (now *Trogonoptera brookiana*), and a new species of flying frog. Most significant were his encounters with the orang-utans. He and the Dayak hunters he employed shot a large number – something about which Wallace had at this stage few qualms. He was also able to make a close study of their habits, in addition to nurturing a very young orang, which he treated – and described – as though it were a human baby. Making his way back to Sarawak, he travelled up the Simunjon River and over the watershed to the Sarawak River, staying in Dayak longhouses on the way. He returned to Singapore with major collections to be shipped to England – some 5,000 insects and orang skins and skeletons. But his mind was also enriched by his observations, and the substantial time spent with other races continued to mould his ideas about species, including man.

Wallace's Line

It was now time to travel further east. He reached Bali (after 20 days in a Chinese-owned schooner) and then Lombok, where he noted that the bird population was entirely unexpected and threw 'great light

LEFT *'Flying frog', an engraving by J. G. Keulemans from an original drawing by Wallace.* OPPOSITE Paradisaea apoda *– greater bird of paradise – a plate from John Gould's* Birds of New Guinea *(1875–88).*

A display from Wallace's personal collection, showing sexual dimorphism. At top left is a specimen of the male Ornithoptera croesus, *which he described as 'the finest butterfly in the world'.*

on the laws of Geographical distribution of Animals in the East'. Bali and Lombok, though no more than 28 km (17 miles) apart, belong to two distinct zoological provinces, of which each island forms the extreme limit. Wallace realized that he had come across the dividing line between the Asian and Australian biological regions – a division marked, eventually, by the name 'Wallace's Line'. This was an astonishing deductive feat, only confirmed by the later geological discovery of tectonic plates.

Wallace moved on to Macassar, the first of several visits to Celebes (Sulawesi) – wonderfully puzzling territory in terms of geographical distribution. But he was fixed on the Ultima Thule of the Aru Islands, where he hoped to find the king bird of paradise and the greater bird of paradise, a voyage of some 1,610 km (1,000 miles) in a native prau. He made himself comfortable in a section of the thatched cabin, 'the snuggest and most comfortable place I have ever enjoyed at sea', and delighted in the pleasant smell of the prau's pure vegetable fibres, which brought to mind scenes of the forest. His descriptions are ecstatic: at the Ke Islands, he found himself in 'a new world', revelling in the 'absolute diversity' of man. In the Aru Islands, he continued to marvel, at the birds of paradise, the rare butterflies and the beauty of the islanders, a people 'superbly adapted' to their environment. He described the moment he caught a specimen of *Ornithoptera poseidon*: 'I trembled with excitement as I saw it coming majestically towards me, and could hardly believe I had really succeeded in my stroke till I had taken it out of the net and was gazing, lost in admiration, at the velvet black and brilliant green of its wings ... its golden body, and crimson breast.' He sailed back to Macassar with his mind teeming and 9,000 specimens of 1,600 species.

Natural Selection and Birds of Paradise

Wallace shifted his base first to Amboyna, where he shared his hut with a 3.6-m (12-ft) long python, and then to Ternate. Exploring the nearby island of Gilolo (Halmahera), and continuing to ponder about man, Wallace found himself, as he shivered with a severe malarial fever, thinking about Malthus's *Principles of Population*. Suddenly the answer to the question of how species change came to him: in every generation the inferior would inevitably be killed off and the superior would remain – that is, 'the fittest would survive'. Back in Ternate, he made a fair copy of his paper and sent it to Charles Darwin, with whom he was in correspondence, for his opinion. Then he prepared for another major voyage, to Dorey in New Guinea.

This proved to be one of the more frustrating legs of his wanderings. In New Guinea two of his men fell ill, and one died. He himself endured sickness, heavy rain and plagues of ants and blowflies. But there was news of his paper's reception, which had been read, with accompanying texts by Darwin, at the Linnaean Society's meeting of

Natives of Aru hunting the greater bird of paradise, an engraving by T. W. Wood from The Malay Archipelago *(1869).*

THE

MALAY ARCHIPELAGO:

THE LAND OF THE

ORANG-UTAN, AND THE BIRD OF PARADISE.

A NARRATIVE OF TRAVEL,

WITH STUDIES OF MAN AND NATURE.

BY

ALFRED RUSSEL WALLACE,

AUTHOR OF

"TRAVELS ON THE AMAZON AND RIO NEGRO," "PALM TREES OF THE AMAZON," ETC.

IN TWO VOLS.—VOL. II.

London:

MACMILLAN AND CO.

1869.

[*The Right of Translation and Reproduction is reserved.*]

A female orang-utan, illustrating the title page of The Malay Archipelago *(1869).*

1 July 1858. The theory of evolution by natural selection was now in the public domain, and Wallace's role – and reputation as a scientific thinker – was incontrovertible. The letters to and from Darwin flowed, and eventually came a copy of Darwin's response, in the shape of *On the Origin of Species*, published in 1859. Wallace acknowledged its mastery with admiration, and quietly put aside his own plan for a theoretical book in favour of completing his study of the relations of animals to time and space. He discovered a new bird of paradise, *Semioptera wallacei*, in Batchian (Bacan), visited Waigiou and Bessir in pursuit of *Paradisaea rubra*, striving to keep specimens alive, and filled in his knowledge of Timor, Java and Sumatra. He finally returned to London on 1 April 1862, bringing with him in triumph – having hand-fed them a daily diet of cockroaches – two birds of paradise, living jewels, for the Zoological Society of London.

Wallace's days as an explorer were over. It was seven years before he published *The Malay Archipelago,* which was gradually recognized as one of the great travel books: lucid, vibrant, insightful and powerfully conveying his sense of wonder at the beauty and diversity of nature. Wallace lived until 1913, and although he never found a regular scientific job – perhaps he was too independent, perhaps slightly suspect because of his socialist leanings and his interest in spiritualism – he produced a stream of influential scientific and popular writing, and ended up with all the official honours the establishment could bestow, crowned by the Order of Merit.

But it was his years as an exploring naturalist that most define his contribution, not so much for the remote places he reached as for his powers of observation. Because he often stayed in one place for a considerable period of time, and because he was deliberately dependent on local resources, he developed an unusual perspective on a world that he saw as a continuum. He questioned the values of modern civilization, and foresaw the dangers, to man and to the natural world, of unchecked development. Reading Wallace, it is impossible not to engage with the questions that surround man's place in nature, and the interdependence and fragility of the natural world.

Frank Kingdon-Ward

PLANT HUNTER IN THE FAR EAST

(1885–1958)

Exploration is days of boredom punctuated with moments of ecstasy.

Frank Kingdon-Ward

There may perhaps be more celebrated explorers than my grandfather, Frank Kingdon-Ward, but he certainly distinguished himself in one sense above all others when compared to many famous travellers – he survived, though only just on several occasions. He was born in Manchester in 1885 and went on his first expedition while still at school, cycling to Oxford over two days, getting soaked to the skin and sleeping under the stars. With his best friend, he formed a club (with two members) and they went on regular adventures. The more discomfort they endured the more successful they considered the trip to be. After 50 years of exploration, interrupted only by two world wars, Kingdon-Ward finally died, in hospital, aged 72.

His father, Harry Marshall Ward, was professor of botany at Cambridge University and distinguished himself with his work on coffee blight in Ceylon (Sri Lanka). As a boy, Frank overheard a conversation between his father and a visiting explorer, and the sentence 'there are places up the Brahmaputra where no white man has ever been' stood out to him above all the rest. On the death of his father, Frank left Cambridge University early and took a teaching post in Shanghai to be closer to the Brahmaputra. In 1909 he accepted an offer to go with an expedition to western China funded by the Duke of Bedford. This was primarily a zoological mission, but Frank also sent back herbarium (dried and pressed plant) specimens to his old university.

Meconopsis betonicifolia, *the Himalayan blue poppy, photographed by Kingdon-Ward and brought back by him in 1924.*

Frank Kingdon-Ward always considered himself to be an explorer first and foremost, even though he is best known today as a plant collector. For him, collecting plants was merely a means to an end, namely to fund the next expedition. For keen horticulturalists in

Britain, and later in America and worldwide, his collecting provided them with a near endless supply of exotic beauty for their gardens. The legendary Himalayan blue poppy, *Meconopsis betonicifolia*, the giant Tibetan cowslip, *Primula florindae*, *Rhododendron wardii* and *Lilium mackliniae* are just four outstanding examples. He also wrote prodigiously. Even after the longest hard day's trek he would sit down at a small table and write in his diary and send letters home. Sadly, he made little money from his many published books and countless articles. Yet these also stand as testament to his life's work, and inevitably form the basis of any biography.

Early Expeditions

Kingdon-Ward's first plant collecting expedition came in 1911 for A. K. Bulley of Bees Seeds; his mission, to go to Yunnan in China and collect new and interesting plants to grow in English gardens. Despite misgivings about his abilities, he rose to the task admirably, bringing back around 200 species, including many new to science. Once, he became lost and separated, surviving for two days on nothing but nectar and some leaves, which gave him stomach cramps. He suffered hallucinations on the second day, and describes stepping over imaginary boulders but falling over real ones. Eventually he was found and continued his journey before returning to England with his precious seeds. He was back in Yunnan in 1913, again for Bees Seeds. In 1914 he went to Burma for one of his most eventful expeditions, being nearly killed on no fewer than three occasions: once when a tree crashed on his tent, then when a storm destroyed his hut, and lastly almost falling off a cliff in the dark. Yet despite this, he continued to collect and explore the region.

On the return journey he met some British officers at one of the furthest outposts of the empire, and was told of the war in Europe. Anxious to enlist as soon as possible, he force marched himself to Fort Hertz, only to pass out from exhaustion, and he was then ill for several days. His war was not illustrious, but not for want of trying. He spent two years training local and unwilling troops in Burma and then another two in Mesopotamia (now Iraq), where the only action he saw was to shoot a crocodile.

In the context of the times, when everyone was racist and disdainful of indigenous populations, when animals were there to be shot, the rarer the better, and someone else's country was simply a resource to be plundered wholesale, Kingdon-Ward can be said to have been a sympathetic traveller. He disliked the habits of some of his contemporaries, who short-changed the locals on deals and took vast trains of

The spectacular scenery of the temperate rainforest at 3,000 m (10,000 ft) in the Mishmi Hills, in the Himalayan region of eastern India, with epiphytic rhododendrons on the trees.

porters through uncharted terrain. In contrast, he travelled light, paid what he promised, was a terrible shot when targeting rare game and rarely wrote bad things about the natives without good cause. He took with him inexpensive western goods, such as cameras and torches, knowing that local chiefs and kings would ask for them as gifts, and he could spare these, but not his best equipment. His 1924 expedition to discover a 'mythical' waterfall was unsuccessful, but 72 years later another expedition searching for the same falls had a guide whose grandfather had worked for Frank. Having grown up hearing stories of the explorer searching for the falls, he was instrumental in the success of the later expedition. *The Riddle of the Tsangpo Gorges*, first published in 1926 and republished in 2001, tells the full story.

A photograph by Kingdon-Ward of a Naga woman in Burma in the 1930s. He took a great interest in anthropology, writing about native peoples copiously and always endeavouring to respect their laws and customs.

A local porter carrying a case of Kingdon-Ward's supplies (date and location unrecorded); he photographed people at least as much as the plants and scenery he encountered.

In 1923 Kingdon-Ward married Florinda Norman-Thompson, but he spent little time at home, despite having two daughters. The marriage lasted 14 years and ended in divorce. Because of the attitudes of the times, Frank had to pretend to have an affair; the decree nisi arrived while he was on another expedition in Burma.

The Second World War and Later Expeditions

During the Second World War Kingdon-Ward was initially occupied in the censor's office in London, translating Chinese documents, but he hated being indoors. Finally, his pleadings to see some action were, at least partially, heeded and he headed off, via

Africa, overland across the Middle East and Asia to Singapore, where he worked out an escape route to India in the event of a Japanese invasion. When it came, he was among the last to leave and nothing was heard of him for 18 months.

When he re-emerged he was engaged in planting hidden fuel and provision dumps in the jungle, and he later trained RAF officers in the art of jungle survival. He was once thrown bodily out of a jeep and landed on the road some distance ahead of the vehicle. After dictating a letter to his sister informing her of his death, he passed out. He was 60 years old. Of course he recovered and the letter was never sent. As the tide of war turned, his expertise was no longer needed and he became 'unemployed', although he took on work for a tea plantation and then for the US air force searching for missing airmen.

In 1947 he remarried. Jean Macklin, unlike his first wife, loved exploration and went with him on all subsequent trips. In 1948 they were in Manipur, India, collecting over 1,000 species. Then they travelled to Mishmi, now part of India, on behalf of the New York Botanical Society in 1949, and in 1950 to the Assam/Tibet border for the Royal Horticultural Society. It was on this trip that the couple experienced

Frank and Jean Kingdon-Ward on expedition. The day did not end when they reached camp: after a long day's march, Kingdon-Ward would sit down and write letters and his diary, and there were also seeds to be packaged and herbarium specimens to dry and press.

an earthquake of magnitude 9.6–9.7 on the Richter scale. It was the largest quake since records had begun and they were only a few miles from the epicentre. In Kingdon-Ward's words 'The mountains round us seemed to be falling into the Lohit Gorge. Some of them were literally rent in half; flayed, the forested sides being peeled off like wet paper, the green mountains turned snow white; the vast curtain of dust coloured the sun copper red.'

Struggling home through the desolate landscape, they ran into some soldiers who had lost all their supplies. Between them, they eventually got back safely, but the expedition had been a disaster. Kingdon-Ward offered to return money to his backers, but they assured him they were simply glad he was alive and well. Despite this terrible setback, he and Jean returned for more. The years 1952/53 saw them in Burma, with two young Burmese botanists; on his 68th birthday Frank climbed to over 3,350 m (11,000 feet); in 1956 they were again in Burma, with a Swedish botanist. It is fitting that in 1930 Kingdon-Ward received the Founder's Medal of the RGS for 'geographical exploration', as well as his botanical work, in China and Tibet.

Kingdon-Ward had a terrible fear of heights; this bridge, which he photographed in an unknown location, is one of the more elaborate – some consisted of just a single rope.

Back in 1911, Kingdon-Ward had written that he was 'tired after 11 hours marching in the rain', but now he described himself as 'exhausted after a five hour climb'. He had contracted malaria in 1909 and suffered many bouts of fever over the years, but all the storms, earthquakes, cliffs, illness and other misadventures too numerous to detail here, had failed to claim him. In April 1958, he suffered a stroke and went into a coma. Two days later he died, aged 72, leaving a 50-year legacy of consistent and methodical exploration, pushing back the boundaries of uncharted territory, making detailed maps and carrying out anthropological studies; but he will be most remembered for adding greater variety and beauty to our gardens.

NEW FRONTIERS

The great age of exploration may be just beginning, in the sense that we are only now starting to realize how little we understand the workings of nature and the intricate relationships between species. There are still also new physical challenges to be met above and beneath the land and the sea. Those chosen for this section have all changed our understanding of the world and the way we interact with it in a significant way through exploring very different aspects.

One young man who, during his brief life, changed our view of an environment and our ability to master it was Gino Watkins. The extreme efforts he and his companions put into setting up a weather station in the interior of Greenland and taking meteorological observations effectively made trans-Atlantic air travel possible. The first man to be propelled into outer space was the son of a carpenter. His humble origins may have helped Yuri Gagarin to be selected by his communist masters as a suitable representative of the proletariat; he became the most famous man in his country. Once it had been shown that man could survive in space, the race was on to go ever further. Machines are now probing the limits of our solar system. One day people will go there, too.

The depths of the oceans are our least-known habitat. The name most associated with developing the equipment to make their exploration possible, the Aqualung, is Jacques-Yves Cousteau. Through his films and books, Cousteau brought the underwater world into the light. His passionate campaigning to protect this most fragile part of our planet is being continued by his eldest son, Jean-Michel Cousteau. Another largely unexplored part of planet earth is the prodigious amount of space beneath the surface. Andrew Eavis, who has been responsible for exploring more caves than anyone alive today, maintains that only 10 per cent of caves which could be entered have so far been explored. The spectacular landscapes being revealed, with breathtaking caverns and fast-flowing rivers, make this area of exploration even more exciting.

At approximately 500 m (1,640 ft) vertical depth, Miao Keng in Chong Ching Province, China, is one of the deepest underground shafts in the world; all the figures seen here are Robert Eavis.

Gino Watkins

AN ADDICTION TO RISK

(1907–1932)

What they experienced in the Arctic was a pure rush.
In that vast empty space of cruel beauty and truth
their lives had a heroic simplicity and nothing
afterwards could come close to matching it.

Jeremy Scott, **Dancing on Ice,** *2008*

An airliner flying from London to the west coast of North America might cross Greenland's icecap at around 13,700 (45,000 ft). High above the weather, it is an untroubled experience, enjoyed during a meal while glancing down at the vast white wilderness below. This was not always so.

In 1930, Henry George 'Gino' Watkins, aged just 23, led a group of 14 young men to Greenland. Their stated aim was to investigate the possibility of an air route over its unexplored icecap, linking Europe to America and paving the way for passenger travel. But their real motives were deeper and more complex. Too young to have fought in the First World War, they found themselves unable to accept the drab dull life that Depression England seemed to offer. They thirsted for adventure, for risk, for the chance to prove their mettle. In the words of one of them, August Courtauld, they wanted 'to do something big'. They took with them two open cockpit biplanes and a wind-up gramophone, and their first action in Greenland was to teach the Inuit to dance the Charleston. The gesture was typical of Gino, whose approach to life and Arctic exploration was essentially lighthearted, though underpinned by ruthless professionalism. He'd first contracted a taste for risk and extreme adventure as a night climber at university in Cambridge, scaling the roofs and towers of the college buildings, then moved on to the Alps. He led his first expedition to the Arctic aged 19, to map the interior of Edge Island (Svalbard). Two years later, he and fellow undergraduate J. M. Scott went to Labrador on a grant from the Royal Geographical Society, to survey the territory's boundaries together with the headwaters of the Hamilton River.

It was while in Labrador that the idea came to Gino to explore an air route linking Europe and America across the icecap. Not only was this the shortest route, but stepping stones existed where a plane could land to refuel. So a commercial passenger route was possible – theoretically.

In July 1930 the British Arctic Air-Route Expedition set sail for East Greenland on *Quest*, Shackleton's old ship on which he'd died. After constructing a base hut, Gino continued north with one aircraft on deck to survey the height of the coastal range, incidentally discovering the highest mountains in the Arctic. Meanwhile Scott and three others, with 28 sledge dogs, set out to establish a weather station at 2,620 m (8,600 ft) in the interior, 225 km (140 miles) from the base camp, where meteorological recordings could be taken and flying conditions monitored throughout the winter.

Effete, slight and blond, and with a taste for jazz, dancing and sports cars, Watkins did not fit most people's ideas of an explorer. He and the others on the expedition were members of the Brideshead generation.

Two men were installed there, duly replaced by another pair. Then at the end of October a party, including Courtauld, started out with supplies to man the station until the following spring. Their journey, beset by blizzards, was ghastly. By the time they reached the station not enough food remained to feed two men through the winter. To abandon the station meant the failure of the expedition. Courtauld volunteered, indeed demanded, to be left alone there until he could be relieved in March. The others returned to base, and two days later 24-hour night shut down on him.

At base, blizzards raged throughout the winter. The group there celebrated Christmas with a feast and a dance. Some were adapting to what Dickens described as the Eskimos' 'domesticity of blood and blubber'. Gino and several of the party took Inuit 'wives' and, to the dismay of the rest, they 'went native'. At least two of the party fathered children. Attempts to supply Courtauld by air proved unsuccessful. In March, Scott with two others set out on foot to relieve him. But by now the station had been buried beneath the snow. During 40 days of continuous storms they searched for it, tramping within yards of where Courtauld lay buried – but failed to find him. The morning after Scott's return to base, crushed by his failure, Gino with two others

One of the de Havilland Moths on the British Arctic Air-Route Expedition; it could be fitted with either floats or skis. At one point it crashed and was repaired with a tail made from the root stump of a Siberian pine, covered with material used by Eskimo women for blouses.

started out to where Courtauld lay entombed, dead or alive. He had now been alone for five months. At the end of March a huge blizzard had buried his tent, sealing the exit. Trapped in his burrow, he had little food and by the end of April only scraps remained. He lay in cold continual dark. On 5 May as he was heating snow for breakfast the primus faltered, and expired. Entombed beneath the ice, it was his 149th day of solitude. But Gino and his party were close. They spotted a dark speck and raced towards it. It was the remains of a tattered flag; by it the tip of the ventilator peeped above the snow. Gino called down it, 'Are you alright?' And a voice came back, tremulous from disuse, but that of a living man.

After more surveys across the icecap and a boat journey around the south coast of Greenland, the party came back to England, with their meteorological data, to great acclaim. But Gino was anxious to return to Greenland to complete the survey and set off again the next summer. In September 1932 the expedition was mapping a fiord for a landing-field, when Charles Lindbergh and his wife flew the route across the icecap they had surveyed. But Gino was then no longer with them. On 20 August he had gone out in his kayak to hunt seals for food for his party and did not return; his body was never found. He was 25 years old. There was an element of wilfulness in his death – only days before he had been almost drowned by a calving iceberg at the same spot. When writing about the expedition later, Scott says the prospect of returning to Depression Britain, to mundanity and a 9 to 5 job (if he was lucky) was so dispiriting to Gino, who was captivated by the Arctic, that he never wanted to go back.

He and all of them were members of the Brideshead generation, sharing its taste for jazz, dancing, sexual ambivalence and frivolity. For them exploration was a heroic quest. Their plan was reckless, clothing absurd, their equipment pitiful by modern standards. Yet, together they had overcome appalling setbacks, experienced conditions described by Arctic experts as 'at the limit of human endurance', been forced to eat their dogs and debate cannibalism to survive. Courtauld, Scott and Gino were awarded the Polar Medal in 1931 at an audience with the king, and Gino received the RGS's Founder's Medal in 1932, but their achievement is marked by the air route they pioneered, which is still in use today.

Christmas 1930 at the base hut (Gino is in the centre). By now several of the party had taken Eskimo 'wives' and 'gone native', to the dismay of the rest. While they celebrated, Courtauld was alone at the icecap station where the temperature was –30°C (–22°F).

Yuri Gagarin

THE FIRST PERSON INTO SPACE

(1934–1968)

Let us not grieve that we shall not participate in distant planetary expeditions.... Great happiness has come our way too: the happiness of the first steps into space. Let those who follow us envy our happiness.

Yuri Gagarin

Yuri Gagarin was a very different kind of explorer from those who had come before him – not just because he was the first person to journey into space, but also because he was not the instigator of his journey. In some respects, he was a passenger on an exploration made possible by others. However, as the eyes and ears of humankind's first leap beyond our planet, his experiences are as important as if he had hand-built his own rocket vehicle.

Born in Klushino, in the former Soviet Union, on 9 March 1934, Gagarin's background gave no indication that he would end up in the history books. The son of a carpenter in an isolated farming collective, Yuri grew up in a village with no running water, no electricity and no contact with the outside world other than a radio. One of four children, Yuri was expected to learn carpentry skills instead of focusing on school, and to follow his father into the family business.

The Gagarin family's lives changed forever with the Nazi invasion of 1941. As the front line of battle crept through the region, the village and everything of value in it was devastated. Surrounded by the invaders before they had time to flee, the family was forced into manual labour by the Nazis and made to dig an earth shelter to live in. There was little food, no schooling and the constant fear of torture or death.

After such a difficult childhood, it is not surprising that Gagarin became a rebellious teenager. To his father's displeasure, the boy had little interest in becoming a carpenter, and eventually confessed to his parents that he was determined to leave the village. He headed for Moscow to study gymnastics in college, only to find that there were no more spaces available. Instead, he had to settle for a brutally tough job in a steel mill. Eventually, he was able to switch to a place at an industrial college, and it was here that the young man finally found his purpose in life. The town had a flying club, and piloting became Gagarin's first love.

A young Yuri Gagarin at the air club where he learnt to fly. Flying was his first love and he became a military pilot before being selected to train for space flight.

Chosen for Space

Gagarin soon abandoned his studies to become a military aviation cadet and devote himself full-time to flying. His first assignment in Murmansk, within the Arctic Circle, was hardly the glamorous flying environment that he had hoped for. Then, in 1960, some mysterious visitors arrived: officials who interviewed dozens of pilots, without saying why. Gagarin was later called to Moscow to undergo medical tests and was finally told the reason behind the interest. He was one of hundreds of pilots being considered for selection as a spacefarer – a cosmonaut.

No one had ever flown in space, so the examiners could only guess what might be needed. Gagarin was a pilot, and young, healthy and psychologically sound. That should be enough. He became one of 20 selected, but was ordered to tell no one – not even his family. Gagarin was moved to a secret training facility just outside Moscow, to begin a rigorous regime of training and testing, both mental and physical.

At first, he and the other trainees were not permitted to see the classified rocket and spacecraft designs that were being prepared. When Gagarin finally did see the spacecraft, he was deeply puzzled. The ball-shaped, shiny object looked nothing like an aircraft. Gagarin was confident and eager to understand its workings, however, and this was noted by the designers and trainers, who were already looking for contenders for the first mission.

It was not long before Gagarin rose to the top of the group, with another pilot – Gherman Titov. Both were well qualified and both were eager to make the first flight.

A spacesuited Gagarin before his flight aboard the Vostok *spacecraft 12 April 1961. On the first test flight the spacecraft was flown automatically and Gagarin did not have to touch the controls. The flight lasted for 79 minutes before returning to earth.*

Titov, however, was more arrogant, and also the son of a teacher. Gagarin had a warm, open personality that was seen as more suitable to the public relations side of the forthcoming assignment, and his family background was viewed as better suited to Soviet propaganda. For the son of a village carpenter to become a cosmonaut proved, it was felt, the equality of life under communism.

Into the Unknown

Just one week before the flight, Gagarin was officially selected, in secret, as the pilot. Titov would be his backup. On the morning of 12 April 1961 both men were awakened in their sleeping quarters. Dressed in their spacesuits, they were taken to the nearby launch pad on the plains of Kazakhstan, where the *Vostok* spacecraft awaited on top of a stubby, modified R-7 rocket.

After he had slid into the spacecraft couch, the hatch was bolted behind Gagarin. He gazed at the controls, familiar to him through training. He would not be expected to touch any of them unless there was an emergency. Gagarin knew how to fly the spacecraft, but on this first, brief test flight, all actions would take place under automatic control. At the appointed moment, propellant surged into the rocket engines, which rumbled into life. The clamps supporting the rocket swung away and it rose, shaking the surrounding grasslands and onlookers with its might. Inside, however, Gagarin felt only a slight vibration and heard little noise. It was hard for him to sense his journey had begun at all, though as he later admitted, 'Of course I was nervous. Only a robot would not have been nervous at such a time and in such a situation.'

The shaking and pressure on Gagarin increased as the rocket picked up speed, but the cosmonaut felt no discomfort. Nine minutes after launch, with a sudden jolt, his spacecraft separated from the last stage of the rocket, and began a gentle drift. Now weightless, Gagarin had become the first human in space. Looking through the small portholes, he saw something no human eyes had ever witnessed before – a sharply curved horizon with a vivid blue band of bright atmosphere, set against the deep black of space. The atmosphere had thin layers of many different colours, which awed him with their beauty.

As *Vostok* gently turned, Gagarin looked down on oceans and islands, cities and forests. Constantly checking his spacecraft gauges, he could see that all was well – there was no need to touch the controls. Curving around the night side of our planet,

The recovery of Gagarin's Vostok *spaceship at the landing site in a field in the Soviet Union. As planned, Gagarin had ejected from the craft and parachuted separately and landed safely elsewhere.*

Gagarin witnessed a spectacular sunset and blinding sunrise. Having almost circled the entire globe in just 79 minutes, it was time to return.

Vostok's retrorockets fired automatically for the plunge back into the atmosphere, and at this point something went wrong. The two remaining segments of the spacecraft did not cleanly separate, and Gagarin tumbled into a dizzying spin, coming close to passing out. Fortunately, the two sections eventually broke free, the tumbling ended and he ejected as planned from his spacecraft, landing by parachute in a field in the Soviet Union.

International Celebrity

Gagarin became a celebrity the instant the flight was made public. He received hero-worship at home and spent months travelling on a gruelling world tour that can only be compared to Beatlemania in its level of intensity and adulation. Here, Gagarin's sunny and friendly personality was his most important asset. The spacecraft, rocket and other details of his flight were still a secret, so Gagarin in person was the representative of his country's great achievement. He won over Cold War enemies and allies alike with his unforced charm, always careful to emphasize that he was a normal person who had been fortunate enough to be part of a huge undertaking.

As the initial euphoria died down, however, Gagarin grew concerned that he was spending too much time on public relations and not enough in training. Unless he acted, he realized, he would fall far behind his colleagues and perhaps never fly in space again. He fought for permission to fly jets, and started a tough regimen of study at an engineering academy. He passed the demanding course, and also took on a jet pilot training programme with an extremely experienced test pilot instructor, Vladimir Seryogin. On 27 March 1968, the two were flying a MiG-15 jet when their plane, apparently pulling out of a steep dive, crashed in a forest; the two aviators died instantly. The accident investigation produced mixed reports, but did rule out any obvious pilot errors on the part of Gagarin and Seryogin. Jet flying is an unforgiving business, and Gagarin became yet another victim while pursuing his dreams.

Gagarin's brief and eventful life showed that people can overcome the most challenging backgrounds and circumstances to make their mark in history. It also demonstrated that the age of great exploration is far from over. Exploring our planet is only the beginning; there are new horizons to be reached and understood.

A postcard celebrating Gagarin's flight and other Soviet space achievements. Gagarin's personality and family background were well suited to Soviet propaganda and he went on a worldwide publicity tour, receiving medals and awards from several countries.

12 АПРЕЛЯ 1961 г. «ВОСТОК»
25.III.1961
12.II.1961
1.XII.1960
15.V.1960
19.VIII.1960
12.IX.1959
4.X.1959
2.I.1959
15.V.1958
4.X.1957
3.XI.1957
СЛАВА!

Jacques-Yves Cousteau

UNDERWATER PIONEER

(1910–1997)

From birth man carries the weight of gravity on his shoulders. He is bolted to earth. But man has only to sink beneath the surface and he is free. Buoyed by water, he can fly in any direction – up, down, sideways. Under water, man becomes an archangel.

Jacques-Yves Cousteau

It is a matter of modern legend that Jacques Cousteau was the first manfish: the first person to explore freely under water, to be accepted by the creatures of the deep, and to report back to the rest of us in stunning images and poetic language, transforming our view of the planet for ever. Cousteau's legendary exploration came about through a near-fatal car accident, in 1936, when he was a 26-year-old naval cadet training to be a pilot. It changed his life.

After eight months in hospital he could walk again, although doctors told him they would have to amputate one arm. Cousteau refused and began his own long, self-designed rehabilitation by swimming daily in the Mediterranean Sea. While swimming, he met Philippe Taillez, who introduced him to the small goggles worn by Japanese pearl divers, and Frédéric Dumas, a champion spear diver. They became the French Riviera's 'Three Muske-mers', swimming and skin-diving daily, filled with a fascination for the marine wonders they were witnessing.

INSPIRATIONS

On the sea's surface Cousteau could watch life unfold below in a jungle of colourful fish. When he raised his head, he saw the traffic of the city of Toulon, and he described the juxtaposition of these worlds as an electric shock, which motivated him to want to go deeper into the sea and to stay longer. Soon after, he met Émile Gagnan, inventor of a demand regulator that fed cooking gas to cars in rationed, wartime France. Cousteau's vision saw beyond this and he wondered if the device could instead deliver air to a diver. Together, Cousteau (already trained as an engineer) and Gagnan experimented with a series of adaptations that finally led, in 1943, to the Aqualung, generally known as SCUBA – the Self-Contained Underwater Breathing Apparatus.

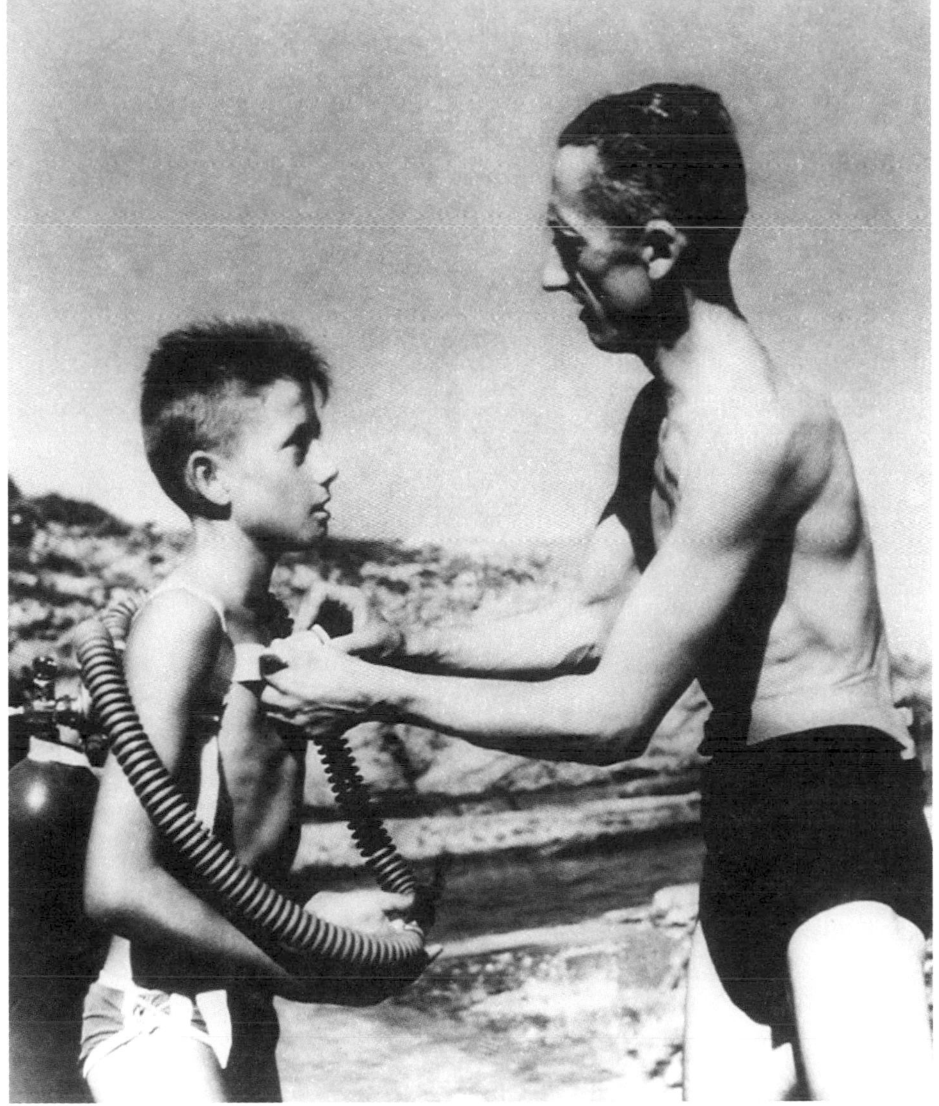

Cousteau adjusts the equipment of a 10-year-old Jean-Michel before one of the family dives in the Mediterranean, near Sanary, France. This version of the Aqualung, which Cousteau co-invented, was one of the first commercially available units produced by Spirotechnique in France.

Along with his insatiable curiosity and intellect, Cousteau was a poet, an engineer and a charismatic communicator. Soon he was surrounded by people as enthusiastic as he was to explore the frontier he had opened. Little was known about the physiology of diving under pressure, of breathing compressed air, of human limits at depth, of embolisms and decompression sickness, and so early undersea exploration using SCUBA was fraught with unexpected hazards.

One of Jacques Cousteau's early passions, besides wanting to fly planes, was cinema, and he was soon at work inventing waterproof cameras that would capture the beauty and wonder he was experiencing and make it available to a worldwide audience. This resulted in *The Undersea World of Jacques Cousteau,* the first underwater documentary series, which began in 1966, continued for 30 years and provided armchair exploration for millions of television viewers worldwide. Cousteau became a household name, synonymous with the ocean and adventure. His film career allowed him to spend decades exploring, making films, pursuing science and campaigning, a tradition that has been continued by his eldest son, Jean-Michel Cousteau.

Innovations and Discoveries

From the beginning, Cousteau was driven by a passion to see more, to go deeper and stay longer, and to do so he needed innovative equipment to meet the new challenges. In 1950 he acquired *Calypso,* a converted Second World War minesweeper that was donated anonymously by the Guinness family to Cousteau for one franc per year. In it, he travelled the globe, transporting many scientists from their laboratories to see their subjects in the real world. By the early 1950s Cousteau had helped to found two research institutions to develop underwater equipment and combine his explorations with scientific research.

Terry Young (left) and Jacques-Yves Cousteau prepare for a dive with the Aqualung and an early version of a dry suit for colder temperatures (1950).

In 1952 Cousteau began work on the first large-scale underwater archaeological expedition at the Grand Congloué islet near Marseille, France. Hundreds of terracotta amphorae were brought to the surface and the crew of *Calypso* were the first to sip wine from the era of Aristotle; they found it a few hundred years past its prime. There were other, far more practical discoveries. In 1954 Cousteau and *Calypso* were commissioned to prospect in the Persian Gulf and discovered the first offshore oil-bearing strata. Then in 1960, his team accomplished the first mapping of a salt dome in the Mediterranean Sea, of interest because of the association of salt domes with underlying hydrocarbons.

Cousteau's passion for the next discovery was always linked to his desire to share his explorations, and so innovations in film and communication continued in parallel with his

Cousteau invented some of the first underwater cameras for still and motion photography. Diving here in tropical waters for The Undersea World of Jacques Cousteau, *he films, as he always did, without using a viewfinder and with an underwater camera housing which he also pioneered.*

travels. He spearheaded the construction of the first integrated, underwater 35mm still camera, named 'Calypso-Phot', the predecessor of the Nikonos underwater camera. In a pioneering event in 1957, he also accomplished the first undersea television broadcast, in the waters off Marseille, which was transmitted all over Europe.

For nearly 30 years, Jacques-Yves Cousteau and his sons, Philippe and Jean-Michel, were involved in filmmaking that made visible to a worldwide audience their underwater explorations. When asked why he had picked a certain location for the next adventure, Jacques was known to reply, 'Because I haven't been there', and when asked what he expected to find he said, 'If I knew that I wouldn't have to go'. But with time his investigations took a more serious turn because of what he was witnessing.

Ecological Awareness

Early in his undersea career, Cousteau took an uncompromising stand against nuclear waste and the hazards of oil pollution. He was instrumental in initiating efforts to

Céline and Fabien Cousteau dive with their father, Jean-Michel, in the Dry Tortugas Ecological Reserve as part of a two-hour film on underwater marine sanctuaries, one of many causes which the Cousteau family continues to champion as part of their legendary heritage.

preserve the Mediterranean Sea, raising the first alarms over the deterioration he saw, caused by land-based sources, tanker oil pollution and ill-managed coastal development. Cousteau sailed the Mediterranean in *Calypso* rallying support and urging standard protocols for water sampling. The alarms he raised resulted in the Regional Seas Programme under UNEP (United Nations Environment Programme) and the 21-country signing of the Barcelona Convention in 1976. With such visibility and influence came responsibility, which Cousteau clearly accepted. Together with his sons, Jean-Michel and Philippe, in 1973 he founded The Cousteau Society in the United States and quickly gained a constituency of hundreds of thousands of followers. Philippe Cousteau, the younger son, was tragically killed in 1979 in an amphibious plane crash, and Jean-Michel stepped in to support and assist his father.

Until his death in 1997, Jacques-Yves Cousteau continued his love affair with the sea, enchanted by its beauty but alarmed by the ignorance and greed that were taking a toll. Long before such issues became headline news, Cousteau warned of over-fishing, habitat destruction, pollution and global warming. While the public seemed to love Cousteau for raising the alarm, they were slower to rally to achieve his goals to protect what he loved – the ocean world. The task of continuing the work fell in part to Jean-Michel, work that was more pragmatic and less visible than that of his legendary father.

The Legacy – and the Future

For over 30 years, Jean-Michel Cousteau has not only continued his father's filmmaking adventures, having produced over 80 films, but also expanded the Cousteau message. Jean-Michel founded Ocean Futures Society and Project Ocean Search, an educational, hands-on adventure that invited students and adults to experience the Cousteau adventure at sea under the guidance of his team of scientists and educators. Continuing under the umbrella of the Ocean Futures Society, the programme is now called Ambassadors of the Environment, and has reached tens of thousands of people with the principles of environmental protection and sustainability.

Trained as an architect, Jean-Michel also brought the Cousteau philosophy to the arena of hotel and resort design. Fiji Island Resort (originally a subject of contention between father and son) began as an attempt to transform coral reef tourism into a sustainable, culturally appropriate, environmentally sound industry. Jean-Michel's design innovations have received the highest awards in the industry for this 'greening' of tourism and tropical reef protection.

Expectations based on the Cousteau tradition will always include new views into the ocean world and the filmmaking tradition has continued, most recently with the Public Broadcasting System-sponsored *Jean-Michel Cousteau: Ocean Adventures* series. The first film, 'Voyage to Kure' on the subject of the vulnerability of the northwestern Hawaiian island group, was a turning point that inspired then US President, George W. Bush, to create the largest protected marine area at the time. 'Call of the Killer Whale' has raised alarms about toxic chemicals used in flame retardants which have invaded the environment, affecting not only killer whales, but also ourselves.

In addition to Jean-Michel, there are four grandchildren who are passionately involved in ocean exploration and the environment: Fabien and Céline, Jean-Michel's son and daughter; and Alexandra and Philippe, Philippe's daughter and son. They are not a family team but four individuals with the sea in their blood, the future in their vision and the inspiration of a legendary explorer in their genes. As Jacques Cousteau noted in his 1980 *Bill of Rights for Future Generations*, 'Why should we preserve a livable planet if not for our children and grandchildren?'.

Andrew James Eavis

FINDING NEW WORLDS UNDERGROUND

(1948–)

Equipment for cave exploring includes: A spare telephone, a telephone trumpet … cords and plumb-line for sounding purposes, a measure, some medicines, a flask of rum … knives, thermometer, barometer, pocket compass, paper squared off for topographical drafting, pencils, provisions and some incense or Armenian paper, which is burned in case there are dead animals putrefying in the depths.

Édouard Alfred Martel, 1898

From an early age I was always going to explore. When I realized later that outer space was not likely to be available to the British in the near future and deep oceans were too specialized, the only exploration available was caves. In 1969, at the age of 21, I spent the summer with the University of Leicester Arctic Norway Expedition, sitting on and under a glacier in northern Norway, the only caver on the trip. When an ice-dammed lake spectacularly emptied, releasing around a cubic kilometre of water in just a few hours, an amazing sub-glacial cave was left behind and I had the chance to get below the glacier.

One of my great inspirational heroes was Édouard Alfred Martel, a French caver who essentially invented the modern activity. In the 1880s Martel was the first to coin the word 'speleology' and the first to explore numerous caves across many different countries, including the first descent of Gaping Gill in the Yorkshire Dales in 1895. He also pioneered early cave photography, specifically to show people both the wonders of caves and that they should be protected. I have spent my life trying to emulate him.

On graduating from Leicester it was only natural that I should do a post-graduate course at Leeds University, since at the time it had one of the finest caving clubs in the world. It is also not surprising that my subject was mining engineering, sponsored by the National Coal Board. Over the next two years, probably at least half my time was spent underground, either coal mining or caving. At Leeds were a number of fanatical cave explorers, including the energetic brothers David and Alan Brook, who undoubtedly have discovered more of Britain than any other living people.

Looking Further Afield

In the early 1970s I went on a number of expeditions to Europe, particularly in France, to the Pierre Saint Martin. This cave in the western French Pyrenees was at that time the deepest known in the world. Getting to the bottom was not easy – over a kilometre of tortuous rift passage led to a series of waterfall pitches, at the base of which the stream disappeared into a narrow crack. Soon after my marriage, I found myself at the bottom with two colleagues, Dick Willis and Paul Everett, trying to enlarge the passage using hand-powered drills and explosives, when we realized the cave was flooding. Dick decided to head for the surface, while Paul thought it was more sensible to find shelter, so I sat with Paul in a small alcove half way up the waterfall system for 55 hours. Eventually the flood waters died down and we were helped to the surface by the rest of our team. One of a number of lucky escapes.

The main river passage in Pierre Saint Martin, a famous and complex cave system in the French Pyrenees: this photograph is taken just before the passage joins a huge cavity called 'the Verna'.

Sarawak Chamber, 1984: the far wall is over 700 m (2,295 ft) from the camera. The photograph was taken by Jerry Wooldridge using a camera mounted on a tripod with at least 10 very large flash bulbs synchronized by radio.

During this period cavers were consumed with breaking the world depth record; only 20 years previously the world's highest place, Mount Everest, had been conquered. Colleagues of mine looked on a map and found some of the most promising high limestone cave country in the world to be in Papua, New Guinea. So the 1975 New Guinea Expedition was born. Dave Brook naturally became the leader and I, somewhat less naturally, as a newcomer to the group, eventually became Deputy Leader and organizer. Although the world depth record was not broken on this trip, over 50 km (31 miles) of cave passage were explored and surveyed by 24 people in 6 months. Every possible organizational mistake was made, but, on the principle of 'you learn by your mistakes', it was excellent training.

After this expedition, the Royal Geographical Society invited myself and four other cavers to join them on their Mulu Expedition in northern Sarawak. At a late

Carlsbad Caverns is a vast system of caves in southeastern New Mexico. The 'Big Room', which is around 1,219 m (4,000 ft) long, 190.5 m (625 ft) wide and 107 m (350 ft) high, is also known as the Hall of the Giants, from the extraordinary formations.

stage in their planning, the RGS had realized the area was cavernous limestone and that cavers should therefore join the scientists. My experiences in Mulu fired my interest in the science of caves and it was an exceptional expedition in many ways – with just five cavers we explored over 50 km (31 miles) of gigantic cave passage. Of great importance also to me as a novice cave expedition leader was learning from the organizational techniques of the leaders, particularly Nigel Winser and Robin Hanbury-Tenison, which, combined with previous lessons, helped me to go on to organize over 20 expeditions to various faraway places, especially Southeast Asia.

It was clear that there were a lot more caves in the area than had been discovered and follow-up expeditions were planned, starting with the first of two trips to Mulu, which I co-led with Ben Lyon. The target of much searching early in the trip in 1980 was an entrance on the other side of the mountain to a blocked passage which had been projected on the map. It was some time before Hans Friederich, a Dutch hydrologist, found a small opening. A few days later Tony White, Dave Checkley and I were lucky enough to explore and survey our way in. First by swimming and then climbing waterfalls and rapids, filmed initially by Sid Perou, the three of us arrived at the top of a boulder pile – the only thing we could see in the darkness was the ground immediately beneath our feet. We turned towards what we hoped would be a wall, and 110 m (360 ft) later we found it – and then followed it for nearly 2 km (1¼ miles). We began to realize we were feeling our way along the edge of a chamber: we had discovered the largest enclosed space known to man, Sarawak Chamber, 2½ times the size of the old Wembley Stadium.

The year 1985 saw me, Tony White and Tim Fogg travelling around the mountains above Wamena in New Guinea, the largest city in the world that is served only by aeroplanes. After getting altitude sickness at nearly 5,000 m (16,400 ft), the three of us split into two teams and covered vast areas. I took a number of local people as helpers, but the fragmented nature of the tribal system meant that in every valley I had to recruit new staff. One of my lowest moments came when, in torrential rain and having been deserted, I was stumbling along carrying three rucksacks. I bumped into an Indonesian from Java who spoke a little English; he produced a business card describing himself as 'landscape gardener'. He was working on a survey for a potential road into the highlands. He took me back to his camp, and ultimately gave me new helpers to get me back to town. I have been back to Irian Jaya on small expeditions a couple of times since then. The scenery and situation are wonderful – alpine grasslands just south of the equator and high, snow-capped hills. The politics are difficult and the caves hydrogeologically juvenile, but there is a lot still to be discovered.

Chinese Caves and Beyond

Official permissions for a trip to China came through after a long wait, and so in 1985 Tony Waltham and I led a joint trip to Guizhou and Guangxi. In both provinces the caves surpassed our wildest expectations. We soon discovered that the gigantic passages had been well trodden by the Chinese until the going became difficult. After that they were completely unexplored.

In Guilin we cemented our relationship with members of the Karst Research Institute, particularly Professor Zhu Xuewen, with whom we formed the China

The expedition team, Guilin, Guangxi Province, China, in 1985. This cave is typical of many in this area, which have been well visited by the Chinese and sometimes used for storage or habitation, but are unexplored beyond any difficult spots.

Traversing upstream in the Di Feng river passage, Chong Ching Province, China Caves Project, 2002. The photograph was taken by Gavin Newman using his non-waterproof camera at the end of a hard upstream swim.

Caves Project. In the years following I have led more than 10 expeditions to China, initially in the south, but more recently in the Yangtze Gorge area, where huge passages, magnificent gorges and underground rivers pepper the landscape. Waterfalls cascade from overhanging cliff faces hundreds of metres high, creating some of the most wonderful and challenging underground environments anywhere in the world. Exploration is continuing in many areas, and there is now a permanent presence of western cavers working with the Chinese in the caves of China.

In 1990 and 1991 came further trips to China with 20 people to explore caves so large that aeroplanes could fly in and out of them. Hundreds of kilometres of passage were surveyed, photographed and scientifically studied. Later in the 1990s we embarked on a great underground adventure in Chong Ching Province, in a system called the Great Crack – 11 km (7 miles) of limestone gorge around 30 m (100 ft) wide and 200 m (650 ft) deep. This unroofed cave then becomes underground for another 10 km (6 miles), passing a skylight which the Chinese say is the largest enclosed valley in the world. At this skylight a hydroelectric tunnel has been constructed to take the water in this system to a power station, leaving the lower passage dry. Upstream, the river makes progress more difficult. Our attempts to advance in an upstream direction were halted after 1.5 km (1 mile) by a vertical wall of water; this was climbed, but the steeply flowing river at the top meant making headway was very slow. An abseil of 200 m (650 ft) at one end of the Great Crack yielded a pleasant campsite at the start of the underground section, albeit one infested by venomous snakes.

Exploring downstream from here has proved to be one of the most challenging encounters underground. Fixed ropes have to be used everywhere to allow the journey to be reversed. The wild white water has so much air in it that it is not buoyant and so even with thick wetsuits and large lifejackets it is impossible to keep your head above water – and the noise! Gavin Newman and I have been the furthest upstream and downstream, with the distance between the points now in the region of 500 m (1,640 ft). Four times we have tried to explore the cave, and each time we have been stopped by inclement weather. A wonderful caving challenge for the future.

My son Robert, with very little encouragement from myself (and possibly some discouragement) has taken up cave exploration. In 2009 he led his third expedition to the White Mountains in Crete hoping to break the 2,000-m (6,560-ft) world depth record. Robert and his generation have plenty of challenges ahead. In my opinion, just 10 per cent of caves that humans can enter have so far been explored. Many limestone regions have not been investigated by cavers at all. In Britain it is possible that the blocking of entrances during ice ages means that 50 per cent of cave passages are still unknown. And in spring 2009 a British/Vietnamese Expedition discovered the largest known cave passage in the world. The golden age of cave exploration may well be yet to come.

CONTRIBUTORS

ROBIN HANBURY-TENISON is a well-known explorer, author, film-maker, conservationist and campaigner. Named by the *Sunday Times* in 1982 as 'the greatest explorer of the past 20 years' and in 1991 as one of the 1,000 'Makers of the 20th Century', and again in 2006, in the *Spectator*, as 'the doyen of British explorers', he has been on over 30 expeditions. He has been a Council Member, Vice-President and Gold Medallist of the Royal Geographical Society and has received many awards. A regular contributor to newspapers and magazines, he has also made several films of his expeditions and written numerous books. He was the editor of *The Oxford Book of Exploration* (1993) and also of *The Seventy Great Journeys in History* (2006), published by Thames & Hudson.

DAVID BOYLE is a fellow of the New Economics Foundation and the author of a number of books on the history and future of money. He has written about Richard the Lionheart's ransom (*Blondel's Song*, 2005) and also about the business rivalry between the early transatlantic pioneers in *Toward the Setting Sun: Columbus, Cabot and Vespucci and the Race for America* (2008).

MILES BREDIN has travelled in and written about Africa for the last 20 years. His biography of James Bruce, *The Pale Abyssinian*, was published in 2000. He lives in Kenya and is writing a novel set in Afghanistan, where he worked between 2006 and 2008.

BILL COLEGRAVE is a venture capitalist and publisher and has travelled in much of Central Asia. His book *Halfway House to Heaven; Unravelling the Mystery of the Source of the Oxus* (2010) follows his expedition to the Pamir and Wakhan Corridor, Afghanistan. He lives in London and on the Cote d'Azur, where he has a boutique hotel.

VANESSA COLLINGRIDGE is a writer, broadcaster and academic specializing in maritime history and the history of maps and ideas. Her historical biographies include *Captain Cook: Obsession and Betrayal in the New World* (2002), which was made into an award-winning international documentary series. She lives in Scotland with her young family.

JEAN-MICHEL COUSTEAU is the eldest son of Jacques-Yves Cousteau and is an explorer, environmentalist, educator and film producer. He has produced over 80 films, received the Emmy, the Peabody Award, the 7 d'Or, and the Cable Ace Award. His organization, Ocean Futures Society, is a non-profit marine conservation and education organization that aims to communicate the ocean's critical bond with humanity and the importance of wise environmental policy. As president, Jean-Michel is a dedicated diplomat for the environment.

DAVID EWING DUNCAN is the author of seven books published in 19 languages, including *Hernando de Soto: A Savage Quest in the Americas* (1995), the worldwide bestseller *Calendar* (1998) and the recently released bestseller *Experimental Man: What one man's body reveals about his future, your health, and our toxic world* (2009). He writes for *National Geographic*, *The New York Times* and others. At UC Berkeley he is the Director of the Center of Life Science Policy. He has won numerous awards including the Magazine Story of the Year from the American Association for the Advancement of Science.

ANDREW JAMES EAVIS has spent over 40 years exploring caves all over the world. To finance his lifestyle, with two others he set up a successful plastic moulding business employing 700 people which he eventually sold in 2007. The business experience helped him with his organization of many caving expeditions. He is currently Chairman of the British Caving Association and President of the World Caving Organization.

FRANCIS FRENCH is the Director of Education at the San Diego Air & Space Museum, California. Among his many books and articles on space history are the award-winning *Into That Silent Sea* (2007) and *In the Shadow of the Moon* (2007), exploring the lives and flights of the earliest space explorers.

CAROLYN GILMAN is a historian of North American frontier history, whose books include *Lewis and Clark: Across the Divide* (2003), *The Grand Portage Story* (1992), *The Way to Independence* (1987) and *Where Two Worlds Meet: The Great Lakes Fur Trade* (1982). She was curator of the National Lewis and Clark Bicentennial Exhibition, which toured the United States in 2004–06. She works for the Missouri History Museum in St Louis and is currently writing a book about the American Revolution on the frontier.

ANDREW GOUDIE is a Professor of Geography at the University of Oxford and the Master of St Cross College. He has worked as a geomorphologist in the world's deserts. He is a Gold Medallist of the Royal Geographical Society, and has been awarded the Mungo Park Medal of the Royal Scottish Geographical Society and the Farouk El-Baz Award of the Geological Society of America. He is the author of *Great Warm Deserts of the World* (2002) and *Wheels across the Desert. Exploration of the Libyan Desert by Motorcar 1916–1942* (2008).

CONTRIBUTORS

CONRAD HEIDENREICH is Professor Emeritus of Geography at York University, Toronto. His numerous books and articles on exploration, mapping, Natives and European/Native relations of early Canada include *Huronia: A History and Geography of the Huron Indians* (1973); he was also co-editor and contributor to the *Historical Atlas of Canada*, Vol. 1 (1987). He is currently working on a new bilingual edition of Champlain's writings to be published by the Champlain Society.

JOHN KEAY is the author of many works on Asian history, including *The Honourable Company* (1991), *Last Post: The End of Empire in the Far East* (1997) and *The Spice Route* (2005). He also writes on the history of exploration: he edited *The Royal Geographical Society History of World Exploration* (1991) and was the author of *Mad About the Mekong: Exploration and Empire in South East Asia* (2005).

JOHN MCALEER is Curator of 18th-Century Imperial and Maritime History at the National Maritime Museum, Greenwich. His research focuses on the history of the British Empire and he is particularly interested in its relationship with the Cape of Good Hope, the Caribbean and Canada. He is the author of *Representing Africa: Landscape, Exploration and Empire in Southern Africa, 1780–1870* (2010).

ALEXANDER MAITLAND is the author of numerous books, including *Speke* (1971) and *A Tower in a Wall: Conversations with Dame Freya Stark* (1982). He worked with Wilfred Thesiger on several books and edited Thesiger's anthology, *My Life and Travels* (2002), as well as writing *Wilfred Thesiger: A Life in Pictures* (2004) and Thesiger's official biography, *Wilfred Thesiger: The Life of the Great Explorer* (2006). Recently he has written the title essay for *Wilfred Thesiger in Africa* to coincide with the centenary exhibition at the Pitt-Rivers Museum Oxford, 2010. He is married and lives in London.

JUSTIN MAROZZI is a travel writer, historian, journalist and political risk and security consultant. He has travelled extensively in the Middle East and Muslim world and recently has worked in conflict and post-conflict environments such as Iraq, Afghanistan and Somalia. His first book, *South from Barbary* (2001), was an account of a journey by camel along the slave routes of the Libyan Sahara. His most recent book is *The Man Who Invented History: Travels with Herodotus* (2008). He is currently working on a biography of Baghdad.

JAMES L. NEWMAN is an Emeritus Professor of Geography in the Maxwell School at Syracuse University. A student of Africa, his most recent books are *The Peopling of Africa: A Geographic Interpretation* (1995), *Imperial Footprints: Henry Morton Stanley's African Journeys* (2004) and *Paths Without Glory: Richard Francis Burton in Africa* (2010).

CLARE PETTITT is Professor of Victorian Literature and Culture in the English Department at King's College London. She is the author of *Patent Inventions: Intellectual Property and the Victorian Novel* (2004), and *'Dr. Livingstone, I Presume?': Missionaries, Journalists, Explorers, and Empire* (2007). She is currently writing a book about the invention of simultaneity in the 19th century.

MILBRY POLK is the Executive Director/Co-Founder of Wings WorldQuest, a non-profit organization that focuses on the discoveries of women explorers (www.wingsworldquest.org). Her books include *Women of Discovery* (with Mary Tiegreen; 2001) and *The Looting of the Iraq Museum, Baghdad* (edited with Angela Schuster; 2005). She is a contributing editor for *The Explorers Journal* and a Fellow of the Explorers Club, the Royal Geographical Society and Honorary Fellow of the Royal Canadian Geographical Society. Her expeditions have been in the Middle East, Asia, the Arctic and Tibet.

RUSSELL POTTER is Professor of English at Rhode Island College. He has written extensively about the 19th-century fascination with the Arctic, and was featured in the 2004 documentary 'The Search for the Northwest Passage', produced by Channel 4. He has lectured in the United States, Canada, Ireland and Britain; his most recent book is *Arctic Spectacles: The Frozen North in Visual Culture, 1818–1875* (2007).

PETER RABY is an emeritus fellow and former Vice-Principal of Homerton College, Cambridge. Among his many books are *Alfred Russel Wallace: A Life* (2001) and a study of Victorian scientific travellers, *Bright Paradise* (1996). Most recently, he has edited the *Cambridge Companion to Harold Pinter* (2009).

PAUL ROSE is a television and radio broadcaster, a field science support expert and published author. His television presenting credits include: 'Oceans', 'Voyages of Discovery', 'Take One Museum' and 'Wind'. He was the Base Commander of Rothera Research Station, Antarctica, for the British Antarctic Survey and was awarded The Polar Medal. For his work with NASA and the Mars Lander project on Mount Erebus, Antarctica, he was awarded the US Polar Medal; he was also awarded the Royal Geographical Society's Ness Award. www.paulrose.org

JOHN ROSS is a Melbourne-based journalist and publisher. He was Editor-in-Chief of *Chronicle of the 20th Century* (Australian edition, 1999) and *Chronicle of Australia* (2000), and co-author of *200 Seasons of Australian Cricket* (1997). He is the author of some 20 books, including *Country Towns* (1975), *One People, One Destiny: The Story of Federation* (2001) and *Voices of the Bush* (2001).

ANTHONY SATTIN is a writer and broadcaster who specializes in Africa and the Middle East, a part of the world he has been travelling in for more than 20 years. His books include the highly acclaimed *The Pharaoh's Shadow: Travels in Ancient and Modern Egypt* (1999) and *The Gates of Africa* (2003), which tells the story of Mungo Park's employers, the African Association. His latest book is *A Winter on the Nile: Florence Nightingale, Gustave Flaubert and the Temptations of Egypt* (2010).

JEREMY SCOTT is the nephew of the explorer Gino Watkins and son of J. M. Scott, another member of the Air-Route Expedition, which is the subject of his book *Dancing on Ice* (2008). After serving in the army, he worked in TV, in New York and London. His scandalous memoir *Fast and Louche: Confessions of a Flagrant Sinner* (2002) resulted in an injunction, two writs for libel, one for contempt of court, and threats of knee-capping, but is now available in paperback.

JULES STEWART is a London-based journalist who has published four books on the British in India. His most recent work, *Crimson Snow* (2008), tells the story of the disastrous First Anglo-Afghan War. His previous books include *The Savage Border: The History of the North-West Frontier* (2007), *The Khyber Rifles* (2005) and *Spying for the Raj* (2006), the story of the Pundits. He has lectured at the Royal Geographical Society, the Jamestown Foundation, the Royal Society for Asian Affairs and other venues.

OLIVER TOOLEY has carefully avoided any form of adventure or danger throughout his life. He became an expert on his grandfather because nobody else did, and to correct errors about him. His pursuits are varied – singing in a Led Zeppelin tribute band, writing fiction and non-fiction and bringing up a family. However, since creating his website about Frank Kingdon-Ward he would love to make at least one journey in the footsteps of his grandfather to see the flowers stretching to the horizon in a sunlit Tibetan valley.

ROBERT TWIGGER, writer and explorer, has been described as a '19th-century adventurer trapped in the body of a 21st-century writer'. In 1998 he discovered a line of menhirs stretching across Kalimantan which he described in his book *Big Snake* (2001). He was the first person to retrace Alexander Mackenzie's exact route, as recounted in his book *Voyageur. Across the Rocky Mountains in a Birchbark Canoe* (2006). He is the author of several other books, including *Lost Oasis: Adventures In and Out of the Egyptian Desert* (2007). In 2009–10 he led the first expedition to cross the Great Sand Sea of the Egyptian Sahara on foot.

SIR JOHN URE is a former British ambassador to Cuba, Brazil and Sweden, having also served as an officer in the Cameronians in Malaya (during the Emergency) and as a diplomat in Russia (during the Cold War), in the Congo (during the Civil War), in Chile and in Portugal (during the revolution of 1974). He was written a dozen historical and travel books which have been widely translated, the latest being *Shooting Leave: Spying Out Central Asia in the Great Game* (2009). He also writes travel articles and book reviews for a number of national publications.

RONALD WATKINS is the author of *Birthright* (1993) and *Unknown Seas: How Vasco da Gama Opened the East* (2003). He has travelled extensively throughout Central America, Europe and East Asia. He works as a writing collaborator and is the author of more than 30 books. He is co-author of the Summit Murder series, mystery novels set on the highest mountains in the world. www.ronaldjwatkins.com

SUSAN WHITFIELD is the director of the International Dunhuang Project at the British Library, making available online archaeological artifacts and manuscripts from the Silk Road, including those acquired by Sir Aurel Stein. She has curated exhibitions on the Silk Road in London, Manchester and Brussels, written many books and articles, including *Aurel Stein on the Silk Road* (2004), and travelled widely in this region.

ISOBEL WILLIAMS is a Fellow of the Royal College of Physicians of London. A medical consultant, she was a specialist in respiratory medicine and much involved in post-graduate medical education. Her curiosity about Antarctica was initially aroused by Edward Wilson's evocative paintings in the medical school she worked in and this fascination remained throughout her medical career. She has written the biography of Wilson, *With Scott in the Antarctic. Explorer, Naturalist, Artist* (2008) and lectures on Antarctic matters.

FURTHER READING

THE OCEANS

Christopher Columbus

Boyle, David, *Toward the Setting Sun: Columbus, Cabot and Vespucci and the Race for America* (New York: Walker Books, 2008)

Casas, Bartolomé de las, *History of the Indies*, trans. Andrée Collard (New York: Harper & Row, 1971)

Fernandez-Armesto, Felipe, *Columbus on Himself* (London: Folio Society, 1992)

Keen, Benjamin (ed. and trans.), *The Life of Admiral Christopher Columbus by his Son, Ferdinand* (London: Folio Society, 1960; 2nd ed., Brunswick, NJ: Rutgers University Press, 1992)

Morison, Samuel E., *Admiral of the Ocean Sea: A Life of Christopher Columbus* (Boston: Little Brown, 1942)

Taviani, Paolo E., *Christopher Columbus: The Grand Design* (London: Orbis, 1985)

Varela, Consuelo, *La Caída de Cristóbal Colón: El juicio de Bobadilla* (Madrid: Marcial Pons, 2006)

Vasco da Gama

Azurara, Gomez Eannes da, *The Chronicle of the Discovery and Conquest of Guinea* (London: Hakluyt Society, 1896)

Correa, Gaspar, *The Three Voyages of Vasco da Gama, and his Viceroyalty, from the Lendas da India* (London: Hakluyt Society, 1869)

Hart, Henry H., *Sea Road to the Indies: An Account of the Voyages and Exploits of the Portuguese Navigators, together with the Life and Times of Dom Vasco da Gama, Capitão-Mór, Viceroy of India and Count of Vidigueira* (New York: Macmillan, 1950)

Howe, Sonia E., *In Quest of Spices* (London: Jenkins, 1946)

Nilakanta Sastri, K. A., *A History of South India from Prehistoric Times to the Fall of Vijayanagar* (London: Oxford University Press, 1966)

Phillips, J. K. S., *The Medieval Expansion of Europe* (Oxford: Oxford University Press, 1988)

Ravenstein, E. G. (trans. and ed.), *A Journal of the First Voyage of Vasco da Gama, 1497–1499* (London: Hakluyt Society, 1898; repr. New York: B. Franklin, 1963)

Watkins, Ronald J., *Unknown Seas: How Vasco da Gama Opened the East* (London: John Murray, 2003)

Ferdinand Magellan

Bergreen, Laurence, *Over the Edge of the World* (New York: Morrow, 2003)

Joyner, Tim, *Magellan* (Camden, ME: International Marine, 1992)

Pigafetta, Antonio, *Magellan's Voyage: A Narrative Account of the First Navigation*, trans. R. A. Skelton (New York: Dover, 1994)

Louis-Antoine de Bougainville

Bougainville, Louis-Antoine de, *The Pacific Journal of Louis-Antoine de Bougainville, 1767–1768*, trans. and ed. John Dunmore (London: Hakluyt Society, 2002)

Bougainville, Louis-Antoine de, *A Voyage Round the World.* [Translated from the French by John Reinhold Forster] (Amsterdam: N. Israel; New York: Da Capo, 1967; orig. ed. London: 1772)

Dunmore, John, *Storms and Dreams. Louis de Bougainville: Soldier, Explorer, Statesman* (Stroud: Nonsuch, 2005)

Kimbrough, Mary, *Louis-Antoine de Bougainville, 1729–1811: A Study in French Naval History and Politics* (Lewiston: E. Mellen Press, 1990)

James Cook

Beaglehole, J. C. (ed.), *The Journals of Captain James Cook on his Voyages of Discovery*, 4 vols (Cambridge University Press for the Hakluyt Society, 1955–74)

Beaglehole, J. C., *The Life of Captain James Cook* (London: A. & C. Black; Stanford: Stanford University Press, 1974)

Collingridge, Vanessa, *Captain Cook: Obsession and Betrayal in the New World* (London: Ebury Press, 2002)

David, Andrew, *The Charts and Coastal Views of Captain Cook's Voyages, Vol. 1, The Voyage of the Endeavour 1768–1771* (London: Hakluyt Society, 1988)

Kaeppler, A. L. and others, *James Cook and the Exploration of the Pacific* (London: Thames & Hudson, 2009)

Robson, John, *The Captain Cook Encyclopaedia* (London: Chatham Publishing, 2004)

Robson, John, *Captain Cook's World: Maps of the Life and Voyages of James Cook, R.N.* (Milsons Point, NSW: Random House, 2000; London: Chatham Publishing, 2001)

http://www.captaincooksociety.com

THE LAND

Hernando de Soto

Duncan, David Ewing, *Hernando de Soto: A Savage Quest in the Americas* (New York: Crown, 1995)

Clayton, Lawrence A., Knight, Vernon Jones Jr. and Moore, Edward C. (eds), *The de Soto Chronicles: Expedition of Hernando de Soto to North America 1539– 1543* (Tuscaloosa: University of Alabama Press, 1993)

Hemming, John, *The Conquest of the Incas* (London: Macmillan; New York: Harcourt Brace Jovanovich, 1970)

Hudson, Charles, *Knights of Spain, Warriors of the Sun: Hernando de Soto and the South's Ancient Cheifdoms* (Athens: University of Georgia Press, 1997)

Lewis and Clark

Ambrose, Stephen E., *Undaunted Courage: Meriwether Lewis, Thomas Jefferson, and the Opening of the American West* (New York: Simon & Schuster, 1996)

DeVoto, Bernard (ed.), *The Journals of Lewis and Clark* (Boston: Houghton Mifflin, 1953)

Gilman, Carolyn, *Lewis and Clark: Across the Divide* (Washington, DC and London: Smithsonian Books, 2003)

Ronda, James P., *Lewis and Clark Among the Indians* (Lincoln and London: University of Nebraska Press, 1984)

Thomas Baines

Baines, Thomas, *Explorations in South West Africa* (London: Longman & Co., 1864)

Baines, Thomas, *Journal of Residence in Africa, 1842–1853*, ed. R. F. Kennedy, 2 vols (Cape Town: 1961–64)

Braddon, Russell, *Thomas Baines and the North Australian Expedition* (Sydney: Collins, 1986)

Carruthers, Jane and Arnold, Marion, *The Life and Work of Thomas Baines* (Vlaeberg: Fernwood Press, 1995)

McAleer, J., *Representing Africa: Landscape, Exploration and Empire in Southern Africa, 1780–1870* (Manchester: Manchester University Press, 2010)

Stevenson, Michael (ed.), *Thomas Baines: An Artist in the Service of Science in Southern Africa* (London: Christie's, 1999)

Wallis, J. P. R., *Thomas Baines of King's Lynn, Explorer and Artist, 1820–1875* (London: Cape, 1941)

Richard Burton

Brodie, Fawn M., *The Devil Drives: A Life of Sir Richard Burton* (New York: W. W. Norton; London: Eyre & Spottiswoode, 1967)

Burton, Isabel, *The Life of Captain Sir Richard F. Burton KCMG, FRGS*, 2 vols (London: Chapman & Hall, 1893)

Burton, Richard, *Selected Papers on Anthropology, Travel, and Exploration*, ed. Norman M. Penzer (London: A. M. Philpot, 1924)

Fortnightly Review, 'Richard Burton', article by Ouida (June 1906)

Lovell, Mary S., *A Rage to Live: A Biography of Richard and Isabel Burton* (London: Little, Brown; New York: W. W. Norton, 1998)

Nain Singh

Barrow, Ian J., *Making History, Drawing Territory: British Mapping in India*, c. *1756–1905* (New Delhi: Oxford University Press, 2003)

Hopkirk, Peter, *Trespassers on the Roof of the World: The Race for Lhasa* (London: John Murray, 1982)

Keay, John, *Explorers of the Western Himalayas, 1820–1895* (London: John Murray, 1996)

Madan, P. L., *Tibet: Saga of Indian Explorers* (New Delhi: Manohar Publishers, 2004)

Markham, Clements R., *A Memoir on the Indian Surveys* (London: Allen & Co., 1871)

Rawat, Indra Singh, *Indian Explorers of the 19th Century* (New Delhi: Ministry of Information and Broadcasting, 1973)

Waller, Derek, *The Pundits: British Exploration of Tibet and Central Asia* (Lexington: University Press of Kentucky, 1990)

Nikolai Przhevalsky

Dubrovin, I. F., *N. M. Prezheval'ski* (St Petersburg, 1890)

Hopkirk, Peter, *The Great Game. The Struggle for Empire in Central Asia* (London: John Murray, 1990; New York: Kodansha, 1992)

Rayfield, Donald, *The Dream of Lhasa: the Life of Nikolay Przhevalsky (1839–88), Explorer of Central Asia* (London: Elek, 1976)

Ney Elias

Black, C. E. D., *A Memoir on the Indian Surveys, 1875–1890* (London: India Office, 1891)

Elias, Ney (ed.), *A History of the Moghuls of Central Asia, Being the Tarikh-i-Rashidi of Mirza Muhammad Haidar, Dughlat*, trans. E. D. Ross (London: Sampson Low & Co., 1895)

Morgan, Gerald, *Ney Elias: Explorer and Envoy Extraordinary in High Asia* (London: Allen & Unwin, 1971)

Francis Younghusband

Allen, Charles, *Duel in the Snows: The True Story of the Younghusband Mission to Lhasa.* (London: John Murray, 2004)

Fleming, Peter, *Bayonets to Lhasa* (London: Rupert Hart-Davis; New York: Harper, 1961)

French, Patrick, *Younghusband: The Last Great Imperial Adventurer* (London: HarperCollins, 1994)

Hopkirk, Peter, *The Great Game. The Struggle for Empire in Central Asia* (London: John Murray, 1990; New York: Kodansha, 1992)

Seaver, George, *Francis Younghusband: Explorer and Mystic* (London: John Murray, 1952)

Verrier, Anthony, *Francis Younghusband and the Great Game* (London: Cape, 1991)

Younghusband, Francis, *The Heart of a Continent: A Narrative of Travels in Manchuria, across the Gobi Desert, through the Himalayas, the Pamirs and Chitral, 1884–94* (London: John Murray, 1896)

Marc Aurel Stein

Hopkirk, Peter, *Foreign Devils on the Silk Road: The Search for the Lost Cities and Treasures of Chinese Central Asia* (London: John Murray, 1980)

Mirsky, Jeanette, *Sir Aurel Stein: Archaeological Explorer* (Chicago: University of Chicago Press, 1977)

Walker, Annabel, *Aurel Stein, Pioneer of the Silk Road* (London: John Murray, 1998)

Whitfield, Susan, *Aurel Stein on the Silk Road* (London: The British Museum Press; Chicago: Serindia, 2004)

RIVERS

Samuel de Champlain

Biggar, H. P. (ed.), *The Works of Samuel de Champlain*, 6 vols (Toronto: Champlain Society, 1922–36)

Fischer, David Hackett, *Champlain's Dream: The Visionary Adventurer Who Made a New World in Canada* (New York: Simon & Schuster, 2008)

Heidenreich, Conrad E., 'The Beginning of French Exploration out of the St Lawrence Valley: Motives, Methods, and Changing Attitudes toward Native People', in Warkentin, G. and Podruchny, C. (eds), *Decentring the Renaissance* (Toronto: University of Toronto Press, 2001), 236–51

Heidenreich, Conrad E., 'Early French Exploration in the North American Interior', in Allen, J. L. (ed.), *North American Exploration: A Continent Defined*, vol. 2 (Lincoln: University of Nebraska Press, 1997) 65–148

Litalien, Raymonde and Vaugeois, Denis (eds), *Champlain: the Birth of French America*, (Montreal-Kingston: McGill Queen's Press, 2004)

James Bruce

Bredin, Miles, *The Pale Abyssinian: A Life of James Bruce, African Explorer and Adventurer* (London: HarperCollins, 2000)

Bruce, James, *Travels to Discover the Source of the Nile*, ed. C. F. Beckingham (Edinburgh: University of Edinburgh Press, 1964; orig. ed. Edinburgh: J. Ruthven, 1790)

Moorehead, Alan, *The Blue Nile* (London: Hamish Hamilton; New York: Harper & Row, 1962)

Alexander Mackenzie

Gough, Barry, *First Across the Continent* (Norman: University of Oklahoma Press, 1997)

Mackenzie, Alexander, *Voyages from Montreal* (London and Edinburgh, 1801)

Morse, Eric, *Fur Trade Canoe Routes of Canada* (Toronto: University of Toronto Press, 1979)

Twigger, Robert, *Voyageur: Across the Rocky Mountains in a Birchbark Canoe* (London: Weidenfeld & Nicolson, 2006)

Woodworth, John and Flygare, Halle, *In the Steps of Alexander Mackenzie* (Prince George, BC: AMVR Association, 1989)

Mungo Park

Boyle, T. C., *Water Music: A Novel* (Boston: Little, Brown; London: Gollancz, 1981)

Hunwick, John O. and Boye, Alida Jay, *The Hidden Treasures of Timbuktu* (London and New York: Thames & Hudson, 2008)

Lupton, Kenneth, *Mungo Park, The African Traveler* (Oxford: Oxford University Press, 1979)

Park, Mungo, *Travels into the Interior of Africa* (London: Eland, 2003)

Sattin, Anthony, *The Gates of Africa: Death, Discovery and the Search for Timbuktu* (London: Harper Perennial, 2004; New York: St Martin's Press, 2005)

John Hanning Speke

Burton, R. F., *The Lake Regions of Central Africa*, 2 vols (London: Longmans, 1860)

Carnochan, W. B., *The Sad Story of Burton, Speke and the Nile; Or was John Hanning Speke a Cad?* (Stanford, CA: Stanford General Books, 2006)

Maitland, Alexander., *Speke and the Discovery of the Source of the Nile* (London: Constable, 1971)

Ondaatje, Christopher, *Journey to the Source of the Nile* (Toronto: HarperCollins, 1998)

Speke, John Hanning, *Journal of the Discovery of the Source of the Nile* (London: Blackwood, 1863)

Speke, John Hanning, *What Led to the Discovery of the Nile* (London: Blackwood, 1864)

David Livingstone

Helly, Dorothy O., *Livingstone's Legacy: Horace Waller and Victorian Mythmaking* (Athens: Ohio University Press, 1987)

Jeal, Tim, *Livingstone* (New Haven and London: Yale University Press, 2001)

National Portrait Gallery, *David Livingstone and the Victorian Encounter with Africa* (London: NPG Publications, 1996)

Pettitt, Clare, *'Dr. Livingstone, I Presume?'. Missionaries, Journalists, Explorers, and Empire* (London: Profile Books; Cambridge MA: Harvard University Press, 2007)

Ross, Andrew C., *David Livingstone: Mission and Empire* (London and New York: Continuum, 2006)

Francis Garnier

Carné, Louis de, *Travels on the Mekong* ('The Political and Trade Report of the Mekong Exploration Commission') (repr. Bangkok: White Lotus, 2000)

Delaporte, Louis and Garnier, Francis, *A Pictorial Journey on the Old Mekong* (vol 3 of 'The Mekong Exploration Commission Report') (repr. Bangkok: White Lotus, 1998)

Garnier, Francis, *Voyage d'exploration en Indo-Chine* (Paris, 1885); English translation: *Travels in Cambodia and Laos and Further Travels in Laos and Yunnan*, 2 vols (Bangkok: White Lotus, 1996)

Keay, John, *Mad about the Mekong: Exploration and Empire in South East Asia* (London: HarperCollins, 2005)

Osborne, Milton, *The Mekong: Turbulent Past, Uncertain Future* (New York: Atlantic Monthly Press, 2000)

Henry Morton Stanley

Driver, Felix, *Geography Militant: Cultures of Exploration and Empire* (Oxford and Malden MA: Blackwell, 2001)

Fabian, Johannes, *Out of Our Minds: Reason and Madness in the Exploration of Central Africa* (Berkeley: University of California Press, 2000)

Hall, Richard, *Stanley: An Adventurer Explored* (Boston: Houghton Mifflin, 1975)

Jeal, Tim, *Stanley: The Impossible Life of Africa's Greatest Explorer* (London: Faber and Faber, 2007)

Newman, James L., *Imperial Footprints: Henry Morton Stanley's African Journeys* (Potomac, VA: Brassey's/Potomac, 2004)

POLAR ICE

Fridtjof Nansen

Nansen, Fridtjof, *The First Crossing of Greenland*, trans. Hubert Gepp (Northampton, MA: Interlink Publishing, 2003)

Nansen, Fridtjof, *Farthest North*, intro. Roland Huntford (New York: Modern Library, 1999)

Shackleton, Edward, *Nansen: The Explorer* (London: H. F. & G. Witherby, 1959)

Edward Wilson

Cherry-Garrard, A., *The Worst Journey in the World* (London: Picador, 1994)

Scott, R. F., *The Voyage of the 'Discovery'*, 2 vols (London: Smith, Elder & Co., 1905)

Scott, R. F., *Scott's Last Expedition*, 2 vols (London: Smith, Elder & Co., 1913)

Williams, I., *With Scott in the Antarctic, Edward Wilson. Explorer, Naturalist, Artist* (Stroud: The History Press, 2008)

Wilson, Edward, *Diary of the 'Discovery' Expedition to the Antarctic Regions 1901–1904*, ed. Ann Savours (London: Blandford Press, 1966)

Wilson, Edward, *Diary of the 'Terra Nova' Expedition to the Antarctic 1910–1912*, ed. H. G. R. King (London: Blandford Press, 1972)

Roald Amundsen

Amundsen, Roald, *The North West Passage: Being the Record of a Voyage of Exploration of the Ship 'Gjöa' 1903–1907* (London: Constable; New York: E. P. Dutton & Co., 1908)

Amundsen, Roald, *The South Pole: An Account of the Norwegian Antarctic Expedition in the 'Fram', 1910–1912*, trans. A. G. Chater, 2 vols (London: John Murray; New York: L. Keedick, 1912)

Amundsen, Roald, *My Life as an Explorer* (London: Heinemann; New York: Doubleday, 1927)

Bomann-Larsen, Tor, *Roald Amundsen* (Stroud: Sutton, 2006)

Wally Herbert

Herbert, Wally, *Across the Top of the World* (London: Longmans, 1969; New York: Putnam, 1971)

Herbert, Wally, *The Noose of Laurels* (London: Hodder & Stoughton; New York: Atheneum, 1989)

Herbert, Wally, *The Polar World: The Unique Vision of Sir Wally Herbert* (Weybridge: Polarworld, 2007)

DESERTS

Heinrich Barth

Barth, Heinrich, *Travels and Discoveries in North and Central Africa*, repr. 3 vols (London: Frank Cass, 1965)

Boahen, A. A., *Britain, the Sahara and the Western Sudan 1778–1861* (Oxford: Clarendon Press, 1964)

Diawara, Mamadou, de Moraes Farias, Paulo Fernando and Spittler, Gerd (eds), *Heinrich Barth et l'Afrique* (Cologne: Rüdiger Köppe Verlag, 2006)

Herrmann, Paul, *The Great Age of Discovery* (New York: Harper, 1958)

Kirk-Greene, A. H. M. (ed.), *Barth's Travels in Nigeria* (London: Oxford University Press, 1962)

Charles Sturt

Blainey, Geoffrey, *The Tyranny of Distance: How Distance Shaped Australia's History* (Melbourne: Sun Books, 1966)

Cannon, Michael, *The Exploration of Australia* (Sydney: Reader's Digest, 1987)

Stokes, Edward, *To the Inland Sea: Charles Sturt's Expedition 1844–45* (Hawthorn: Hutchinson, 1986)

Sturt, C. N., *Two Expeditions into the Interior of Southern Australia, during the years 1828, 1829, 1830 and 1831*, 2 vols (London: Smith, Elder & Co., 1833)

Sturt, C. N., *Narrative of an Expedition into Central Australia during the Years 1844, 5 and 6*, 2 vols (London: T. & W. Boone, 1849)

Gertrude Bell

Bell, Gertrude, *The Desert and the Sown* (London: Virago, 1985; Mineola: Dover, 2008)

Bell, Gertrude, *Amurath to Amurath* (London: Heinemann, 1911)

Howell, Georgina, *Daughter of the Desert: The Remarkable Life of Getrude Bell* (London: Macmillan, 2006); *Gertrude Bell: Queen of the Desert, Shaper of Nations* (New York: Farrar, Strauss & Giroux, 2007)

Wallach, Janet, *Desert Queen* (London: Weidenfeld & Nicolson, 1996; New York: Anchor Books, 2005)

Winstone, H. V. F., *Gertrude Bell* (London: Cape; New York: Quartet, 1978)

Gertrude Bell archive: http://www.gerty.ncl.ac.uk/

Harry St John Philby

Meulen, D. van der, *The Wells of Ibn Sa'ud* (London: John Murray, 1957)

Monroe, Elizabeth, *Philby of Arabia* (London: Faber, 1973)

Philby, H. St J. B., *Arabian Days* (London: Hale, 1948)

Philby, H. St J. B., *A Pilgrim in Arabia* (London: Hale, 1946)

Philby, H. St J. B., *Forty Years in the Wilderness* (London: Robert Hale, 1957)

Ralph Bagnold

Bagnold, R. A., *Libyan Sands: Travel in a Dead World* (London: Hodder & Stoughton, 1935)

Bagnold, R. A., *Sand, Wind and War. Memoirs of a Desert Explorer* (Tucson: University of Arizona, 1990)

Gordon, John W., *The Other Desert War. British Special Forces in North Africa, 1940–1943* (New York: Greenwood, 1987)

Goudie, Andrew, *Wheels Across the Desert. Exploration of the Libyan Desert by Motor Car 1916–1942* (London: Silphium, 2008)

Kelly, Saul, *The Hunt for Zerzura. The Lost Oasis and the Desert War* (London: John Murray, 2002)

Wilfred Thesiger

Maitland, Alexander, *Wilfred Thesiger: The Life of the Great Explorer* (London: HarperPress, 2006)

Philby, H. St J. B., *The Empty Quarter* (London: Constable, 1933)

Thesiger, Wilfred, *Arabian Sands* (London: Longmans Green, 1959)

Thesiger, Wilfred, *The Marsh Arabs* (London: Longmans, 1964)

Thesiger, Wilfred, *The Life of My Choice* (London: Collins, 1987)

Thomas, Bertram J., *Arabia Felix: Across the Empty Quarter of Arabia* (London: Jonathan Cape, 1932)

LIFE ON EARTH

Alexander von Humboldt

Botting, Douglas, *Humboldt and the Cosmos* (London: Jospeph; New York: Harper & Row, 1973)

Hein, Wolfgang-Hagen (ed.), *Alexander von Humboldt: Life and Work*, trans. John Cumming (Ingelheim am Rhein: C. H. Boehringer Sohn, 1987)

Humboldt, Alexander von, *Personal Narrative of a Journey to the Equinoctial Regions of the New Continent*, abridged and trans. Jason Wilson (London: Penguin, 1995)

Kellner, L., *Alexander von Humboldt* (London and New York: Oxford University Press, 1963)

Marianne North

Birkett, Dea, *Spinsters Abroad: Victorian Lady Travellers* (Oxford: Basil Blackwell, 1989)

Lees-Milne, A., 'Marianne North', *Journal of the Royal Horticultural Society*, 98 (6), June 1964, 231–40

North, Marianne, *Recollections of a Happy Life*, ed. and intro. Susan Morgan (Charlottesville: University of Virginia Press, 1993; orig. ed. London: Macmillan, 1892)

North, Marianne, *Some Further Recollections of a Happy Life* (London: Macmillan, 1893)

North, Marianne, *A Vision of Eden*, ed. G. Bateman, 4th ed. (London: Royal Botanic Gardens, Kew and HMSO, 1993)

Polk, Milbry and Tiegreen, Mary, *Women of Discovery* (New York: Clarkson Potter, 2001)

Ponsonby, L., *Marianne North at Kew Gardens* (London: Webb and Bower, 1990)

Alfred Russel Wallace

Berry, Andrew (ed.), *Infinite Tropics: An Alfred Russel Wallace Anthology* (London and New York: Verso, 2002)

Knapp, Sandra, *Footsteps in the Forest: Alfred Russel Wallace in the Amazon* (London: Natural History Museum, 1999)

Raby, Peter, *Alfred Russel Wallace, A Life* (London: Chatto & Windus; Princeton: Princeton University Press, 2001)

Wallace, Alfred Russel, *Travels on the Amazon and Rio Negro*, 2nd ed. (London: Ward Lock, 1889)

Wallace, Alfred Russel, *The Malay Archipelago: The Land of the Orang-utan and the Bird of Paradise*, ed. John Bastin (Oxford: Oxford University Press, 1989)

Wilson, J. G., *The Forgotten Naturalist: In Search of Alfred Russel Wallace* (Kew, Victoria: Arcadia, 2000)

Frank Kingdon-Ward

Kingdon-Ward, Frank, *Frank Kingdon-Ward's Riddle of the Tsangpo Gorges: Retracing the Epic Journey of 1924–25 in South-East Tibet*, ed. Kenneth Cox (Woodbridge: Antique Collectors' Club, 1999)

Kingdon-Ward, Frank, *The Land of the Blue Poppy. Travels of a Naturalist in Tibet* (Cambridge: Cambridge University Press, 2009)

Kingdon-Ward, Frank, *A Plant Hunter in Tibet* (Bangkok: White Orchid, 2006)

Kingdon-Ward, Frank, *Burma's Icy Mountains* (Bangkok: White Orchid, 2006)

Lyte, Charles, *Frank Kingdon-Ward. The Last of the Great Plant Hunters* (London: John Murray, 1989)

NEW FRONTIERS

Gino Watkins

Chapman, F. Spencer, *Watkins' Last Expedition* (London: Chatto and Windus, 1934)

Chapman, F. Spencer, *Northern Lights: The Official Account of the British Arctic Air-Route Expedition, 1930–1931* (London: Chatto and Windus, 1932)

Lindsay, Martin, *Those Greenland Days* (London: Blackwood, 1932)

Scott, J. M., *Gino Watkins* (London: Hodder & Stoughton, 1935)

Scott, Jeremy, *Dancing on Ice* (London: Old Street Publishing, 2008)

Yuri Gagarin

Burchett, Wilfred and Purdy, Anthony, *Cosmonaut Yuri Gagarin, First Man in Space* (London: Gibbs & Phillips, 1961)

Burgess, Colin and Hall, Rex, *The First Soviet Cosmonaut Team: Their Lives, Legacy and Historical Impact* (New York: Springer, 2009)

French, Francis and Burgess, Colin, *Into That Silent Sea: Trailblazers of the Space Era 1961–1965* (Lincoln: University of Nebraska Press, 2007)

Hall, Rex and Shayler, David, *The Rocket Men: Vostok and Voskhod, The First Soviet Manned Spaceflights* (New York and Chichester: Springer, 2001)

Jacques-Yves Cousteau

Cousteau, Jacques-Yves, *The Silent World*, with Frédéric Dumas (New York: Harper; London: Hamish Hamilton, 1952)

Cousteau, Jacques-Yves, *The Living Sea*, with James Dugan (New York: Harper & Row; London: Hamish Hamilton, 1963)

Cousteau, Jacques-Yves, *World Without Sun*, ed. James Dugan (New York: Harper & Row; London: Heinemann, 1965)

Cousteau, Jacques-Yves and Cousteau, Phillipe, *The Shark: Splendid Savage of the Sea* (Garden City, NY: Doubleday; London: Cassell, 1970)

Cousteau, Jacques-Yves and Richards, Mose, *Jacques Cousteau's Amazon Journey* (New York: Abrams, 1984)

Cousteau, Jacques-Yves and Schiefelbein, Susan, *The Human, the Orchid and the Octopus* (New York: Bloomsbury, 2007)

Andrew James Eavis

Brook D. B. (ed.), 'The British New Guinea Speleological Expedition, 1975', *Transactions of the British Cave Research Association*, 3, 1976

Brook, D. B., *Caves of Mulu* (London: Royal Geographical Society, 1978)

Howes, Chris, *To Photograph Darkness* (Gloucester: Alan Sutton, 1989)

Shaw, Trevor R., *History of Cave Science: The Exploration and Study of Limestone Caves, to 1900* (Sydney Speleological Society, 1992)

http://www.chinacaves.org.uk/

http://www.mulucaves.org/

SOURCES OF QUOTATIONS

p. 7 C. P. Cavafy, 'Ithaca', from *Collected Poems*, trans. Edmund Keeley and Philip Sherrard (London: Hogarth Press, 1975); p. 20 quoted in F. Fernández-Armesto, *Columbus on Himself* (London: Folio Society, 1992) p. 158; p. 28 quoted in M. Kaplan, *The Portuguese: The Land and Its People* (New York: viking, 1991), p. 29; p. 32 Antonio Pigafetta, *The First Voyage Round the World, by Magellan. Translated from the accounts of Pigafetta, and other contemporary writers*, trans., with notes and introduction, Lord Stanley of Alderley (London: Hakluyt Society, 1874), p.101; pp. 33, 36, 37 Antonio Pigafetta, *Magellan's Voyage: A Narrative Account of the First Circumnavigation*, trans. R. A. Skelton (New Haven: Yale UP, 1969); pp. 40, 43 Louis-Antoine de Bougainville, *A Voyage Around the World*, trans. J. R. Forster (London, 1772); p. 46 J. C. Beaglehole (ed.), *The Journals of Captain James Cook on His Voyages of Discovery*, 4 vols (London: CUP, 1955–74), vol. II, p. 322; p. 56 James Elroy Flecker, 'The Golden Journey to Samarkand', 1913, *Collected Poems* (London: Secker & Warburg, 1916); p. 60 E. G. Bourne (ed.), *Narratives of the Career of Hernando de Soto in the Conquest of Florida as Told by a Knight of Elvas* ..., trans. Buckingham Smith (New York: A. S. Barnes & Co., 1904), Vol. 2, p. 162, www.americanjourneys.org/aj-024/; pp. 64, 69, 70 Bernard DeVoto (ed.), *The Journals of Lewis and Clark* (Boston: houghton Mifflin, 1953); p. 72 quoted in J. P. R. Wallis, *Thomas Baines of King's Lynn, Explorer and Artist, 1820–1875* (London: Cape, 1941), p. 158; p. 72 Roderick Murchison, quoted in J. P. R. Wallis, *Thomas Baines of King's Lynn, Explorer and Artist, 1820–1875* (London: Cape,1941), p. xvii; p. 72 Thomas Baines, *Journal of Residence in Africa, 1842–53*, ed. R. F. Kennedy, 2 vols (Cape Town, 1961–64), vol. 1, p. 9; p. 72 Thomas Baines, *Journal of Residence in Africa, 1842–53*, ed. R. F. Kennedy, 2 vols (Cape Town, 1961–64), vol. 1, p. 10; p. 74 Quoted in Jane Carruthers and Marion Arnold, *The Life and Work of Thomas Baines* (Vlaeberg: Fernwood Press, 1995), p. 50 and p. 171; p. 75 Thomas Baines, *The Victoria Falls, Zambesi River*... (London: Day & Son, 1865), p. 3; p. 75 RGS, JMS/2/35/a, Thomas Baines to Sir George Cathcart, 13 April 1853; p. 77 RGS, CB5/33, 'Victoria Falls of the Zambesi: A series of oil paintings'; p. 78 Thomas Baines, *Explorations in South West Africa* (London: Longmans & Co., 1864), p. 34; p. 78 Thomas Baines, *Journal of Residence in Africa, 1842–53*, ed. R. F. Kennedy, 2 vols (Cape Town, 1961–64), vol. 1, p. 1; p. 79 Murchison: RGS, CB5/33, 'Victoria Falls of the Zambesi: A series of oil paintings'; p. 79 Baines, quote in J. P. R. Wallis, *Thomas Baines of King's Lynn, Explorer and Artist, 1820–1875* (London: Cape, 1941), p. 188; p. 79 RGS, JMS/2/35/a, Thomas Baines to Sir George Cathcart, 13 April 1853; p. 80 Richard F. Burton *The Kasîdah Of Hâjî Abdû El-Yezdî* (1880); p. 83 'Discovery...' Richard F. Burton, *The Carmina of Caius Valerius Catullus* (London, 1894); p. 85 Lord Derby, quoted in *The New York Times*, 21 August 1921; p. 86 'Pay, pack, and follow', Isabel Burton, *The Life of Captain Sir Richard F. Burton KCMG, FRGS*, (London: Chapman & Hall, 1893), Vol. 2, p. 569; p. 86 'Now that I know...' Isabel Burton, *The Life of Captain Sir Richard F. Burton KCMG, FRGS*, (London: Chapman & Hall, 1893), Vol. 2, p. 442; pp. 87, 92 Sir Clements Markham, *A Memoir of the Indian Survey* (London: Allen & Co., 1871); p. 102 Francis Younghusband, *The Heart of a Continent* (London: John Murray, 1896); p. 106 quoted in Peter Hopkirk, *Foreign Devils on the Silk Road: The Search for the Lost Cities and Treasures of Chinese Central Asia* (London: John Murray, 1980); p. 116 H. P. Biggar (ed.), *The Works of Samuel de Champlain* (Toronto: Champlain Society, 1922–36); pp. 121, 123 James Bruce, *Travels to Discover the Source of the Nile* (Edinburgh: J. Ruthven, 1790); p. 130 Mungo Park, *Travels in the Interior Districts of Africa* (London, 1799); p. 136 J. H. Speke, *Journal of the Discovery of the Source of the Nile* (London: Blackwood, 1863); p. 142 David Livingstone, *Livingstone's African Journal, 1853–1856*, ed. I. Schapera (London: Chatto & Windus, 1963); p. 153 Francis Garnier, *Voyage d'exploration en Indo-Chine* (Paris, 1885); English translation 2 vols: *Travels in Cambodia and Laos and Further Travels in Laos and Yunnan* (Bangkok: White Lotus, 1996); p. 158 A. J. Mounteney Jephson, *The Diary of A. J. Mounteney Jephson: Emin Pasha Relief Expedition, 1887–1889*, ed. Dorothy Middleton (Cambridge: CUP, 1969); p. 169 Fridtjof Nansen, *Farthest North* (London: Newnes, 1898), p. 58; p. 174 R. F. Scott, *Scott's Last Expedition, Vol. I, Journals of Captain R. F. Scott* (London: Smith, Elder & Co., 1913); p. 189 Wally Herbert, *The Polar World* (Weybridge:Polarworld, 2007); pp. 196, 199, 201, 202 Heinrich Barth, *Travels and Discoveries in North and Central Africa* (London: Longman, Brown, Green, Longmans & Roberts, 1857–58); p. 204 C. N. Sturt, *Narrative of an Expedition into Central Australia during the Years 1844, 5 and 6* (London: T. & W. Boone, 1849); pp. 206, 207 C. N. Sturt, *Two Expeditions into the Interior of Southern Australia, during the years 1828, 1829, 1830 and 1831* (London: Smith, Elder & Co., 1833); p. 208 C. N. Sturt, *Narrative of an Expedition into Central Australia during the Years 1844, 5 and 6* (London: T. & W. Boone, 1849); p. 210 Gertrude Bell, Diary, 21/1/1902: Gertrude Bell Archive, Newcastle University, www.gerty.ncl.ac.uk/; p. 210 'I have known...' quoted in Georgina Howell, *Gertrude Bell: Queen of the Desert, Shaper of Nations* (New York: Farrar, Strauss & Giroux, 2007); p. 213 caption, Getrude Bell, letter, 7/3/1914: Gertrude Bell Archive, Newcastle University, www.gerty.ncl.ac.uk/; p. 214 'Confound...' quoted in Georgina Howell, *Gertrude Bell: Queen of the Desert, Shaper of Nations* (New York: Farrar, Strauss & Giroux, 2007); p. 214 'They are...' Gertrude Bell, letter, 16/8/1922: Gertrude Bell Archive, Newcastle University, www.gerty.ncl.ac.uk/; p. 215 Harry St J. Philby, *Arabian Days* (London: Hale, 1948); p. 221 R. A. Bagnold, *Libyan Sands* (London: Hodder & Stoughton, 1935); p. 222 *The Times*, 3 January 1931; p. 223 *Geographical Journal* 82, p. 120; p. 225 Wilfred Thesiger, *The Life of My Choice* (London: Collins, 1987); p. 227 Wilfred Thesiger, *Arabian Sands* (London: Longmans Green, 1959); p. 232 Francis Darwin (ed.) *The Life and Letters of Charles Darwin*, vol. 2 (New York: Basic Books, 1959), p. 422; p. 233 letter of Alexander von Humboldt to J. F. Blumenbach, June 1795; pp. 234, 235, 237, 239 Alexander von Humboldt, *Personal Narrative of a Journey to the Equinoctial Regions of the New Continent* (London: Penguin, 1995); pp. 240, 244 Marianne North, *Recollections of a Happy Life* (London: Macmillan & Co., 1892); p. 245 Marianne North, *Some Further Recollections of a Happy Life* (London: Macmillan & Co., 1893); p. 248 'should civilized man...' A. R. Wallace, *The Malay Archipelago* (London: Macmillan & Co., 1869); p. 248 'I should like...' A. R. Wallace, *My Life* (London: chapman & Hall, 1908), p. 248; p. 249 letter of A.R.Wallace to Samuel Stevens, first published in *Annals and Magazine of Natural History*, 5 February 1850; p. 250 'a good...' A. R.Wallace, *Travels on the Amazon and Rio Negro* (London: Ward Lock, 1889), p. 145; p. 250 'almost at ...' letter of Richard Spruce to John Smith, 25 December 25 (R.B.G. Kew), quoted in Peter Raby, *Alfred Russel Wallace* (London: Chatto & Windus, 2001), p. 77; p. 252 A. R. Wallace, *Contributions to the Theory of Natural Selection* (London: Macmillan & Co., 1871); pp. 253–54 A. R. Wallace to Samuel Stevens, 21 August 1856 (Cambridge University Library), quoted in Peter Raby, *Alfred Russel Wallace* (London: Chatto & Windus, 2001), p. 113; p. 254 A. R. Wallace, *The Malay Archipelago* (London: Macmillan & Co., 1869), p. 411; p. 255 A. R. Wallace, *The Malay Archipelago* (London: Macmillan & Co., 1869), p. 434; p. 263 F. Kingdon-Ward, 'The Assam Earthquake of 1950', *The Geographical Journal*, Vol. 119, No. 2 (1953), pp. 169–82; p. 266 Jeremy Scott, *Dancing on Ice* (London: Old Street Publishing, 2008); p. 267 Charles Dickens, 'The Lost Arctic Voyagers', *Household Words*, 9 December 1854, p. 392; pp. 270, 273 quoted in Kevin W. Kelley (ed.), *The Home Planet* (Reading, MA: Addison Wesley, 1988); p. 276 quoted in Ross R. Olney *Men Against the Sea* by (New York: Grosset & Dunlap, 1969); p. 282 quoted in Trevor R. Shaw, *History of Cave Science: The Exploration and Study of Limestone Caves, to 1900* (Sydney Speleological Society, 1992)

SOURCES OF ILLUSTRATIONS

a: above; b: below

1 Courtesy of the American Philosophical Society; 2 British Library, London; 6 National Maritime Museum, Greenwich, London (BHC1932); 8, 9, 11 © Royal Geographical Society, London; 12 Scott Polar Research Institute, University of Cambridge; 13 Fridtjof Nansen/National Library of Norway, Oslo, The Picture Collection; 14 from Heinrich Barth, *Travels and Discoveries in North and Central Africa...* (London: Longman, Brown, Green, Longmans & Roberts, 1858); 17 Bibliothèque nationale de France, Paris; 18 akg-images/Gilles Mermet; 19 Georg-August-Universität Göttingen, Ethnographic Collection. Photo Harry Haase; 21a Museo Navale di Pegli, Genoa; 21b, 22 Agosto, courtesy Palazzo Tursi, Genoa; 23 Museo Naval, Madrid; 25 British Library, London; 26 © AISA; 29 akg-images; 31 The Art Archive/Science Academy Lisbon/Gianni Dagli Orti; 34-35 Biblioteca Estense, Modena; 36–37 Courtesy Lilly Library, Indiana University, Bloomington, Indiana; 39 Bibliothèque nationale de France, Paris; 41 National Library of Australia, Canberra (6045157); 43 National Library of Australia, Canberra (9454368); 44 Bibliothèque nationale de France, Paris; 45 Courtesy of Hordern House Rare Books; 46 Museum of New Zealand, Te Papa Tongarewa, Wellington; 47 © Crown Copyright and/or database rights. Reproduced by permission of the Controller of Her Majesty's Stationery Office and the UK Hydrographic Office (www.ukho.gov.uk); 48 Peter Mazell (after S. Parkinson), 'View of the great peak & the adjacent country on the west coast of New Zealand'. National Library of Australia, Canberra (8391515); 49 Natural History Museum, London; 50 National Library of Australia, Canberra (8391494); 53 Natural History Museum, London; 54 National Maritime Museum, Greenwich, London (BHC2375); 57 Reproduced with the kind permission of the Director and the Board of Trustees, Royal Botanic Gardens, Kew; 58 from Richard F. Burton, *Personal Narrative of a Pilgrimage to el-Medinah & Meccah* (London: Longman, Green, Longman, and Roberts, 1855); 59 © Royal Geographical Society, London; 61 British Museum, London; 62 Library of Congress, Geography and Map Division, Washington, D.C.; 63 Library of Congress, Washington D.C.; 65 Courtesy of the American Philosophical Society; 66 Joslyn Art Museum, Omaha, Nebraska, 1986.49.214. Gift of Enron Art Foundation; 68 Collection of the New-York Historical Society, 1971.125. Gift of the Heirs of Hall Park McCullough; 69 Joslyn Art Museum, Omaha, Nebraska. Gift of Enron Art Foundation; 71 Missouri Historical Society, St Louis, William Clark Papers, Voorhis #2. Gift of Julia Clark Voorhis in memory of Eleanor Glasgow Voorhis; 73, 74, 76, 77 © Royal Geographical Society, London; 78 Reproduced with the kind permission of the Director and the Board of Trustees, Royal Botanic Gardens, Kew; 79 © Royal Geographical Society, London; 81 from Richard F. Burton, *Personal Narrative of a Pilgrimage to al-Madinah & Meccah* (London: Tylston & Edwards, 1893); 82 from Richard F. Burton, *Goa, and the Blue Mountains; or Six Months of Sick Leave* (London: Richard Bentley, 1851); 83 National Portrait Gallery, London; 84, 85 from Richard F. Burton, *The Lake Regions of Central Africa: A Picture of Exploration* (London: Longman, Green, Longman, and Roberts, 1860); 87, 88–89 © Royal Geographical Society, London; 90–91 © The British Library Board, London (Add. Or. 3013); 92, 94 © Royal Geographical Society, London; 95, 96 from Nikolai Przhevalsky, *Mongolia i strana tangutov* (*Mongolia and the Land of the Tanguts*) (St. Petersburg: 1875); 99, 100–01 © Royal Geographical Society, London; 103 © The British Library Board, London (Mss Eur F197/674(1)); 105 © Royal Geographical Society, London; 107 The British Library, London (Stein Photo 392/23(12)); 108 © The Trustees of the British Museum, London; 111 © The British Library Board, London (Or.8210/P.2); 113 © Royal Geographical Society, London; 114 from Francis Garnier, *Voyage d'Exploration en Indo-Chine* (Paris: Hachette, 1885); 115 Yale Center for British Art, Paul Mellon Collection, USA/The Bridgeman Art Library; 117 Library and Archives Canada (NL 15316); 118 Library of Congress, Geography and Map Division, Washington, D.C.; 119 Library and Archives Canada (NL 6643); 120 John Carter Brown Library at Brown University, Providence, Rhode Island; 121 National Portrait Gallery, London; 123 Courtesy of the Lewis Walpole Library, Yale University, New Haven; 124, 125 Cushing Memorial Library and Archives, Texas A&M University; 127 National Gallery of Canada, Ottawa; 128 © Royal Geographical Society, London; 129 The National Archives, UK; 131 R. Caillé, *Travels through Central Africa to Timbuctoo*, 1830; 132, 133, 134 Courtesy Anthony Sattin; 135 National Portrait Gallery, London; 137, 139, 140, 141, 143, 144, 145, 146 © Royal Geographical Society, London; 147 from David Livingstone, *Missionary Travels and Researches in South Africa* (London: John Murray, 1857); 148, 149, 150 © Royal Geographical Society, London; 152, 155 from Francis Garnier, *Voyage d'Exploration en Indo-Chine* (Paris: Hachette, 1885); 156 Bibliothèque nationale de France, Paris; 159 Stanley Archives, collection King Baudouin Foundation, under trust of RMCA Tervuren, Belgium; 160, 161, 162 © Royal Geographical Society, London; 163 from Henry Morton Stanley, *How I found Livingstone; travels, adventures, and discoveries in central Africa; including four months' residence with Dr. Livingstone* (London: S. Low, Marston, Low, and Searle, 1872); 165 Stanley Archives, collection King Baudouin Foundation, under trust of RMCA Tervuren, Belgium; 167 © Royal Geographical Society, London; 168, 169 Fridtjof Nansen/National Library of Norway, Oslo, The Picture Collection; 170 © Royal Geographical Society, London; 171, 173 Fridtjof Nansen/National Library of Norway, Oslo, The Picture Collection; 175 © Royal Geographical Society, London; 176, 177 Scott Polar Research Institute, University of Cambridge; 178, 179 © Royal Geographical Society, London; 180 Scott Polar Research Institute, University of Cambridge; 182, 184, 185 Photographer unknown/National Library of Norway, Oslo, The Picture Collection; 186 Fram Museum, Oslo; 187 National Library of Australia, Canberra (23814300); 188 © Bettmann/Corbis; 189, 190, 191, 192 Courtesy Herbert Collection; 194 Gertrude Bell Archive, Newcastle University; 195, 197 © Royal Geographical Society, London; 198, 200, 202, 203a, 203b from Heinrich Barth, *Travels and Discoveries in North and Central Africa...* (London: Longman, Brown, Green, Longmans & Roberts, 1858); 205 National Library of Australia, Canberra (2377285); 206 National Library of Australia, Canberra (2377287); 207 National Library of Australia, Canberra (5263644); 209, 210, 212, 213a, 213b, 214 Gertrude Bell Archive, Newcastle University; 216, 217, 218, 219, 220, 222, 223 © Royal Geographical Society, London; 226 Pitt Rivers Museum, University of Oxford (2004.130.12990.1); 227 Pitt Rivers Museum, University of Oxford (2004.130.17285.1); 229 Pitt Rivers Museum, University of Oxford (2004.130.19462.1); 231 © Royal Geographical Society, London; 234 Natural History Museum, London; 235 © Royal Geographical Society, London; 236 akg-images; 239 © Royal Geographical Society, London; 241, 242, 243 Reproduced with the kind permission of the Director and the Board of Trustees, Royal Botanic Gardens, Kew; 244 Private collection; 245, 247 Reproduced with the kind permission of the Director and the Board of Trustees, Royal Botanic Gardens, Kew; 249 Private collection. Copyright A. R. Wallace Memorial Fund; 250 Natural History Museum, London; 252 from A. R. Wallace, *The Malay Archipelago, land of the Orang-Utan and the Bird of Paradise: a narrative of travel, with studies of Man and Nature* (London: Macmillan & Co., 1869); 253, 254 Natural History Museum, London; 255, 256 from A. R. Wallace, *The Malay Archipelago, land of the Orang-Utan and the Bird of Paradise: a narrative of travel, with studies of Man and Nature* (London; Macmillan & Co., 1869); 257, 258, 260, 261, 262, 263 © Royal Geographical Society, London; 265 Robbie Shone; 267 Private collection; 268, 269 Scott Polar Research Institute, University of Cambridge; 271, 272, 273 RIA Novosti/aviation-images.com; 275 © Rykoff Collection/Corbis; 277 Private collection; 278 Popperfoto/Getty Images; 279 Kobal Collection; 280 © Carrie Vonderhaar, Ocean Futures Society/KQED; 283 Andy Eavis; 284 Jerry Wooldridge; 285, 287 Andy Eavis; 288 Gavin Newman

INDEX

Page numbers in *italic* refer to illustrations

INDEX

INDEX

INDEX